Houghton
Mifflin
Harcourt

STECK-VAUGHN

PRE GED® TEST PREPARATION

SOCIAL STUDIES

- Instruction at manageable reading levels and practice of basic skills aligned to the 2014 GED® Test content areas

- Emphasis on social studies practices and critical thinking skills

- Pretest and posttest assessments identify strengths and weaknesses

- Complete answers and explanations

Houghton
Mifflin
Harcourt

ii

CONTENTS

CONTENTS

How to Use This Book

The purpose of this book is to help you develop the foundation you need to pass the *GED® Social Studies* test.

Throughout the four units of the book, you will learn a variety of thinking and reading skills. You will also learn several graphic skills, such as reading timelines, maps, political cartoons, and graphs. These skills will not only help you as you work through this book, but they are crucial to success on the GED®.

Pretest and Posttest

The Pretest is a self-check of what you already know and what you need to study. After you complete all of the items on the Pretest, check your work in the Answers and Explanations section at the back of the book. Then fill out the Pretest Evaluation Chart. This chart tells you where each skill is taught in this book. When you have completed the book, you will take a Posttest. Compare your Posttest score to your Pretest score to see your progress.

Units

Unit 1: U.S. History. This unit covers such history skills as reading historical and political maps, understanding photos, and using timelines. The articles you read will increase your knowledge of major events in the history of the United States.

Unit 2: Geography and the World. In this unit you will learn about important events in the world's history. You will learn about cultural and economic realities for various people. You will also learn such skills as comparing and contrasting, summarizing, and drawing conclusions from tables and graphs.

Unit 3: Civics and Government. In this unit you will learn about selected contents in political science. You will read diagrams and study political cartoons. You will also read about how laws are made and the roles of local, state, and federal governments.

Unit 4: Economics. This unit focuses on skills in economics. You will use graphic illustrations such as tables, line graphs, and circle graphs. You will gain an understanding of our economy by reading articles about fundamental economic concepts, supply and demand, world trade, and money management.

Lessons

Each unit is divided into lessons. Each lesson is based on the Active Reading Process. This means doing something before reading, during reading, and after reading. By reading actively, you will improve your reading comprehension skills.

The first page of each lesson has three sections to help prepare you for what you are about to read. First, you will read some background information about the passage presented in the lesson. This is followed by the Relate to the Topic section, which includes a brief exercise designed to help you relate the topic of the reading to your life. Finally, Reading Strategies will provide you with a pre-reading strategy that will help you to understand what you read and a brief exercise that will allow you to practice using that strategy. These are the activities you do before reading. Vocabulary words important to the lesson are listed down the left-hand side of the page.

The articles you will read are about interesting topics in social studies. As you read each article, you will see two Skills Mini-Lessons. Here you learn a reading or graphic skill, and do a short activity. After completing the activity, continue reading the article. These are the activities you do during reading.

After reading the article, you answer fill-in-the-blank, short-answer, or multiple choice questions in the section called Thinking About the Article. Answering these questions will help you decide how well you understood what you read. The final question in this section relates information from the article to your own real-life experiences.

Social Studies at Work

Social Studies at Work is a two-page feature in each unit. Each Social Studies at Work feature introduces a specific job and describes the skills the job requires. It also gives information about other jobs in the same career area.

Mini-Tests and Unit Reviews

Unit Reviews tell you how well you have learned the skills covered in each unit. Each Unit Review includes a Social Studies Extension activity that provides an opportunity for further practice. Mini-Tests follow each Unit Review. These timed practice tests allow you to practice your skills with the kinds of questions that you will see on the actual GED® tests.

Use this Pretest before you begin Unit 1. The Pretest will help you determine which content areas in social studies you understand well and which you must practice further. Read each article and study the graphics—map, timeline, graph, diagram, and cartoon. Then answer the questions on each page.

Check your answers on pages 224–225. Mark the number of correct answers you have in each content area on the chart on page 13. Use the chart to figure out which content area(s) to work on and where to find practice pages in this book.

The Elevation of the United States

United States Elevation Map

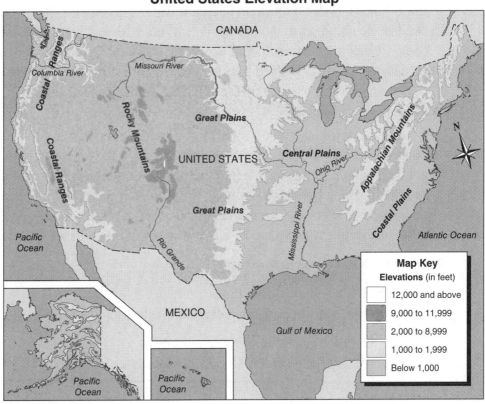

▶ Circle the letter of the best answer.

1. What is the elevation of the Coastal Plains?

  A. Below 1,000 feet

  B. 1,000 to 1,999 feet

  C. 2,000 to 8,999 feet

  D. 9,000 to 11,999 feet

Desert Regions

Nearly every continent has at least one desert region. When people think of deserts, they often picture hot, dry, sandy, empty lands. Hot deserts are usually found at low latitudes and low elevations. The Sahara, a desert region in North Africa, is hot.

Indeed every desert is very dry with few or no plants at all. But not all deserts are hot. Some are cold. Cold deserts include the Gobi, a desert in northeastern Asia. Cold deserts are found at higher latitudes and higher elevations. The Gobi's elevations range from 3,000 to 5,000 feet above sea level. Although many deserts have sand, most of them do not. Only five percent of the Gobi, for example, has sand.

Deserts are home to many different plants and animals. Desert plants and animals have adapted to the harsh environment. Desert plants have tough skins and few or thick leaves so they can keep any water they absorb. Some desert animals, like the mourning dove and the desert rat, are active at night when temperatures are cooler. Other animals need little water to survive. For example, kangaroo rats never actually drink water. Instead they get their water from the seeds they eat. Another desert animal, the camel, can live off fat stored in its hump and can go for long periods without water.

People have also found ways to live in the desert, just as they have in every other environment. Some people move from place to place with herds of camels, goats, or sheep. Other people farm in the desert although it is nearly impossible to do so. These daring farmers must bring water to their fields from a distant underground spring or river. People have found oil and other natural resources in the desert. They often build cities in the desert, near the valuable resources.

● **Circle the letter of the best answer.**

2. Which is an opinion from the article?
   A. It is nearly impossible to farm in the desert.

   B. Only five percent of the Gobi has sand.

   C. People build cities near natural resources.

   D. Some desert animals are active at night.

The Nomadic Life

Mongolia, located in Asia, has a harsh environment that can be unpredictable. Most of the country, around 90%, is considered pasture or desert wasteland. Only about 1% of the land can be used to grow crops. Yet, over 2 million people live there. Many of them live in urban areas such as the capital, Ulaanbaatar. But Mongolia is also home to one of the world's last remaining nomadic cultures.

Pastoral nomadism makes it possible to support many people in the harsh Mongolian environment. Pastoral refers to pasture. So, pastoral nomadism is the practice of nomadic peoples following their livestock from pasture to pasture, typically moving two to four times each year. Once they have exhausted the resources in an area, they move to the next. This allows the resources to recover. The nomadic people depend on their livestock for meat and milk. Other than allowing their animals to graze, they do little that impacts their environment. They live in felt tents called gers, which are easily moved but have the comforts of home. Solar panels often provide electricity for lights and televisions.

The nomadic lifestyle, however, is not easy. Recently, very harsh winters have killed many millions of animals. Climate change and desertification threaten pastures. Faced with these difficult challenges, many nomadic people are moving to cities looking for a better life. Sadly, they leave behind a nomadic culture that has existed for thousands of years.

▶ **Circle the letter of the best answer for each question.**

3. How do nomadic people help sustain the land on which they live for the future?
   A. They use the milk and meat of their animals.

   B. They use few modern conveniences such as cars.

   C. They do not make any changes to their environment.

   D. They move frequently which allows the land to recover.

4. What enables many nomadic people in Mongolia to use modern conveniences?
   A. lightbulbs

   B. solar panels

   C. gers

   D. televisions

Go on to the next page.

U.S. Immigration Policy

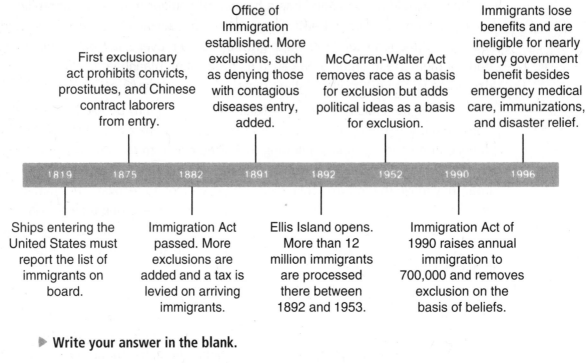

Office of Immigration established. More exclusions, such as denying those with contagious diseases entry, added.

First exclusionary act prohibits convicts, prostitutes, and Chinese contract laborers from entry.

McCarran-Walter Act removes race as a basis for exclusion but adds political ideas as a basis for exclusion.

Immigrants lose benefits and are ineligible for nearly every government benefit besides emergency medical care, immunizations, and disaster relief.

1819   1875   1882   1891   1892   1952   1990   1996

Ships entering the United States must report the list of immigrants on board.

Immigration Act passed. More exclusions are added and a tax is levied on arriving immigrants.

Ellis Island opens. More than 12 million immigrants are processed there between 1892 and 1953.

Immigration Act of 1990 raises annual immigration to 700,000 and removes exclusion on the basis of beliefs.

▶ **Write your answer in the blank.**

5. Public policy on immigration became exclusionary in _____ when Chinese contractors were excluded from entering the United States.

6. In 1929, the National Origins Act set an annual immigration quota of 150,000. Public policy on immigration has changed since then and the number of immigrants that

may come to the United States each year has increased by _____.

▶ **Circle the letter of the best answer for each question.**

7. How did changes in public policy on immigration likely affect the culture of the Chinese already living in the United States?
   A.   They likely tried to pretend they were not Chinese.
   B.   They likely tried to introduce Americans to their culture.
   C.   They likely maintained their Chinese traditions.
   D.   They likely tried to become more "American."

8. When were exclusions on immigration based on beliefs removed?
   A.   before the Office of Immigration was established
   B.   before immigrants lost benefits
   C.   before race was removed as an exclusion
   D.   before Ellis Island opened

The American Revolution

The start of the American Revolution forced people in North America to take sides. Those who wanted to be free from Britain were called Patriots. Those who were loyal to Britain were called Loyalists. Most African Americans faced a hard choice. Many were enslaved. They chose the side that offered them their freedom.

Even before the colonies declared their independence, African Americans were taking sides. African-American soldiers fought in all the early battles of the war. Then in November 1775, Patriot leaders said African Americans could no longer serve in the Patriot army. Those who had already joined were sent home. Slave owners did not want any African Americans to have guns. They were afraid African Americans would use the guns to fight against slavery.

Then, the British promised to free any slave who joined their army. Many slaves accepted the offer. As a result Patriot leaders changed their minds. However, they decided to allow only free African Americans, not slaves, to join their army. In December 1777, George Washington took his army of about 9,000 men to Valley Forge, Pennsylvania. By the spring of 1778, Washington had fewer than 6,000 soldiers. Many deserted, while others died of cold or hunger.

Washington desperately needed more soldiers. So the Patriot leaders finally decided to allow enslaved African Americans to enlist. By the end of the war, 5,000 African Americans had taken part in the American Revolution. They came from every state and fought in every major battle. The efforts of African-American soldiers during the war helped convince people who lived in the northern states that slavery should not be allowed.

▶ **Circle the letter of the best answer for each question.**

9. Which piece of evidence from the article supports the inference that George Washington originally did not want African Americans serving in the army?
   A. Most African Americans fought on the side of the British.
   B. Patriot leaders said African American soldiers could no longer serve in the army.
   C. Washington desperately needed more soldiers.
   D. By the spring of 1778, George Washington had fewer than 6,000 soldiers.

10. What event permitted enslaved African Americans to join the Patriots' army?
   A. the start of the American Revolution
   B. Britain's decision to free slaves who joined its army
   C. the loss of so many soldiers at Valley Forge
   D. African-American participation in earlier battles

Go on to the next page.

Women's Right to Vote

Women's Suffrage in the United States

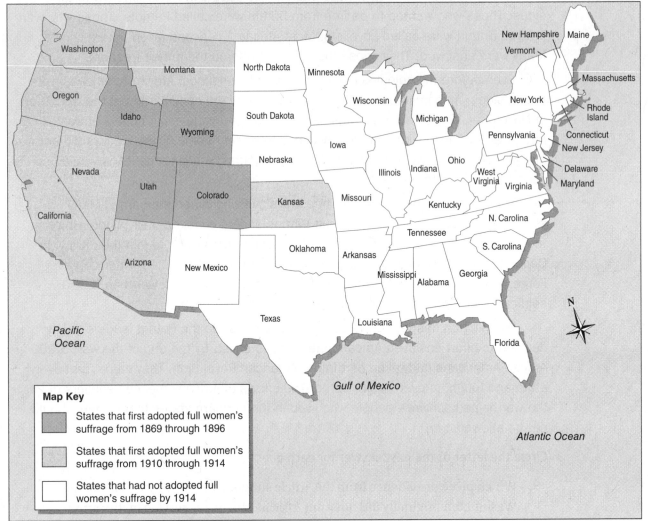

Map Key

States that first adopted full women's suffrage from 1869 through 1896

States that first adopted full women's suffrage from 1910 through 1914

States that had not adopted full women's suffrage by 1914

▶ **Write your answer in the blank.**

11. Based on the map, in 1914 there were _____ states that had not adopted full women's suffrage than there were states that had.

Civil Rights

For many years after the Civil War, African Americans worked for equal rights. In the North and the South, they faced **discrimination.** White Americans did not treat them as if they had the same rights that whites did. In many states, schools were segregated. As a result, African American and white children could not attend the same school. African Americans were not allowed to live in many neighborhoods or to hold certain jobs. Some state laws even kept African Americans out of such places as restaurants, public swimming pools, movie theaters, and hotels.

In August 1963, nearly one hundred years after the Civil War ended, more than 250,000 Americans marched down the streets of Washington, D.C. They included white Americans and African Americans from every state and several foreign countries. They demanded that Congress finally pass a civil rights bill that would end discrimination in the United States.

Dr. Martin Luther King, Jr., was among the marchers. He was an African-American minister who was well known for his inspiring sermons. King captured the mood of the day. He said to the crowd, "I have a dream that one day this nation will rise up and live out the true meaning of its creed: 'We hold these truths to be self-evident; that all men are created equal.'"

President John F. Kennedy supported King's cause. He called on Congress to pass a strong civil rights bill. Kennedy did not live to see the bill become law. After Kennedy's death, Congress passed the Civil Rights Act of 1964. It protected the right of all citizens to vote. It outlawed discrimination in hiring and education. It also ended segregation in public places.

▶ **Circle the letter of the best answer.**

12. What do you think the word *segregated* means based on the way it is used in the fourth sentence?

    A.   located in different areas

    B.   open to all races

    C.   separate for whites and African Americans

    D.   discriminated against by the government

Electing a President and Vice President

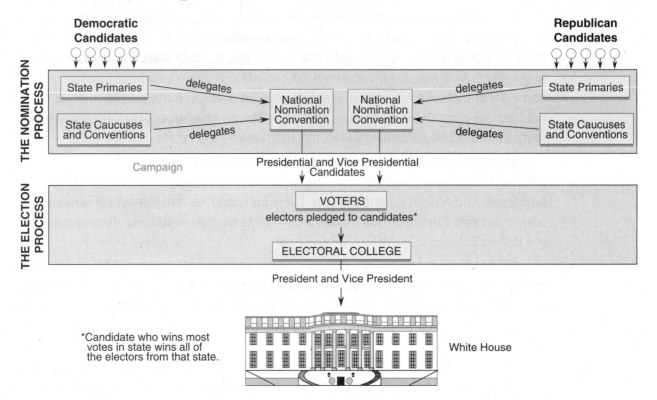

▶ Circle the letter of the best answer for each question.

13. From which source are delegates chosen to represent the Democratic and Republican parties at their nominating conventions?

    A. state primaries

    B. national conventions

    C. the electoral college

    D. national elections

14. Based on the information provided in the diagram, which group directly elects the president and vice president?

    A. the voters for the national candidates

    B. party delegates from the national conventions

    C. electors of the Electoral College

    D. party caucus of each political party

Taxes

Government in the United States provides citizens with many goods and services. To pay for these, it collects taxes from individuals and businesses. Taxes are generally collected on income, sales, and property. Taxes collected in the United States usually follow one of two basic tax principles.

One is the benefit principle. This says that those who benefit the most should be the ones taxed. It also says that they should pay in proportion to the amount of benefit they receive. Gasoline taxes are an example of benefit taxes. Those people who use the most gasoline pay the most gasoline taxes. People who do not own a car do not pay any gasoline tax.

The second tax principle is the ability-to-pay principle. This says that those who have the most income should pay a higher rate of taxes than those who make less money. Most income taxes are based on this principle. The federal government, state governments, and some city governments charge income taxes using this principle. This idea comes from the belief that people with higher incomes can afford to pay higher taxes. So Americans pay different percentages based on their income. A single person in 2002 with $25,000 in taxable income paid 10 percent on the first $6,000 and 15 percent on the rest, or $3,450 in federal income taxes. A person with $50,000 of taxable income paid $9,846, or 10 percent on the first $6,000, 15 percent on $27,950, and 27 percent on the rest. A single person with $308,000 of taxable income in 2002 paid $95,085—close to one-third of this income, in federal income tax.

Many Americans object to the ability-to-pay principle. They argue that everyone should pay the same percentage of his or her income in federal tax. Such a tax is called a flat tax.

▶ **Write the answer to the question.**

15. If you were a representative to the United States Congress that was debating new tax laws, would you argue in favor of or against a flat tax? Explain your position using evidence from the article. You may wish to use the income examples given and calculate a flat tax for each to compare.

The Global Economy

▶ **Circle the letter of the best answer.**

16. Which word would the cartoonist most likely use to describe the global economy?

A. strong

B. fragile

C. indestructible

D. unshakable

Natural Rights Philosophy

Natural law is a cornerstone of the U.S. Constitution. The framers of the Constitution did not write it to grant people rights, but rather to guarantee the rights they believed people already had. Many philosophers wrote about natural rights as the colonies were being founded and systems of government were being put into place. From natural rights philosophy evolved the theory of popular sovereignty, which states that government is given its authority by the people. John Locke and Alexander Hamilton were both influential in this movement.

"To understand political power right, and derive it from its original, we must consider, what state all men are naturally in, and that is, a state of perfect freedom to order their actions, and dispose of their possessions and persons, as they think fit, within the bounds of the law of nature, without asking leave, or depending upon the will of any other man."

John Locke, *The Second Treatise of Civil Government,* 1690

"Hence also, the origin of all civil government, justly established, must be a voluntary compact, between the rulers and the ruled; and must be liable to such limitations, as are necessary for the security of the absolute rights of the latter; for what original title can any man or set of men have, to govern others, except their own consent? To usurp dominion over a people, in their own despite, or to grasp at a more extensive power than they are willing to entrust, is to violate that law of nature, which gives every man a right to his personal liberty; and can, therefore, confer no obligation to obedience."

Alexander Hamilton, 1775

▶ **Circle the letter of the best answer.**

17. How are the two passages related?
   A. Hamilton uses Locke's ideas to propose how government should work.

   B. Locke uses Hamilton's ideas to support his theory for natural law.

   C. Hamilton disregards Locke's ideas in his statements.

   D. Locke disregards Hamilton's ideas in his statements.

Go on to the next page.

Entrepreneurship in the United States

People start new businesses every day. They also close businesses every day. Starting and running a business requires resources, dedication, and customers. Many factors can make or break a business. An entrepreneur may have a fantastic idea and lots of resources, but if the location of his or her business is hard to find, then fewer customers will be able to find it. Or an entrepreneur may have everything he or she needs but if the business is started just before the economy goes downhill, then it is not likely to survive.

The graph shows the number of businesses that were less than one year old each year between 1994 and 2010.

Number of Establishments Less Than 1 Year Old, March 1994–March 2010

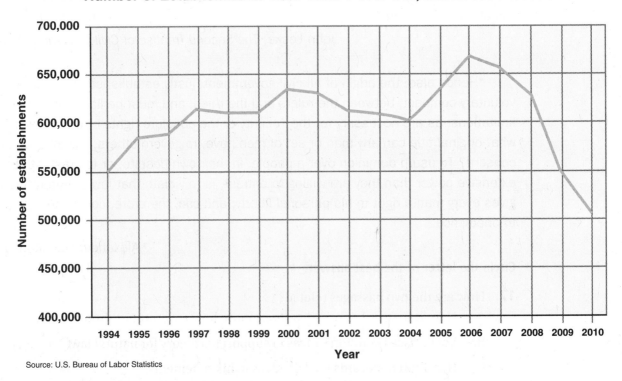

Source: U.S. Bureau of Labor Statistics

▶ **Circle the letter of the best answer.**

18. Which is true about the data in the graph?
   A. It shows causation.

   B. It shows correlation.

   C. It shows both causation and correlation.

   D. It shows neither causation nor correlation.

Pretest Evaluation Chart

The chart below will help you determine your strengths and weaknesses in the four content areas of social studies.

Content Area	Pretest Question	Total Correct	Practice Pages
U.S. History (Pages 14–77)	9, 10 12	_____ out of 3	Pages 22–27 Pages 58–63
Geography and the World (Pages 78–129)	1 2, 3, 4	_____ out of 4	Pages 92–97 Pages 116–121
Civics and Government (Pages 130–175)	5, 6, 7, 8 11 13, 14 17	_____ out of 8	Pages 161–166 Pages 143–148 Pages 149–154 Pages 137–142
Economics (Pages 176–209)	15 16, 18	_____ out of 3	Pages 155–194 Pages 177–182

Total Correct for Pretest _____ out of 18

▶ **Directions**

Check your answers on pags 224–225. In the Questions column, circle the number of each question that you answered correctly on the Pretest. Count the number of questions you answered correctly in each content area. Write the amount in the Total Correct blank in each row. (For example, in the U.S. History row, write the number correct in the blank before *out of 3*). Complete this process for the remaining rows. Then add the five totals to get your Total Correct for the whole Pretest.

If you answered fewer than 15 questions correctly, look more closely at the four content areas of social studies listed above. In which areas do you need more practice? Each content area makes up a part of this book. Look for the page numbers of that section in the chart's right-hand column. Then complete that part of the book for further practice.

U.S. history tells an exciting story of native peoples and of immigrants from around the world; of everyday citizens and their leaders; of soldiers, teachers, farmers, and inventors. It is the story of how Americans have shaped—and continue to shape—this nation.

Name a historic event that has happened in your lifetime and one that

happened long ago. _____

_____

Thinking About U.S. History

You may be surprised to discover how much you already know about U.S. history. Think about what you learned in school, have read in newspapers, or heard on the television news.

Check the box for each fact that you already know.

- ☐ Christopher Columbus was an early explorer of the Americas.
- ☐ The Declaration of Independence declared the American colonists free of Great Britain's control.
- ☐ The Civil War led to the end of slavery in the United States.
- ☐ The first motion pictures were made by Thomas Alva Edison.
- ☐ There have been two world wars.
- ☐ The *Apollo 11* mission put the first Americans on the moon.

Write two other facts that you know about U.S. history.

_____

_____

Previewing the Unit

In this unit, you will learn:

- how European nations gained and then lost colonies in North America
- why Americans fought each other in the 1860s
- how reformers changed American society
- why the United States became involved in the world wars and some conflicts that followed
- how changes in the way we share information have shaped the modern world

Lesson	1	**Establishing Colonies**
Lesson	2	**Revolution and a New Republic**
Lesson	3	**The U.S. Civil War and Reconstruction**
Lesson	4	**The Reform Movement**
Lesson	5	**World War I**
Lesson	6	**World War II**
Lesson	7	**The Cold War**
Lesson	8	**Civil Rights**
Lesson	9	**Post 9/11 Foreign Policy**

ESTABLISHING COLONIES

Vocabulary

immigrant

migrate

pueblo

conquistador

mission

colony

indentured servant

The first people to come to North America traveled east from Asia long ago. Over time, they spread across the land and eventually inhabited all parts of North and South America. They were the original Americans—the Native Americans.

Many years later, Europeans sailed across the Atlantic Ocean. Spanish explorers, who were looking for riches, conquered Native Americans in the southern part of North America. Other Europeans settled along the Atlantic coast. The mixing of these cultures helped shape what would become the United States of America.

Relate to the Topic

This lesson is about the Americans who lived here first and the ones who came later. Think about your own background.

Where did each of your parents' families originally come from?

How has your family background affected your life?

Reading Strategy

SKIMMING **Skimming** means to look quickly over something to get the main idea. A good way to do this is to start with the **title,** or name, of an article. The title will give you a general idea about what the writer will discuss. Read the title on page 17. Then answer the questions.

1. Which groups of people will the writer discuss?

   Hint: What words describe the people?

2. What do you think is the basic difference between the two groups?

   Hint: In what order does the writer present the groups?

Native and New Americans

The United States is a land of **immigrants.** Immigrants come to a region or country where they were not born in order to live there. Scientists believe that the original Americans came at least 27,000 years ago. They may have walked from Asia to North America across land that today is underwater. Nearly 500 years ago, Europeans sailed to the eastern shores of what would become the United States of America. Even today immigrants from many parts of the world travel to America.

The Original Americans

Small bands of Asian hunters followed animals across a land bridge where water now separates Siberia and Alaska. These people and their descendants **migrated,** or gradually moved, across the continent from the Pacific Ocean to the Atlantic Ocean and south to South America. Over thousands of years, the hunters changed to fit their environment. They learned to farm and settled in villages. Groups in different areas developed their own crafts, language, and religion.

One group in North America was the Anasazi. From 100 B.C. to about A.D. 1300, these people lived in what is now the southwestern United States. They managed to raise corn, squash, and beans in a very dry climate. They built large **pueblos,** or settlements with apartment-like buildings made of sandy clay called *adobe*. Anasazi buildings are believed to be the oldest in what today is the United States.

By the 1400s, some groups of Native Americans in what are now Mexico and Central America had empires with elaborate cities. The cities had canals, pyramids, temples, and markets. The Aztec people built the great city of Tenochtitlán, which was located where Mexico City stands today. In 1500, this Aztec city had about 300,000 people, which was twice the number of people that lived in London, England, at the time.

In the eastern woodlands of North America, many nations of American Indians shared the region's thick forests and rich soil. Groups often disagreed over farmland and hunting grounds. In what is now New York, Indians from five nations often trespassed on one another's land. Trespassing led to fighting. Tired of war, the nations finally decided to work together. About 1570, they formed the Iroquois League. Each nation governed itself but also chose members to serve on a Great Council. The council made decisions on important matters, such as trade and war.

European Explorers and Traders

The first Europeans to visit North America were sailors from Scandinavia. They reached Newfoundland about A.D. 1000 but did not stay. European exploration and settlement of the Americas did not really begin until Spain sent Christopher Columbus on a voyage in 1492. He was looking for a sea route from Europe to Asia. He wanted to trade for Asian spices. Instead he found the Americas, or what Europeans called *the New World*.

Europeans soon realized that the New World was full of riches. Spanish **conquistadors** (conquerors), driven by dreams of gold and silver, looted the rich empires of Mexico and South America. At first the Native Americans did not resist because they thought the Spaniards were gods. Later the Native Americans were unable to resist because so many had died from European diseases.

In North America, the explorers found little gold. Nevertheless, Roman Catholic priests who came with the Spanish explorers built missions in what are now Mexico, Texas, California, and Florida. A **mission** is a settlement centered around a church. The priests who ran the missions were called *missionaries*. The Spanish missionaries invited Native Americans into their missions and taught them about Christianity. Many missionaries thought the Native Americans were savages and tried to make them give up their ways.

The English, French, and Dutch also searched for a water route through the Americas to the markets of Asia. In this search, they explored the northern regions of North America. By 1610, France had a profitable fur trade with Native Americans in what is now Canada.

▶ Reading a Historical Map A map can show how different groups moved from one place to another. A map key can indicate when each move took place. Look closely at the map below. How many years before the English did the Spanish establish a settlement in what is now the eastern United States?

   A. 42 years   B. 55 years

Some European Voyages to North America

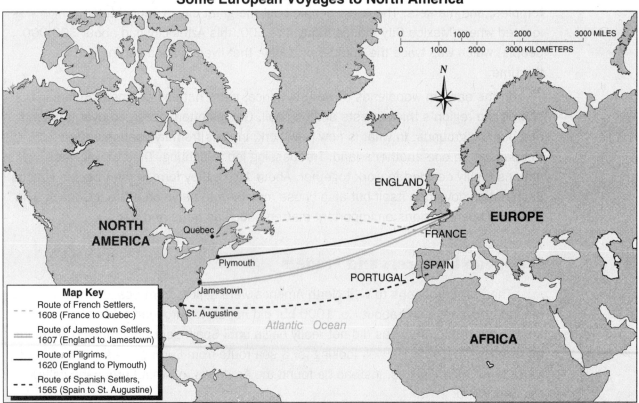

New Americans

The English began their settlement of North America in the early 1600s. Their **colonies** lasted longer and grew larger than many other European settlements. Most English who settled in North America came for religious, political, or economic reasons.

The first long-lasting English settlement in North America was Jamestown, Virginia. Three ships carrying 144 settlers landed there in 1607. That first winter, the settlers faced disease, starvation, and attacks by Native Americans. In time, however, they learned to grow food crops and tobacco.

In 1620, the *Mayflower* set sail from Plymouth, England, with 73 men and boys and 29 women and girls. They were seeking religious freedom from the official Church of England. Their ship landed along the coast of Massachusetts. These settlers, who called themselves *Pilgrims*, also had a difficult first year. Almost half of them died. But a Native American named Squanto taught the survivors how to plant corn, catch fish, and find their way in the wilderness.

Later, a religious group known as Puritans started the Massachusetts Bay Colony. They permitted only followers of their religion to live in their settlements. So some colonists who wanted religious freedom left Massachusetts and set up the colonies of Rhode Island in 1644 and New Hampshire in 1662. Quakers, another religious group, founded Pennsylvania in 1681. They welcomed Spanish Jews, Irish Catholics, and German Lutherans.

As news of these colonies returned to England, more people came to North America looking for land and freedom. Those who had no money to pay their way became **indentured servants.** They promised to work for two to seven years in exchange for their passage to the colonies. Convicted criminals served their sentences in the colonies as indentured servants. Africans were kidnapped and also forced to work in America as indentured servants. By the 1660s, however, colonies were passing laws that made slaves of African-American servants.

Gradually, the 13 British colonies developed their own way of life. This strained their ties with England. By the 1770s, some colonists were ready for independence.

▶ Sequencing Events The **sequence** of events is the order in which things happen. This is also called chronological order. Specific dates and words like *first, second, next,* and *finally* provide clues to the order of events. Reread the paragraphs under "New Americans." Then number the names of the colonies below in the order that they were established.

_____ Pennsylvania

_____ Massachusetts

_____ Virginia

_____ Rhode Island

Thinking About the Article

Practice Vocabulary

▶ **The words below are in the passage in bold type. Study the way each word is used. Then complete each sentence by writing the correct word.**

immigrants	migrated	pueblos
conquistadors	missions	indentured servants

1. The Spanish _____ came to America seeking wealth.

2. Europeans with little money became _____ to pay their way to America.

3. Scientists believe that over many generations the first Americans slowly _____ across North and South America.

4. Spanish priests invited Native Americans to live and learn at the

   _____ .

5. The Anasazi lived in settlements known as _____ .

6. _____ from many parts of the world have moved to North America for a better life.

Understand the Article

▶ **Write the answer to each question.**

7. Immigrants and immigration are topics often argued in the United States today. How would you describe the author's viewpoint on immigrants?

   _____

8. Why did each group of immigrants come to North America?

   _____

9. What difficulties did settlers have in establishing a colony in Jamestown?

   _____

10. The author states that later Native Americans could not resist the Spanish because of European diseases. How could population statistics about Native Americans provide evidence to support this claim?

    _____

    _____

Apply Your Skills

▶ **Circle the letter of the best answer for each question.**

11. Look at the map on page 18. Based on the map, which of the following statements describes the beginnings of European settlement?

    A. European settlers moved west across North America over a long period.

    B. Early English settlements lay north of Spanish settlements.

    C. French settlers arrived about 40 years before the English.

    D. The Spanish first landed in Asia on their way to North America.

12. Review the article, and then select the most recent event below.

    A. The Anasazi raised corn, beans, and squash in what today is the southwestern United States.

    B. The Aztecs in Mexico built an empire with a great city.

    C. The first Americans migrated across a land bridge from Asia.

    D. The English settled at Jamestown, Virginia.

13. Use data for the Jamestown Colony and the group from Plymouth, England that settled in Massachusetts. What was the average number of settlers that came to America with an expedition?

    A. 144

    B. 123

    C. 73

    D. 29

Connect with the Article

▶ **Write your answer to each question.**

14. The Pilgrims and Squanto were better neighbors than later colonists and Native Americans. Give two reasons why you think this was the case.

_____

_____

_____

15. At one time or another, members of your family moved to North America. Why do you think they came?

_____

_____

_____

REVOLUTION AND A NEW REPUBLIC

Vocabulary

prime minister

legislature

boycott

exports

repealed

imports

minutemen

appeasement

The years from 1688 to 1812 were a time of war. France, Spain, and Great Britain fought one another for control of Europe and the Americas. In 1763, Great Britain won a seven-year war with the French in North America.

Great Britain had created one of the largest empires in the world, but the nation was deeply in debt. British King George III decided that his American colonies must help pay the bill. The colonists disagreed and started down the road to war with Great Britain.

Relate to the Topic

This lesson is about the conflict between Great Britain and its American colonies. Describe how this kind of conflict could be similar to conflicts between parents and their teenage children.

_____

_____

_____

Reading Strategy

SKIMMING   A title usually gives the main topic of an article. **Headings** are the names of sections within the article. Headings are set in smaller type than the title, and tell you what details that support the main topic are discussed in each section. Read the title and headings on pages 23 through 25 and skim the text. Then answer the questions.

1. Name three places that the writer will discuss. _____

_____

Hint: Look for words that name places rather than things.

2. What do the words "revolt" and "revolution" suggest about the article?

_____

_____

Hint: Think about how you would use these words.

A New Nation

After Great Britain's long war with France, the British Parliament became more involved in its American colonies. The colonists, who had done as they pleased for many years, did not welcome this new interest. Parliament pushed and the colonists pushed back. In time, the disagreements grew more serious. They led to a war known as the American Revolution.

Great Britain faced a huge bill after the war with France. Nearly half the debt was from the fighting in North America. Therefore Parliament decided that Americans should help pay the bill. Britain's **prime minister,** or head of the Parliament, realized that enforcing some old trade laws in the colonies might help the Treasury.

The money raised from these laws was still not enough to pay the bill. More taxes would raise money, but people in Great Britain already were paying high taxes. So in 1765 Parliament passed the Stamp Act. Colonists who bought certain items or documents had to buy stamps that proved they had paid the tax on those items. Without a stamp that proved they had paid the necessary tax, items like marriage licenses, newspapers, and playing cards were considered stolen or illegal. This angered the colonists who did not have any representatives in Parliament. Therefore they believed that Parliament had no right to tax them. They felt that only a colony's **legislature,** or lawmakers, had that right.

Parliament said its members acted in everyone's interest, including that of the colonists. But the colonists did not accept this. They protested, "No taxation without representation." They **boycotted,** or refused to buy, British products. British merchants suffered when colonists refused to buy their **exports.** These were the products made in Great Britain and sold in the colonies. One year later, Parliament **repealed,** or did away with, the Stamp Act. Colonists celebrated with bonfires and parades. But, the British Parliament continued to add new taxes. The colonies protested the new taxes, and Great Britain sent troops to the colonies to enforce the laws. Soon, conflict erupted into violence. On March 5, 1770, the British opened fire on the colonists after being taunted by them. The British killed three colonists and wounded eight others. This clash is called the Boston Massacre.

▶ Identifying Cause and Effect Every event has at least one cause and one effect. The cause is <u>why</u> something happened. Words like *because, since,* and *reason* signal a cause. The **effect** tells <u>what happened</u> as a result of the cause. Words such as *so, therefore,* and *as a result* signal an effect. Reread the second paragraph under "A New Nation." Then circle the letter of the effect of Great Britain's debt.

   A. Parliament passed new taxes for the colonies.

   B. Britain fought a seven-year war with France.

Revolt and Revolution

A month after the clash in Boston, Parliament repealed all the taxes except the tea tax. British lawmakers wanted to remind the colonists that Parliament had the right and power to tax the colonists. Unexpectedly, the colonists boycotted tea. On the night of December 16, 1773, a group of colonists in Boston dressed up like Native Americans, boarded British ships and dumped more than three hundred chests of British tea into Boston's harbor. This protest against the tea tax became known as the Boston Tea Party.

The British were outraged. In 1774, Parliament passed new laws to punish the colonists. Colonists called the laws the Intolerable Acts because Americans thought the laws made life unbearable.

Events Leading to the American Revolution

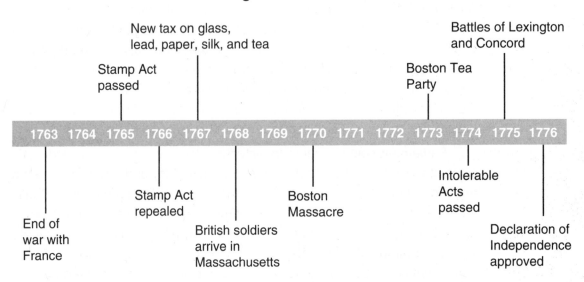

Because of the Intolerable Acts, representatives from 12 of the 13 colonies met in Philadelphia, Pennsylvania, in 1774. They called the meeting the First Continental Congress. The delegates were still willing to remain part of Britain, but they wanted the harsh laws repealed. The colonists also wanted Parliament to know it could not tax them. The delegates voted to meet again in May 1775. But, before they would meet again, the American Revolution began on the night of April 18, 1775 with the Battles of Lexington and Concord. When the Second Continental Congress met again in May 1775, they elected George Washington as Commander in Chief of the Continental Army. Over the next year, fighting between the colonies and Britain broke out in earnest.

By June 1776, the Continental Congress was prepared to declare independence from Britain. Thomas Jefferson wrote the first draft of the Declaration of Independence in June of that year. An eloquent writer and staunch advocate of liberty, Jefferson was just 33 years old at the time. Later, he would become president of the United States.

George Washington's strategy throughout the war was to harass the British, only engaging in battle when necessary. This well-calculated strategy allowed him to conserve the strength of his army. In 1781, with the aid of the French, Washington forced the British to surrender. The colonies were free. They had already adopted the Articles of Confederation on November 15, 1977, which established a loose system of confederate states and a weak central government. In 1781, the Articles were ratified by all the states. However, it soon became clear that a stronger central government was necessary. On March 4, 1789, the Articles of Confederation were replaced by the United States Constitution. George Washington served as the first president of the United States. The next twenty years were spent growing and changing as a new nation. Many believed in Manifest Destiny—the inevitability of expansion of the United States to the Pacific and beyond. This concept was often used to justify the annexation of new territories. However, disputes over land continued.

Growing Pains

The United States and Britain would meet on the battlefields again, however, in the War of 1812. France and Britain had been fighting off and on since the 1790s. When Britain began interfering in America's trade with France, the United States declared war against Britain in 1812. The Americans hoped to quickly reassert independence. Instead, they were thwarted by a series of defeats that included the dramatic burning of the White House and Capitol building in 1814, but they continued fighting.

But, by the end of that year, the Treaty of Ghent ended the war. Neither side gained anything and the Native Americans were supposedly restored their rights, privileges, and possessions. But in reality, this was a turning point for U.S. Indian policy. Historically, Native Americans had most often sided with the French or the British. So as not to encourage strong alliances between them, the United States followed a policy of **appeasement** with the Native Americans, in which they simply tried to avoid conflict. But in the War of 1812, Native Americans fought with the British against the Americans. After the war, the United States adopted a policy of removal— they negotiated over 200 treaties that resulted in Native Americans losing their land. Ninety-nine of these agreements created reservations west of the Mississippi River.

▶ Reading a Timeline A **timeline** shows when a series of events took place. It also shows the order of events. It helps you figure out the time between events as well as cause-and-effect relationships. Look at the timeline on page 24. Then answer the questions.

1. In what year were the colonies first taxed by Britain? _____

2. In what year were protesting colonists killed in Boston? _____

3. Was the Declaration of Independence approved before or after the Battles of

Lexington and Concord? _____

Thinking About the Article

Practice Vocabulary

▶ **The words below are in the passage in bold type. Study the way each word is used. Then complete each sentence by writing the correct word.**

exports	**legislature**	**boycotted**
repealed	**appeasement**	**minutemen**

1. Colonists protested the Stamp Act by refusing to buy British
_____.

2. Parliament _____ the Stamp Act in 1766.

3. Each colony had its own _____ , which made laws for its people.

4. The _____ wanted the colonists to help pay Great Britain's war debt.

5. The U.S. Native American policy prior to the War of 1812 was one of
_____.

6. British trade was hurt after the colonists _____ goods from Great Britain.

Understand the Article

▶ **Write the answer to each question.**

7. How did the colonists react to the Stamp Act?

_____

_____

8. What role did Thomas Jefferson play in the American Revolution?

_____

9. Which detail from the article supports the author's opinion of George Washington as a wise, patient man?

_____

10. The author stated that after the Articles of Confederation were ratified it soon became clear a stronger central government was needed. Why do you think a stronger central government was needed?

_____

_____

Apply Your Skills

▶ **Circle the letter of the best answer for each question.**

11. Which event caused the British to pass the Intolerable Acts?

    A.   the colonial boycott of British products

    B.   the Boston Massacre

    C.   the enforcement of the tea tax

    D.   the Boston Tea Party

12. When discussing the Native Americans' rights, which word from the article implies that the author is biased toward Native Americans?

    A.   restored

    B.   historically

    C.   supposedly

    D.   negotiated

13. Who were the actual losers in the War of 1812?

    A.   The French

    B.   The Americans

    C.   The Native Americans

    D.   The British

Connect with the Article

▶ **Write your answer to each question.**

14. What are your thoughts on the concept of Manifest Destiny? Do we still see traces of it today?

_____

_____

_____

15. Using the American Revolution as an example, how do you think people today might react if laws are enforced unfairly over a long period of time?

_____

_____

_____

THE U.S. CIVIL WAR AND RECONSTRUCTION

Vocabulary

cash crop

Union

Confederacy

abolitionist

Emancipation Proclamation

discrimination

ratify

In the early 1800s, the United States doubled its territory. Each region—the North, the South, and the new West—developed its own character. In the North, many farm workers moved to cities, where they could find work at textile mills. In the South, enslaved African Americans worked long hours on plantations. The cotton that they picked went to mills in the North and in Europe. Other Americans migrated to western lands. There they built towns, farms, and plantations of their own.

These different ways of life led to disagreements. The disagreements became so serious that they threatened to tear the United States apart.

Relate to the Topic

This lesson is about why Americans during the 1860s fought one another in a war that split the country. Think of a time when you and a friend disagreed about an issue that was very important to you. Describe how you tried to resolve your difference. If the issue is unresolved, describe how you feel about it now.

Reading Strategy

SKIMMING TITLES AND HEADINGS   In most informational reading, the title and headings can add to your understanding of the text. They can also help you preview a passage. Skim the title of the article and the headings. Then answer the questions.

1. What do you think the article is about based on the title?

   Hint: Complete this sentence: The title is about _____.

2. Based on a heading, name a topic that you think the writer might discuss in the article.

   Hint: Skim all of the headings first.

Differences Lead to War

In the North, many people were leaving farms to become factory workers. There was a shift from an agricultural society to one dominated by factories and machinery. This shift was known as the Industrial Revolution, and it was just beginning in the United States. Thousands of job-seeking immigrants arrived through northern seaports. By 1860, the North's population was nearing twenty million.

The South's eleven million people included four million enslaved African Americans. Many white Southerners depended on slave labor to grow cash crops, such as tobacco and cotton. A **cash crop** is grown to be sold rather than for personal use. Most Southerners did not hold slaves, but those who did were the South's leaders.

The Many-Sided Slavery Issue

In Congress and in newspapers throughout the country, Americans debated the issue of slavery. Many Northerners saw slavery as immoral. Southern plantation owners feared financial ruin if slavery was outlawed.

The most heated debates centered on whether new states in the West should allow slavery. Congress created plans in 1820 and 1850 to answer this question. But, neither the North nor the South was satisfied. Abraham Lincoln, who was against the expansion of slavery, was elected the United States President in 1860. Several states soon left the United States to form a new nation. In 1861, the Civil War began.

The Civil War was fought between 23 northern states, called the **Union,** and 11 southern states, called the **Confederacy.** Southerners in the Confederacy no longer wanted to be part of the United States. Most Northerners did not think the South had a right to declare itself a separate country. African Americans hoped the Civil War would end slavery.

Before the war, fifteen states allowed slavery. Four of these slave states stayed in the Union. They were called the border states. When Lincoln asked for volunteers to fight for the Union, thousands of free African Americans rushed to sign up. But Lincoln thought the Union might lose the border states to the Confederacy if he allowed African Americans to fight. So the armed forces turned away African-American volunteers. Lincoln explained his war goals in a letter to a New York newspaper:

> My paramount object in this struggle is to save the Union, and is not either to save or destroy slavery. If I could save the Union without freeing any slave I would do it; and if I could save it by freeing all the slaves, I would [do] it; and if I could do it by freeing some and leaving others alone, I would also do that.

▶ Understanding the Main Idea The main idea of a paragraph is often stated in a topic sentence. It is usually the first sentence in a paragraph but is sometimes the last. It tells what the paragraph is about. Underline the topic sentence from Lincoln's letter. Then circle the letter of the statement below that best describes his main idea.

   A. The Civil War must save the Union.

   B. The Civil War must destroy slavery.

The Emancipation Proclamation

Lincoln wanted a quick end to the war. **Abolitionists**—people opposed to slavery—were pressuring him to free enslaved African Americans. However, Lincoln thought he should wait for a Union victory before announcing any decision. In September 1862, the North won a battle at Antietam in Maryland. Five days later, Lincoln issued a written statement. It said that on January 1, 1863, all slaves in states fighting against the United States would be "forever free." This action was called the **Emancipation Proclamation.** Lincoln was still concerned that the border states might leave the Union, so he was very clear that he had not freed the enslaved people in those states. But the war took on a new meaning. African Americans and white Northerners who were against slavery celebrated.

The proclamation did not end slavery in the Confederacy. Lincoln knew that the South would have to be defeated before all the people there would be free. The proclamation also did not end discrimination. **Discrimination** is the unequal and unfair treatment of a person or group. Even free African Americans in the North did not enjoy the same rights that Whites enjoyed. For example, in most states, African Americans could not vote or attend public schools. However, the Emancipation Proclamation opened the door for African Americans to join the military. By the end of the war, about 200,000 African Americans served in the Union army and navy. Many of them had escaped from slavery in the South.

The South surrendered in April 1865, ending the Civil War. African Americans had won their freedom. However, the fight to end discrimination in the United States was just beginning.

Civil War Amendments and Reconstruction

Although the Emancipation Proclamation had freed slaves in many states, the question of slavery on the national level was still unanswered at the end of the Civil War. The Thirteenth Amendment to the United States Constitution formally abolished slavery. It was ratified by the states on December 6, 1865. **Ratify** means the states made the Thirteenth Amendment official by voting for it. As a condition of regaining representation in the federal government, former Confederate states were required to ratify the amendment.

This was only one of many conditions placed on the former Confederate states by the federal government. Congress implemented Reconstruction—a plan to reorganize the Southern states so they could be readmitted to the Union. In addition, Reconstruction worked to change the social order so that blacks and whites could live together in a society without slavery. Reconstruction lasted from 1866 to 1877. The South generally did not welcome Reconstruction and felt it was humiliating. However, many African Americans took advantage of their new opportunities.

One of the new freedoms African Americans enjoyed was citizenship. On July 9, 1868, the Fourteenth Amendment was ratified. The Fourteenth Amendment granted citizenship to all citizens "born or naturalized in the United States," including former slaves. Additionally, the amendment included Reconstruction provisions such as prohibiting former Confederate states from compensating former slave owners for the emancipation of their slaves. Again, the former Confederate states were required to ratify the Fourteenth Amendment to regain their representation in the federal government.

The Fifteenth Amendment prohibited states from not allowing citizens to vote based "on account of race, color, or previous condition of servitude." Some states tried to get around this by instituting voter qualifications that applied to everyone. However, poll taxes and literacy tests clearly discriminated against African Americans who could not afford to pay in order to vote and who had not received a formal education as slaves.

Reconstruction officially ended in 1877 with the inauguration of President Rutherford B. Hayes. In a disputed election, he had gained the support of Southern Democrats by promising to end the harsh Reconstruction policies in the South. Although Reconstruction ended, difficult relationships between whites and African Americans did not.

Confederate forces under General Robert E. Lee prepare to attack Union forces in Pickett's Charge during the Battle of Gettysburg, on July 3, 1863.

▶ **Identifying Point of View in a Historic Context** Writers express their point of view using words. Artists use pictures to show how they feel. Look at the picture above. It shows a part of the Battle of Gettysburg called Pickett's Charge. On July 3, 1863, Confederate forces attacked Union forces, but were defeated. Which detail in the picture suggests that the artist sided with the South?

　　A.　Confederate flags are near the center of the picture.

　　B.　The faces of Union soldiers are clearly shown.

　　　Check your answers on page 226.

Thinking About the Article

Practice Vocabulary

▶ The words below are in the passage in bold type. Study the way each word is used. Then complete each sentence by writing the correct word or words.

cash crop	Union	Confederacy	abolitionists
Emancipation Proclamation		discrimination	ratify

1. Eleven southern states left the _____ and

   formed the _____ .

2. In 1862, President Lincoln announced the _____ .

3. _____ tried to persuade President Lincoln to end slavery.

4. Even free African Americans in the North suffered from

   _____ .

5. In order to rejoin the Union, Southern states had to

   _____ several amendments.

6. Abraham Lincoln's major concern was preserving the

   _____ .

7. An example of a(n) _____ is tobacco.

Understand the Article

▶ Write the answer to each question.

8. Why did plantation owners defend slavery?

   _____

9. How does President Lincoln's quotation in the New York newspaper differ on the subject of slavery from how the article discusses slavery and the Civil War?

   _____

10. How was the Fifteenth amendment directly connected to the Fourteenth Amendment?

   _____

   _____

11. How did the Union military change after the Emancipation Proclamation?

   _____

Apply Your Skills

▶ **Circle the letter of the best answer for each question.**

12. What would the author's view point on Reconstruction likely have been if the author had been living in the South during Reconstruction?

A. The author would likely have felt Reconstruction was needed for the North but not the South.

B. The author would likely have been very angry about Reconstruction.

C. The author would likely have been supportive of Reconstruction.

D. The author would likely have felt that Reconstruction was important.

13. Which Civil War amendment had the purpose of giving freed slaves a voice in government?

A. the Thirteenth Amendment

B. the Fourteenth Amendment

C. the Fifteenth Amendment

D. the Sixteenth Amendment

14. Which best describes the Industrial Revolution?

A. a shift from an urban to a rural society

B. a shift from an agriculture to manufacturing

C. a shift from cash crops to crops for personal use

D. a shift from slave labor to indentured servant labor

Connect with the Article

▶ **Write your answer to each question.**

15. Why do you think people in the South felt humiliated by Reconstruction?

_____

_____

_____

16. What would be your plan for Reconstruction if you had been part of the government at the end of the Civil War?

_____

_____

_____

_____

_____

LESSON 4

THE REFORM MOVEMENT

Vocabulary

child labor

apprentice

master

reformer

literate

In colonial times, a family worked as a team. All family members—even children—shared the work. They tended to animals, planted crops, cooked meals, and cleaned the house and barns together. Children worked six days a week from sunup to sundown. Few went to school.

In the 1800s, Americans began leaving their farms. They found jobs in growing cities and new factory towns. Business owners encouraged their workers' children to work, too. Soon children were doing work that was as hard or as dangerous as the work that adults were doing. In addition, child workers earned only a fraction of an adult's pay. The situation cried out for change.

Relate to the Topic

This lesson is about how some Americans in the early 1900s wanted laws to protect children in the workplace. Write a sentence or two about your early work experiences. How old were you when you first earned money? When did you start your first job? How many hours did you work each week? On what did you spend your wages?

_____

_____

_____

_____

Reading Strategy

RELATING TO WHAT YOU KNOW   There are several ways to help yourself make sense of informational reading. One way is to compare the facts with what you already have read or learned about the topic. Read the paragraph that begins the article on page 35. Then answer the questions.

1. What do you already know about this topic? _____

_____

Hint: When or where might you have heard the term child labor?

2. Write one fact that is new to you. _____

_____

Hint: What dates and other numbers does the writer mention?

34   *Check your answers on page 227.*   UNIT 1   U.S. HISTORY

Child Labor

As factories spread throughout the United States, so did the practice of **child labor,** or in other words, using children as workers. By 1890, one million children had jobs. In the South, most child laborers worked in textile mills, where cotton was made into cloth. In Chicago, many children worked in the meat-packing industry. In New York, they worked in the garment industry. By 1900, more than 1.7 million Americans under 16 years of age had jobs.

Learning a Trade

Child labor was not a new idea. Learning from skilled masters was a common practice in ancient Egypt, Greece, and Rome. It was still the way young people learned a trade in Europe when the American colonies were founded.

During colonial times, many children were working as apprentices by the time they were 12 years old. An **apprentice** is someone who learns a trade, or skill, from an expert called a **master.** Apprentices learned how to make clothing from master tailors. They learned how to make shoes from master cobblers. Hatmakers, blacksmiths, silversmiths, and other skilled business people all trained apprentices. Apprentices worked long, hard days. Being an apprentice was an opportunity for a boy to get ahead. Girls, on the other hand, rarely had the chance to become apprentices.

At the age of 12, Benjamin Franklin became an apprentice to his older brother, James. The older brother was a printer. James agreed to teach Benjamin how to become a good printer. He also provided Benjamin with food, clothing, and a place to live. He promised to take care of Benjamin if he became ill. In return Benjamin had to work hard for five years. He also had to promise not to give away any of his master's printing secrets.

When Franklin finished his apprenticeship at age 17, he had valuable skills. His skills made him capable of contributing to a business. Because he had a trade, he would earn more wages than someone with no special skills. When he could not find work in Boston or New York, he moved to Philadelphia. Within weeks, he was working for a printer. By the time he was 22, he had enough experience to start his own printing shop. Franklin became one of Philadelphia's most respected business leaders.

▶ Comparing and Contrasting. To **compare** people, events, or things is to show how they are alike. The words *also, as well as,* and *like* signal a comparison. To **contrast** is to show how people, events, or things are different. Words that signal a contrast include *however, on the other hand, unlike, although,* and *yet.* Reread the second paragraph under "Learning a Trade." In one sentence, the phrase *on the other hand* signals a contrast. Which two groups are being contrasted?

A. apprentices and masters
B. boys and girls

A Child's Life

Factory owners in the 1800s had jobs that needed little or no training. A ten-year-old child could often handle the work. In fact, some factory owners hired only children. They claimed that children could do certain jobs better than adults. Children ran errands, helped machine operators, and cleaned. Factory owners also paid children less than adults. Unskilled adult workers made about one dime per hour, which came to one dollar for a ten-hour day. Children worked for as little as 50 cents a day.

By the mid-1800s, many states had free public schools. In 1850, nearly 3.3 million children went to elementary schools. Most parents wanted their children to go to school. But because factory jobs paid adults so little, some parents needed their children to work, too. Before 1900, most workers made only about $400 to $500 per year. Yet the basic cost of living was about $600. Many parents could not pay their family's living expenses without the money their children earned. They could not afford to let their children go to school.

Children worked in factories, but they also worked in other places. Some worked in coal mines. Others worked in country stables. Some worked on city sidewalks, selling newspapers or shining shoes. Many children still worked on farms. They harvested berries, tobacco, sugar beets, and other vegetables. However, children in factories and mines worked under the most dangerous and unhealthy conditions. In paint factories, child workers breathed in toxic fumes. In the garment industry, young laborers hunched over sewing machines and developed curved spines. In coal mines, boys as young as nine years old inhaled coal dust all day.

Many children worked in the textile industry. The white objects in the photograph are large spools of thread.

© Houghton Mifflin Harcourt • Image Credits: National Archives and Records Administration

The Push for Reform

People who work to change things for the better are called **reformers.** In the 1890s and early 1900s, many Americans worked hard to improve the lives of children. These reformers wanted laws that set a minimum working age. They also wanted to limit the number of hours children could work. They felt children should be kept out of dangerous jobs. Most reformers believed that every child should have the chance to go to school.

Reformers worked to make people aware of the conditions that children faced in the workplace. Some reformers created the National Child Labor Committee. This group hired people to investigate factories and mines. One of these investigators was Lewis Hine. He wrote about the children he met and took photos of them at work. In 1908 he took the photo shown on page 36.

Factory owners hired guards to keep Hine away. The owners did not want anyone to take photos of their workers. They were afraid to let people see what conditions were like. But Hine found ways to get inside the factories. He often disguised himself as a Bible salesman or a fire inspector. Sometimes, he pretended to be a photographer eager to take pictures of the latest machines. He always kept his notebook hidden in a pocket. He used his notes to write many articles. His photographs, however, were more powerful than any words he wrote.

Several states passed laws to protect children as the result of the work of Hine and others. For example, the Illinois Factory Act of 1893 stopped employers from hiring children under 14 to work more than eight hours a day. By 1914, every state but one had child-labor laws with a minimum age limit. The age was 12 in several states in the South, 15 in South Dakota, and 16 in Montana. Most laws also banned children from working until they were **literate,** which means they could read and write.

Often states failed to enforce their laws. As a result, many Americans demanded a national law that the United States government and its federal agents would enforce. But business people across the nation disapproved of any such law.

Several times, Congress passed child-labor laws, but the Supreme Court ruled them unconstitutional. In 1925, reformers even proposed a Constitutional amendment that would limit child labor. However, the amendment failed to win enough support. Finally, in 1938 Congress passed a national child-labor law. The law made it illegal for most businesses to hire children under the age of 16. Children under the age of 18 could not work at dangerous jobs. But the law failed to protect all children. For example, it did not include farm workers. It also failed to stop child labor during World War II. When adults left their jobs to join the armed forces, states ignored the law and allowed young teenagers to work long hours.

▶ Understanding a Photo As proof of the need for laws to protect children, Hine used photos like the one on page 36. Which charge would the details in the photo support?

    A. Child workers lack adult supervision.

    B. Children work in unhealthy conditions.

Thinking About the Article

Practice Vocabulary

▶ **The words below are in the passage in bold type. Study the way each word is used. Then complete each sentence by writing the correct word.**

child labor	apprentice	master
reformers	literate	

1. _____ was common from the nation's beginning.

2. In order to make people aware of the conditions that children faced in the workplace, _____ created the National Child Labor Committee.

3. From ancient times, the best way for a young person to learn a skill was to study under a(n) _____.

4. In the early 1900s, many immigrants moved to the United States and needed to become _____ in English.

5. A(n) _____ spent years learning a trade from an expert.

Understand the Article

▶ **Write the answer to each question.**

6. Suppose that in 1914, five of the states in the south had a minimum age limit of 12. What was the median minimum age limit for child laborers in these southern states, South Dakota, and Montana?

   _____

7. Is the following statement from the article a fact or an opinion? "In the garment industry, young laborers hunched over sewing machines and developed curved spines?"

   _____

8. Why did many factory owners hire children?

   _____

9. Why did factory owners try to keep Lewis Hine from visiting their factories?

   _____

Apply Your Skills

▶ **Circle the letter of the best answer for each question.**

10. What type of correlation would a line graph that shows the average minimum age limit each year from the late 1800s to the early 1900s show if age is graphed on the *y*-axis and the year is graphed on the *x*-axis?

    A. positive correlation

    B. negative correlation

    C. no correlation

    D. maximum negative correlation

11. Look again at the photograph on page 36. Which phrase best describes the working conditions?

    A. no fresh air

    B. dirty workplace

    C. dangerous tasks

    D. unsafe machinery

12. Which sentence states a true contrast between apprentices in colonial times and child workers in the early 1900s?

    A. Both apprentices and boys in coal mines worked long hours.

    B. Masters and factory owners supplied their workers with clothing.

    C. An apprentice earned better wages than a child worker in a factory.

    D. An apprentice learned more valuable skills than a factory worker.

Connect with the Article

▶ **Write your answer to each question.**

13. There is an old saying that "one picture is worth a thousand words." How does this saying apply to Hine's photograph on page 36?

    ....

    ....

14. Many teenagers have part-time jobs in which they work 20 to 30 hours a week during the school year. To help protect young workers, suggest two guidelines for an employer of teenagers.

    ....

    ....

WORLD WAR I

The early 1900s was a time of great change around the world. Many nations were growing and changing because of advances in science and industry. These changes led to conflicts between countries, which eventually led to World War I.

World War I was very different from any other war in history. It was the first war in which poisonous gas was used. It was also the most devastating war at the time in terms of the number of casualties, soldiers who died in combat. Nearly 9 million soldiers were killed.

Vocabulary

sphere of influence

alliance

imperialism

nationalism

militarism

neutral

stalemate

Relate to the Topic

This lesson is about World War I, its causes, and its outcomes. Write a sentence or two about a conflict you have had and how it was resolved.

What was the cause of the conflict?

_____

_____

How was it resolved?

_____

_____

Reading Strategy

USING VISUALS   Informational text often uses visuals to help explain concepts or show ideas. Knowing how to use these visuals can help you to better understand the information in an article. Look at the visual on page 42.

1. What information is shown on the map?

_____

Hint: Look at the map key.

2. How does looking at the map help you to better understand the information in the article?

_____

Hint: Is there information on the map that is not in the article?

The First World War

In the forty years before World War I, western countries and the countries in their **spheres of influence** were in a time of change. A sphere of influence is the territory over which one nation has political or economic influence. Scientific and industrial revolutions had changed life dramatically. But these changes naturally led to conflicts. Countries became nervous about maintaining their authority. They also wanted to expand their wealth and territories. While doing this, countries also looked to form **alliances** with other countries they could rely on in times of war. An alliance is a formal agreement between two or more nations to cooperate for specific purposes.

The start of World War I is easy to identify. A Serbian nationalist assassinated Archduke Ferdinand of Austria-Hungary on June 28, 1914. This event touched off what would become World War I. After the assassination, countries in Europe quickly joined sides by strengthening existing alliances or forming new ones. Imperialism, nationalism, and militarism around the world at that time were factors in the war, too.

Imperialism is a policy of extending a nation's power and control. Governments operating under imperialism try to spread their power and influence. Imperialism is what led European nations to colonize new areas during colonial times. Most countries at the time wanted more wealth and territory. By getting new territories, they could increase their sphere of influence.

Many countries at this time also had a strong sense of **nationalism**. Nationalism is the feeling of pride that people have in their country. This feeling often comes with a belief that their country is better and more important than others. As part of nationalism and imperialism, countries of this time were building up their militaries in case of war. **Militarism** is a policy in which it is very important to have a prepared military. So, while the assassination sparked the fire for World War I, the practice of imperialism, nationalism, and militarism practiced by so many nations fueled the fire.

Alliances

Natural alliances formed between countries in Europe. Many agreements had already been set in place before World War I began. Not all agreements were honored when World War I started. As far back as 1882, Germany, Austria-Hungary, and Italy formed the Triple Alliance. They all signed a document promising each other military assistance in time of war. There were other alliances made as well. But, by the time of World War I, not all alliances were still together. Italy, for example, decided to fight with Britain, and against Germany and Austria-Hungary, in the war.

The two "sides" in World War I were known as the Allied Powers and the Central Powers. A map of Europe shows that the Central Powers of Germany, Austria-Hungary, Bulgaria, and Turkey were surrounded by the major Allied Powers of Britain, France, Italy, and Russia. Many smaller countries in the Balkans also joined the Allied Powers as did Morocco and Algeria in northern Africa. Some countries remained **neutral**, that is they did not get involved, during the war. Norway, Sweden, and Denmark did not become involved. Neither did Spain.

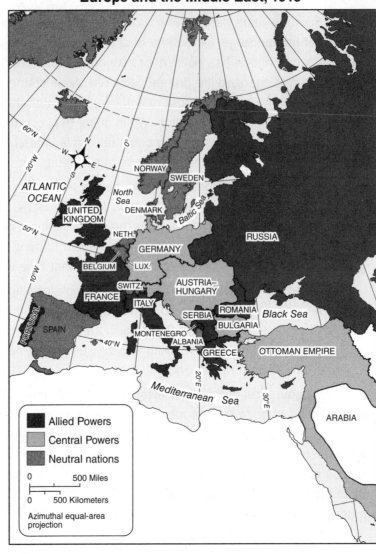

Europe and the Middle East, 1915

▶ **Using a Map** A map may show political information or geographic information, or both. This map shows the countries involved in World War I, so it is a political map. The countries that fought for the Allied Powers are shown in black and the countries that fought for the Central Powers are shown in light gray. Which side had more countries fighting together?

    A. the Allied Powers

    B. the Central Powers

The Russian Revolution

The countries involved in the war believed it would be over quickly. But it continued for four years. The war was at a **stalemate**, or standstill, for much of the time. This stalemate made life in many of the countries difficult. In Russia, for example, food was scarce. Many Russians felt that the government had failed them in the war. This led to the Russian Revolution of 1917. The old government was overthrown, and a new communist government took power.

The United States and World War I

The United States did not enter World War I at the beginning of the war. It tried to remain neutral, and not to get involved. The main reason the United States entered the war was because Germany was attacking passenger and merchant ships in the Atlantic Ocean, including American ones. This angered President Woodrow Wilson. He asked Congress to declare war on Germany. The United States entered World War I on December 7, 1917 on the side of the Allies.

Shortly after the United States entered the war, President Wilson outlined his plans for ending the war. He wanted to bring a "just and secure peace." His plans are known as Wilson's Fourteen Points. The points included ideas about how to divide up territories. They also included ideas about freedom of the seas and free trade. These points were about how to prevent such a war from happening again. The fourteenth point suggested creating a League of Nations to protect "the integrity of great and small states alike."

On June 28, 1919, the Treaty of Versailles, which was the peace agreement between Germany and the Allied Forces, was signed and ended World War I. Wilson tried to include his fourteen points in the Treaty of Versailles. He was unable to get any of the points included, except for the formation of the League of Nations. Although the Treaty of Versailles ended the war, it did not solve many of the issues that started the war in the first place.

Neutrality Acts

Several years after the war ended, the United States wrote a series of new laws to keep the United States from becoming involved in another war. These laws were known as the Neutrality Acts. They prevented the United States from becoming involved with countries that were hostile.

▶ MAKING INFERENCES When you make an inference, you use information you know to come up with an idea. What can you infer might have happened if Russia had not been part of an alliance in World War I?

    A. Russia would have been defeated because the country was weak from a revolution.

    B. Russia would have won because the new government was stronger than the old government.

Check your answers on page 228.

Thinking About the Article

Practice Vocabulary

▶ **Use the bold type words from the article. Study the way each word is used. Then complete each sentence by writing the correct word or words.**

sphere of influence	**alliance**	**nationalism**	**imperialism**
militarism	**neutral**	**stalemate**	

1. Countries that were not part of either _____ in World War II were most likely _____.

2. _____ is a strong pride in one's country while _____ is the building up of a country's military.

3. Countries that practiced _____ were trying to build their wealth.

4. A country's _____ often extended beyond its borders.

5. World War I lasted longer than expected because it was at a(n) _____.

Understand the Article

▶ **Write your answer to each question.**

6. How did the alliance system make World War I into a *world* war?

_____

7. What detail supports the claim that nationalism could be dangerous?

_____

8. Which word best describes what was happening for most of World War I? _____ How did this affect the Russian Revolution?

_____

9. How does the author portray Woodrow Wilson? Cite evidence from the article to support your answer. _____

_____

10. The Neutrality Acts were passed in the 1930s. Why do you think the government may have felt it was necessary at that time to pass them?

_____

Apply Your Skills

▶ **Circle the letter of the best answer for each question.**

11. What was the purpose of the League of Nations?

    A.   to ensure peace among nations

    B.   to protect countries from alliances

    C.   to punish German, Austria-Hungary, and Serbia for the war

    D.   to control the governments of the Central Powers

12. The author would have the most credibility if this article were found in which source?

    A.   a textbook

    B.   a government website

    C.   a newspaper

    D.   a magazine

13. Which of the following would a country most likely practice to be seen as a country that will protect itself?

    A.   imperialism

    B.   nationalism

    C.   militarism

    D.   neutrality

Connect with the Article

▶ **Write your answer to each question.**

14. Do you feel there is nationalism in the United States today? Explain how it affects or does not affect our relationships with other countries.

_____

_____

_____

15. Would you have agreed with the Neutrality Acts if you had been living in the United States in the 1930s? Why or why not?

_____

_____

_____

WORLD WAR II

Only 21 years after the end of World War I, countries across the globe clashed again. By the late 1930s, Germany, Italy, and Japan had built up their armed forces. They began threatening their neighbors.

As in World War I, the United States was not involved at the start of World War II. Many Americans in the 1930s felt that isolationism was a good policy. **Isolationism** is a policy of staying out of the affairs of other countries. The nation still was recovering from the serious economic problems of the Great Depression and concerned with its own well-being. President Franklin D. Roosevelt had created programs that helped people keep their farms, get jobs, and stay in business. Putting people to work boosted the economy. World War II, however, helped American industry really regain its strength.

Vocabulary

isolationism

Nazism

Fascism

totalitarianism

internment camps

Holocaust

decolonization

Relate to the Topic

This lesson is about how Americans fighting overseas and working in factories at home helped win World War II. Write a sentence or two about being part of a team. Have you been a member of a sports team or any other type of group effort? What united the team? Why do you think your team accomplished what it did?

_____

_____

_____

_____

Reading Strategy

SCANNING A GRAPH Social studies materials often use graphs to illustrate information. You can scan, or quickly look over, a graph to find out what kinds of information it includes. **Scanning** is another way to preview something. Scan the title, labels of the graph, and key of the graph on page 49. Then answer the questions.

1. What information does the graph illustrate?

_____

_____

Hint: Look at the title and the words along the side.

2. What years does the graph cover?

_____

Hint: Look at the numbers along the bottom.

War-Time Opportunities

On December 7, 1941, Japanese planes bombed the American fleet in Pearl Harbor, Hawaii. The next day the United States declared war on Japan. Thousands of young workers left their jobs to join the armed forces. This meant fewer workers in factories. Yet war production required millions of skilled workers. Enemy bombs had destroyed many weapons factories in other Allied countries. As a result, the American defense industry had more work than ever. The defense industry produced weapons, planes, and other military supplies.

American factories had to make military supplies for American troops and the rest of the Allies—the British, the French, and the Soviets. The Allies fought together against the Axis Powers—the Germans, the Italians, and the Japanese. Germany followed **Nazism**, which was the belief that the white race was better than all other races. Italy was now a fascist country. **Fascism** is a system in which the government is ruled by a dictator. Japan had characteristics of **totalitarianism**, in which the government controls every aspect of the lives of its people.

The Doors Open

For years, American employers had discriminated against African-American workers. Many companies in the defense industry had policies against hiring any African Americans. Others had labor unions that did not welcome African-American members. Labor unions help workers get higher wages and better work rules from employers.

African-American leaders wanted to end discrimination in the workplace. They planned a march on Washington, D.C., in 1941 to get the attention of President Roosevelt and the nation. Leaders of the march wanted to convince Roosevelt that African Americans had a right to be treated as most white Americans were treated.

One week before the scheduled march, Roosevelt issued a presidential order. It was the first time since the Reconstruction era (right after the Civil War) that the federal government took action against discrimination. The order required that factories with defense contracts end discrimination in hiring and promoting employees. Defense contracts are agreements that a government makes with companies so that they will produce goods needed by the military. To keep their defense contracts, these companies could no longer refuse to hire or promote workers because of race or religion. This opened the door for both African Americans and women.

▶ **Summarizing Information** When you summarize, you shorten a large amount of information into its major points. Reread the text under the heading "The Doors Open." Which statement best summarizes that information?

    A. A need for workers during World War II opened doors for minorities and women.

    B. Women faced discrimination in labor unions before World War II.

Major Events in the War

African Americans were not the only group discriminated against in the United States during World War II. Thousands of Japanese Americans were sent to **internment camps** run by the government. It did not matter if they were American citizens or not. After the Japanese attacked Pearl Harbor, Japanese Americans were instantly viewed with distrust. Japanese Americans were forced to leave their homes and businesses by executive order. The camps were prison-like. Amazingly, the residents eventually formed communities with schools, newspapers, gardens, musical groups, and sports teams. The Japanese Americans remained very loyal to the United States despite their situation and more than 300,000 Japanese American men enlisted in the armed forces.

As terrible as internment camps were for Japanese Americans, they were nothing compared to the horrors of concentration camps in Europe. The Nazis in Germany had a plan called the "Final Solution." The plan was to eliminate all European Jews. Nazis considered this as a necessary step in preserving the white German race, referred to as *Aryan*. The Nazi's persecution and murdering of approximately six million Jews is known as the **Holocaust**.

Early in World War II, Germany controlled territory in large parts of Europe. In May, 1942, the British attacked Germans in Germany for the first time and, over the next few years, many German cities were reduced to rubble. Germany surrendered on May 8, 1945. The United States dropped atomic bonds on the cities of Hiroshima and Nagasaki in Japan in August, 1945, killing 120,000 people. The Japanese surrendered on September 2, 1945. Approximately 55 million were killed around the world during World War II.

After World War II, the process of **decolonization** began. Colonies became independent of their colonizing countries. Some transitions were peaceful, while others were violent. Both the United States and the Soviet Union had taken positions against colonialism. This pressured European countries into giving their colonies independence.

A Changing Labor Force

World War II brought great changes to the United States labor force. Americans produced twice as many military supplies as Germany, Italy, and Japan combined. During 1939, American workers made about 6,000 planes. In 1944 they made almost 100,000 planes. American workers made military supplies in less time than ever before. The time for making an aircraft carrier was cut from 35 months to 15 months. Factories were open day and night.

Working for the Allies' victory was an experience many workers would never forget. A welder in New York explained the change. She said: "Rosie the Riveter was the woman who got up early in the morning when it was still dark and went to work and came in smiling, drinking coffee, working hard, finding herself as a new person."

Yet, many of these new workers were unemployed within a year after the war ended. The GI bill, passed in 1944, provided benefits to World War II veterans. These included grants for college tuition, job training, and hiring privileges. As veterans were rehired for their old jobs, about four million women either lost of left their jobs. Three-fourths of the women workers during the war were married, and many husbands did not want their wives working outside the home.

Neither women nor African Americans were willing to return to the way things were before the war. They now knew what it was like to have good jobs. They had enjoyed the benefits of a good wage. An African-American woman years later recalled the feeling:

A lot of blacks . . . decided they did not want to go back to what they were doing before. They did not want to walk behind a plow. They wouldn't get on the back of the bus anymore.

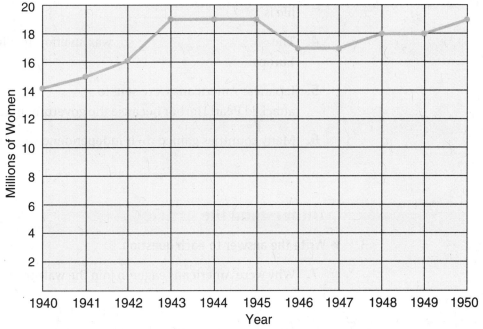

Women in the Labor Force, 1940–1950

To encourage more women to work in the war effort, the government launched the "Rosie the Riveter" campaign.

▶ Reading a Line Graph A **line graph** usually shows how something has changed over time. According to the graph above, which statement best sums up what happened between the beginning of World War II and the height of the war in 1943?

A. The number of women in the labor force increased.

B. The number of women in the labor force decreased.

Check your answers on page 229.   **49**

Thinking About the Article

Practice Vocabulary

▶ The words below are in the passage in bold type. Study the way each word is used. Then complete each sentence by writing the correct word.

internment camps	nazism	totalitarianism
fascism	Holocaust	decolonization

1. _____ was the belief that the Aryan race was superior to other races.

2. In _____ , the government is controlled by a dictator.

3. A system of government in which the government controls all aspects of life is _____ .

4. The _____ was an effort to eliminate the Jews in Europe.

5. Japanese Americans were sent to _____ after Japan attacked Pearl Harbor because the government did not trust them.

6. Many countries gained their independence through

_____ .

Understand the Article

▶ Write the answer to each question.

7. Why were Americans eager to join the wartime labor force?

_____

8. How do you think World War I may have influenced isolationism in the 1930s?

_____

_____

9. How did the GI bill affect the millions of women who had gone to work during the war?

_____

10. Imagine the graph on page 49 showed men in the labor force instead of women. How would it look different? Explain why.

_____

Apply Your Skills

▶ **Circle the letter of the best answer for each question.**

11. Which country was not a member of the Axis Powers in World War II?

    A. Japan

    B. France

    C. Italy

    D. Germany

12. Look at the line graph on page 49. Which statement best summarizes what the changes on the graph show?

    A. Many women were unwilling to return to the way life was before the war.

    B. World War II affected the wages of American factory workers.

    C. Former soldiers returned to their old jobs after the war.

    D. No job seemed too tough for women.

13. Look at the line graph on page 49. Which of the following could be a cause for the dip in the number of women in the labor force in 1946?

    A. women leaving to have children

    B. men heading off to war

    C. women not wanting to work

    D. men returning to their jobs

Connect with the Article

▶ **Write your answer to each question.**

14. How might you have reacted if you were a Japanese American in an internment camp during World War II?

    _____

    _____

15. Since World War II, there have been other instances of genocide, in which an entire group of people has been singled out and killed, like the Jews in the Holocaust. Do you think the United States has a responsibility to intervene in these situations? Explain your answer.

    _____

    _____

    _____

THE COLD WAR

The Soviet Union, the United States, Great Britain, and France were Allies during World War II. Afterward, however, they had very different ideas about how to treat the defeated Germany. The Soviet Union took over East Germany. The United States, Great Britain, and France controlled West Germany. The Allies even divided Berlin, Germany's capital.

The Soviet Union wanted control over even more of Europe. The other Allies wanted all European countries to become independent. These differences led the Soviet Union and the United States into a tense struggle for world power called the Cold War.

Vocabulary

capitalism

communism

containment

Cold War

blockade

Relate to the Topic

This lesson is about how world politics changed after World War II, leading to the Cold War and major events of the Cold War. Think about what you have heard or seen about the Cold War. Then write two facts that you know about the war.

_____

_____

_____

Reading Strategy

SKIMMING HEADINGS   **Headings** in informational text are helpful in identifying main points in an article. You can skim the headings to find out what kind of information will be included in the article. Skim the headings in the article on the following pages. Then write two questions that you expect the article to answer based on the headings.

_____

_____

_____

_____

Check your answers on page 230.

The Race for World Power

World War II had left much of the Soviet Union's western lands in shambles. The Soviet people were starting over. Many had lost not only family members but also their homes during the war. With so much destruction, the Soviet leaders and people were bitter. They wanted to punish Germany. The Soviets believed that a weak Germany was their best protection against another war. So they stripped East Germany of its factories and other resources. The Soviets also wanted to control their eastern European neighbors, some of whom had once belonged to Russia.

The Cold War

After World War II, the United States, Great Britain, and France were still allies. They believed that a rich Germany was the best protection against another war. These Allies worked to return West Germany to normal. Americans gave West Germans financial help to rebuild their shops, factories, homes, and a capitalist economy. **Capitalism** is an economic system in which the means of production are owned privately, not by the government.

The Soviet Union had a different point of view. It wanted to force its communist system on all of eastern Europe. **Communism** is both a political system and an economic system. A small group of people, those who lead the Communist Party, run the government. The party also controls the economy and most property.

Eventually the Soviets gained control of Poland, Czechoslovakia, Hungary, Romania, Bulgaria, and Albania. They made sure each country, including East Germany, had a communist government. In 1949, the West made West Germany an independent nation. The Soviets soon made East Germany an independent nation, too, but they continued to control its leaders and those of other eastern European countries. The Soviets also helped Communists in China, the Soviets' neighbor to the east. The Chinese Communists gained control of China in 1949.

Some Americans feared that the Communists might take over the world. In 1947, the United States announced a policy called **containment.** This policy was designed to stop communism from spreading without going to war. Instead, the United States sent military and economic aid to help threatened countries fight the Communists themselves.

From 1945 to 1989, the United States and the Soviet Union struggled for world power in what has been called the **Cold War.** The two countries' military forces never fought each other directly, even though tensions were often high.

Fighting Communism

One way the United States fought against Communism was to help democratic countries that were under threat of communism. The Truman Doctrine, in 1947, provided for military, political, and economic aid. This was different than the policy of avoiding involvement in foreign affairs. President Truman argued that American security depended on stopping the spread of Soviet totalitarianism.

In 1947, Secretary of State George C. Marshall proposed a plan to rebuild Europe. In March 1948, Congress passed the Marshall Plan. The plan gave more than $12 billion to rebuild Western Europe. It allowed Western Europe to develop industries again, which put people back to work. It was good for America's economy because Western Europe became a market for American goods. Economists have debated just how much the Marshall Plan helped. Whether or not it did, Secretary of State Marshall received a Nobel Prize for peace for his efforts.

Worsening Relations

In June, 1948, relations between the United States and the Soviet Union worsened. When Germany was divided between Britain, France, the United States, and the Soviet Union, each country took a part of Berlin as well. East Berlin was controlled by the Soviet Union. West Berlin was divided between France, Britain, and the United States. But Berlin was surrounded by East Germany. For this reason, there was conflict over whether West Berlin should remain divided by the Allies, or come under Soviet control. In addition, France, the United States, and Britain had been planning to create a new German state from their zones. They planned to introduce the *Deutschmark*, a form of money, to West Berlin. When the Soviets found out, they created a **blockade** of West Berlin. They blocked roads, railroads, and water routes to the city. No supplies could get into the city. The United States and Britain responded by airlifting food and fuel into the city. At one point during the blockade, an aircraft landed every 45 seconds at Tempelhof Airport in West Berlin. The United States and Britain proved they could get around the blockade, so the Soviet Union finally lifted it. In all, the blockade lasted from June 24, 1948 until May 12, 1949.

New Alliances

The Berlin Blockade and other events in 1947 and 1948 caused the United States to be concerned for the security of Western European nations. In 1949, the United States, Canada, and several Western European nations created the North Atlantic Treaty Organization, or NATO. NATO's goal was to provide security against the Soviet Union. The countries of NATO agreed that an attack against one of them would be considered an attack against all of them. Today, NATO is still the largest peacetime military alliance in the world. It even includes some former Soviet states.

The Federal Republic of Germany (West Germany) became part of NATO in 1955. This worried the Soviet Union. So the Soviet Union and several Eastern European countries formed the Warsaw Pact. It was a political and military alliance just like NATO. The Warsaw Pact supposedly was organized around decisions being made by all members. However, the Soviet Union controlled most of the decisions.

▶ **Drawing Conclusions** To draw conclusions, you must identify what facts are important. Then you judge or decide what the facts tell you about the subject. A judgment made from examining facts is a conclusion. Which of the following facts supports the conclusion that the Soviet Union blockade of West Germany did not achieve its goals?

    A. East Berlin was part of the Soviet Union.

    B. The United States and Britain proved they could get around the blockade.

Cold War Presidents

The United States had several presidents during the Cold War. Lyndon B. Johnson became president in 1963 after President John F. Kennedy was assassinated. Johnson challenged the United States to "build a great society, a place where the meaning of man's life matches the marvels of man's labor." In 1965, the Great Society program became Johnson's plan for Congress. It included money for conservation, beautification, and protection of the right to vote. Medicare, which is government health insurance for the elderly, was also part of Johnson's Great Society.

Richard Nixon was the next president after Johnson. President Nixon succeeded in reducing tensions with the Soviet Union. He had summit meetings with Soviet leader Leonid Brezhnev. They made a treaty to limit nuclear weapons. Unfortunately, Nixon is best remembered for the Watergate scandal. During the 1972 presidential campaign, there was a break-in at an office. It was tied to officials on Nixon's re-election committee. When it was discovered that Nixon tried to sidetrack the investigation, it became likely that Congress would try to remove him from office. Instead, he resigned.

The Berlin Wall

During the 1980s, President Ronald Reagan and Soviet leader Mikhail Gorbachev met at several summits that helped bring the Cold War to a close. The Soviet Union's grasp on Eastern Europe lessened with the collapse of the Berlin Wall in 1989. Communist governments in Eastern Europe began falling. Then in December, 1991, the Soviet Union broke peacefully apart into many separate nations. Russia is the largest and most powerful of these countries.

▶ **Using Visuals** Historical images can help give you a better view of what was happening at a certain time in history. Which statement best describes the mood in the photograph of the Berlin Wall?

    A. The Berlin Wall helped create an atmosphere of cooperation.

    B. The Berlin Wall was an unfriendly reminder of the Cold War.

Check your answers on page 230.

Thinking About the Article

Practice Vocabulary

▶ **The words below are in the passage in bold type. Study the way each word is used. Then complete each sentence by writing the correct word or words.**

communism   containment   Cold War

capitalism   blockade

1. In the _____ , Soviets and Americans opposed each other without any direct military conflict between them.

2. Americans thought that the _____ policy was the answer to stopping the spread of communism.

3. Americans participated in _____ , while the Soviet point of view was one of _____ .

4. The Soviets cut off access to Berlin during the Berlin

_____ .

Understand the Article

▶ **Write the answer to each question.**

5. Why did the Soviets try to control other European countries?

_____

6. How are the Marshall Plan and the Truman Doctrine examples of the United States becoming a world power?

_____

7. How is an article written by a Soviet citizen in 1955 likely to be different from this article?

_____

8. Which alliance was the Soviet Union a part of during the Cold War?

_____ Why was it formed?

_____

9. Why was Germany divided at the end of World War II?

_____

_____

Apply Your Skills

▶ **Circle the letter of the best answer for each question.**

10. Which best describes the author's view point on the Great Society?

    A.   The author feels it was too hard to achieve.

    B.   The author feels that it was a wise plan with excellent ideas.

    C.   The author feels that the plan was too costly.

    D.   The author feels that it was a wasteful plan.

11. Which word from the paragraph about Richard Nixon shows the author feels he did some very good things in addition to the Watergate scandal?

    A.   unfortunately

    B.   sidetrack

    C.   remove

    D.   scandal

12. Which event was partly responsible for the falling of communist governments in Eastern Europe?

    A.   the break up of the Soviet Union

    B.   President Nixon's resignation

    C.   the Marshall Plan

    D.   the fall of the Berlin Wall

Connect with the Article

▶ **Write your answer to each question.**

13. Why do you think the United States and the Soviet Union had different attitudes toward Germany after World War II?

_____

_____

_____

14. Think about the Truman Doctrine and the Marshall Plan. Do you think it was the responsibility of the United States to provide assistance? How do you think things might have ended up differently if the United States had not provided assistance?

_____

_____

_____

CIVIL RIGHTS

Vocabulary

segregation

intermarriage

suffrage

constitutionality

NAACP

After the Civil War, the Civil War amendments guaranteed African Americans citizenship and protected their right to vote. Laws, however, must be enforced to be effective. Often these laws were ignored. Even in the northern states where abolitionists had worked to outlaw slavery, African Americans still faced discrimination.

It took decades for African Americans to achieve equality. Sadly, even with full legal rights, African Americans still face discrimination in the United States.

Relate to the Topic

This lesson is about civil rights. These are the basic rights of citizens that are protected by law. Think about the Bill of Rights. Write down as many civil rights as you can.

_____

_____

_____

_____

Reading Strategy

USING A TITLE TO PREVIEW   The title of an article can help you identify the main topic and focus your reading. Read the title at the top of page 59.

1. What is the main topic of the article according to the title?

_____

Hint: What is the most important word or words in the title?

2. How does knowing the main topic help you to think about what you will read?

_____

Hint: What information will you look for as you read?

The Fight for Civil Rights

Jim Crow Laws

From after the Civil War in the 1880s until the 1960s, many states in America enforced segregation. **Segregation** is separation. Racial segregation is separation of people based on race. Racial segregation was enforced through "Jim Crow" laws. Jim Crow was a black character in minstrel shows at the time. These laws had legal punishments. For example, one could be punished for associating with a person from another race. Common Jim Crow laws included forbidding **intermarriage**. In intermarriage, the spouses are of two different races. Many businesses were ordered to keep their black and white customers separated too.

Other Jim Crow laws were very specific. In Georgia, for example, an amateur African American baseball team was not allowed to play baseball within two blocks of a playground devoted to the white race. This was also true of white baseball teams— they could not play within two blocks of a park for African Americans. So, on the surface, the laws were "equal." But in reality, there were many more parks for whites than there were for African Americans and the parks for whites were nicer. Jim Crow laws didn't only separate, they discriminated.

Segregation and Jim Crow laws also kept African American and white children in separate schools. Again, the reality of this was that schools for African Americans were of poor quality compared to schools for whites.

Women's Suffrage and Civil Rights

Although civil rights are often thought of in relation to African Americans in the Untied States, women fought for civil rights as well. The women's rights movement had begun in the mid-1800s. However, the Civil War interrupted the women's rights movement. After the war, the Fourteenth Amendment defined *citizens* and *voters* as *male*. Freed slaves gained the right to vote, but not women. When the war ended, the women's rights movement picked up steam again. The first women's rights convention in the United States was held in Seneca Falls, New York in 1848.

The American Equal Rights Association was formed. Its goal was universal suffrage. **Suffrage** is the right to vote. Slowly, progress was made. By 1913, women had gained the right to vote in nine states. In 1918, President Wilson gave his support to women's suffrage. In 1919, the Nineteenth Amendment was passed through Congress. On August 26, 1920, the Nineteenth Amendment was adopted after being ratified by the states. Women had gained the right to vote.

▶ Identifying Cause and Effect Every event has at least one cause and one effect. An event may also have multiple causes and multiple effects. The cause is *why* something happened and the effect is *what* happened. Reread the paragraphs under "Jim Crow Laws." What was an effect of the racial segregation that was enforced by Jim Crow laws?

   A. African Americans felt inferior.   B. African Americans felt superior.

Court Cases

The Civil Rights Act of 1875 made it a crime for an individual to discriminate against a person. However, the Supreme Court struck down the 1875 act in 1883. They said that the Fourteenth Amendment did not give Congress authority to prevent discrimination by private individuals. They felt that people who had been racially discriminated against should take it up with the states, not the federal government. But state governments were passing Jim Crow laws. In Louisiana, one of these laws required separate compartments on trains for whites and African Americans. The railroads did not like the law because it cost them money to create separate train cars.

In 1891, a group of young black men in New Orleans formed a group to test the **constitutionality** of the separate cars law. Constitutionality is the characteristic of being constitutional. They hired a lawyer and took their case to the Louisiana Supreme Court. The court decided that the law was unconstitutional when applied to travel between states. The group decided to test the result. They had Homer Plessy, a man who was seven-eighths white and one-eight African American, ride a train on June 7, 1892. He seated himself in a white compartment. A train conductor challenged him and he was arrested. He was charged with breaking the state law.

The case went to court in Louisiana where Judge John H. Ferguson ruled against Homer Plessy. Plessy took the case to the United States Supreme Court, hoping the Supreme Court would rule in his favor. But, the Supreme Court ruled in favor of Ferguson and segregation under state law was allowed to continue.

People kept working, however, to end discrimination. The **Civil Rights Movement** took hold in the 1950s. Through nonviolent resistance, marches, protests, and boycotts, they brought attention to racial inequality. They started to receive national attention in newspapers, on the radio, and on television. They also worked hard to fight segregation through the court system.

The Civil Rights Movement

Their efforts paid off when in 1954, the United States Supreme Court made a decision in the case of *Brown vs. Board of Education*. It was actually five cases put together under one name. Each of the cases challenged the constitutionality of racial segregation in public schools. The Supreme Court decided that separate schools were "inherently unequal." They felt racial segregation in public schools violated the Equal Protection Clause of the Fourteenth Amendment. The decision was unanimous—all of the justices decided in favor of Brown. A year later, the court ordered the states to integrate their schools, and to do so quickly.

Chief Justice Earl Warren presided over the Supreme Court from 1953 to 1969. Previously, the court had been more concerned with economic rights and not civil rights. During Chief Warren's time, the court ruled on several cases that dealt with civil rights.

The Supreme Court decision that public schools must be integrated was a huge victory for the Civil Rights Movement. Many other hard fought victories followed. In December, 1955, African American woman Rosa Parks refused to give up her seat for a white man on a bus in Montgomery, Alabama. She was an **NAACP** activist. NAACP was the National Association for the Advancement of Colored People. The NAACP was a major force in the Civil Rights Movement. Rosa Parks' actions led to a bus boycott in Montgomery. The boycott lasted until December, 1956 when the NAACP won a Supreme Court case to desegregate the bus system.

Ending discrimination was easier said than done. Rosa Parks refusal to giver up her bus seat to a white man led to a boycott of the Montgomery Alabama bus system.

Martin Luther King, Jr. is the most well-known civil rights leader. He was living in Montgomery, Alabama at the time of the Rosa Parks incident. He led the Montgomery Improvement Association, which led the bus boycott. He promoted nonviolent resistance including sit-ins and protests. He was an excellent speaker and organizer. He organized the March on Washington that took place on August 28, 1963. More than 200,000 people gathered around the Lincoln Memorial. It was here that King gave his famous "I have a dream" speech.

The work of King and other civil rights leaders led to the passage of the Civil Rights Act of 1964. It gave the federal government the power to enforce desegregation. It also outlawed discrimination in publicly owned facilities. It was followed by the passage of the Voting Rights Act of 1965. It protected the right to vote through various laws. These federal acts helped to undo the Jim Crow laws of the various states. Unfortunately, racial discrimination still exists in the United States, but it no longer has the support of the government.

▶ DRAWING CONCLUSIONS When you draw conclusions, you identify important facts. Then you decide what the facts tell you about the subject. The judgment you make is called a conclusion. Reread the first paragraph on page 60. You can conclude that the federal government allowed the states to resolve issues of discrimination at the state level.

Which fact supports this conclusion?
A. State governments were passing Jim Crow laws.
B. The Supreme Court struck down the 1875 act.

Check your answers on page 231.

Thinking About the Article

Practice Vocabulary

▶ **The words below are in the passage in bold type. Study the way each word is used. Then complete each sentence by writing the correct word or words.**

segregation	intermarriage	suffrage
constitutionality	NAACP	

1. The task of the Supreme Court is often to decide the

    _____ of a law.

2. Jim Crow laws enforced racial _____ by prohibiting

    things like _____.

3. The _____ won a Supreme Court case to desegregate
    the bus system in Montgomery, Alabama.

4. The right to vote is known as _____.

Understand the Article

▶ **Write your answer to each question.**

5. Who or what enforced Jim Crow laws? _____ How did
    Jim Crow laws affect African Americans?

    _____

6. How do you think women's suffrage affected the Civil Rights Movement?

    _____

7. What part of the Fourteenth Amendment did the Supreme Court cite in its

    decision on *Brown vs. Board of Education*? _____
    From what you know about the Supreme Court decision, what do you
    think this part of the Amendment stated?

    _____

8. How do you think that most people who were in favor of Jim Crow laws
    justified the laws?

    _____

9. How was the Supreme Court under Chief Justice Warren different from
    Supreme Courts of the past?

    _____

10. What did Rosa Parks mean to the Civil Rights Movement?

    _____

Apply Your Skills

▶ **Circle the letter of the best answer for each question.**

11. In the case of *Plessy vs. Ferguson*, who was the defendant?

A. a Louisiana judge

B. an African American man

C. a train conductor

D. a group of young African American men

12. Which word from the article supports the idea that the author has a very positive view of Martin Luther King, Jr.?

A. promoted

B. famous

C. excellent

D. well-known

13. Which was a result of *Plessy vs. Ferguson*?

A. Schools were desegregated.

B. Train cars no longer had to be separate.

C. Jim Crow laws were allowed to continue.

D. The Supreme Court of Louisiana was stripped of its power.

Connect with the Article

▶ **Write your answer to each question.**

14. How might the Civil Rights Movement have been different if the members of the Supreme Court had been more conservative during the 1950s and 1960s?

_____

_____

_____

_____

15. Do you think discrimination still exists in the United States today? If so, how do you think it can be changed?

_____

_____

_____

_____

Check your answers on pages 231–232.

POST 9/11 FOREIGN POLICY

Vocabulary

foreign policy

Taliban

insurgent

preemption

diplomacy

emerging nation

economic security

entrepreneurship

The way the United States has related to other countries around the world has changed many times throughout our country's history. Relationships with other countries are important for global stability and economic security.

The United States Department of State is charged with maintaining relationships with other countries. The Department of State tries to advance freedom for Americans and people around the world.

Relate to the Topic

This lesson is about foreign policy since 2001. Foreign policy, or how the U.S. deals with other countries, has changed over the years depending on world events. Events in 2001 had a large impact on U.S. foreign policy. What happened on Sept. 11, 2001? How do you think these events affected most Americans?

_____

_____

_____

Reading Strategy

PREVIEWING A POLITICAL CARTOON   Social studies materials sometimes contain political cartoons. A political cartoon is a special type of cartoon that presents an opinion about a controversial topic. Look at the cartoon on page 66. Then answer the questions.

1. What do the sticks of dynamite represent?

_____

Hint: What is dynamite used for?

2. What does the political cartoon try to show?

_____

Hint: What anniversary is being celebrated?

How 9/11 Changed the United States

On the morning of September 11, 2001, four airplanes were hijacked in the United States. Two of these planes were deliberately flown into the upper floors of the North and South Tower of the World Trade Center in New York City. Another plane was flown into the Pentagon in Washington, D.C. A fourth plane was in route to Washington, D.C. Passengers on that plane found out about the crashes of the other three planes. The passengers fought the hijackers and the plane crashed into a field about 20 minutes by air from Washington, D.C. It is believed that the hijackers would have flown the plane into the Capitol building.

The planes that hit the World Trade Center towers crashed within 20 minutes of each other. As many as 18,000 people were in the World Trade Center towers at the time. Most of them made it out of the towers safely. The jet fuel from the planes added fuel to the fires from the impacts. The fires weakened the towers and they both collapsed. Nearly 3,000 people from 93 different nations were killed in the attacks.

A terrorist group called Al-Qaeda was responsible for the attacks. They are an Islamist extremist terrorist group. One of their goals at the time was to overthrow governments in the Middle East that do not follow the strict religious political and social order that they follow. The United State has supported many of these governments. The attacks were meant to weaken the United States so it would not support these governments.

The United States is too big and strong for a small terrorist organization to attack. So they attacked symbols of America's economic power—the Twin Towers of the World Trade Center.

A new tower—One World Trade Center, has been built on the site. It is the tallest building in the Western Hemisphere at 1,776 feet tall. The height is symbolic as 1776 was the year the colonies declared independence from Britain.

War on Terror

The events of September 11, 2001 definitively changed **foreign policy** in the United States. Foreign policy is a policy or policies that a nation follows when it deals with another nation or nations. After September 11, fighting the "War on Terror" became a main goal. Security was seen as a major concern because there had not been an attack on U.S. soil since the World War II attack on Pearl Harbor in 1941. President George W. Bush addressed Congress and the nation on September 20, 2011:

> "We will direct every resource at our command—every means of diplomacy, every tool of intelligence, every instrument of law enforcement, every financial influence, and every necessary weapon of war—to the destruction and to the defeat of the global terror network."

The United States began its war on terror on Oct 7, 2001. The U.S. launched airstrikes in Afghanistan against Al-Qaeda and the Taliban. The **Taliban** was the extreme Islamic government that had been in place in Afghanistan since 1996. The Taliban provided safety for Al-Qaeda and its leader Osama bin Laden.

The United States had asked the Taliban to hand over Osama bin Laden but they refused. By December 9, 2001, the United States had ousted the Taliban from power. A new Afghan government, backed by the United States, was put in place. The United States and Afghan forces continued to fight insurgents. An **insurgent** is a person who forcefully opposes a government.

The Iraq War

President Bush adopted a policy of preemption after 9/11. **Preemption** is the concept of launching an attack in order to prevent a suspected attack. In simple terms, if you believe someone is going to attack you, you attack them first. **Diplomacy**, or negotiating, was no longer the first plan in foreign relations.

According to the Bush administration, Iraq allegedly had weapons of mass destruction. Iraq also supported Al-Qaeda. These two issues made disarming Iraq a priority. The United Nations worked to make this happen through diplomacy, but the United States grew restless and gave Saddam Hussein, Iraq's leader, 48 hours to leave the country. The United States attacked Iraq on March 20, 2003. Within months, the United States had taken over Iraq. Saddam Hussein was caught in December, 2003 and turned over to the Iraqis. In December 2006, he was executed.

The Bush administration implied that the Iraq War would be short and straightforward.

Unfortunately, conflict continued in Iraq for many years. U.S. troops finally left Iraq in 2011. No weapons of mass destruction were ever found. The Iraq War put stress on the relationships of the United States with other countries. Many countries did not agree with the decision of the United States to invade Iraq. They felt that more time should have been given to diplomacy. It is estimated that the wars in Iraq and Afghanistan cost the United States $4 trillion to $6 trillion.

▶ **Interpreting Political Cartoons** A political cartoon expresses an opinion. The artist uses symbols to express his or her views. Labels give important information. Study the cartoon above. What do the sticks of dynamite signify?

    A. The Iraq War hostilities ended ten years ago.

    B. The Iraq War is still going on after ten years.

Foreign Policy Today

Today the U.S. Department of State and the U.S. Agency for International Development (USAID) have a shared mission to "shape and sustain a peaceful, prosperous, just, and democratic world, and foster conditions for stability and progress for the benefit of the American people and people everywhere."

The United States is the largest economy in the world. In 2013, the Gross Domestic Product of the United States was $16.2 trillion. By 2018, it is expected to be $21.1 trillion. As such, economics plays a major role in foreign policy today. **Emerging nations,** countries that are on their way to becoming industrialized, measure themselves in terms of economic power. Most conflicts are rooted in economics. Throughout history, nations have fought over resources. The more economically stable a country is, the more politically and socially stable it is likely to be.

In the decade after September 11, America's foreign policy focused on the places where the United States faced the greatest danger, such as Iraq and Afghanistan. Moving ahead, the United States plans to focus on places that present opportunities. For example, focusing on new free trade agreements and foreign markets provides opportunities for the U.S. economy to grow. It also provides opportunities for the United States to influence the economies of other nations. The U.S. has an interest in the stability of other countries.

Economic security directly affects our national security. **Economic security** is the state of having a stable income to support a standard of living for now and into the future. A country that is economically secure is also more likely to be politically stable. The U.S. State Department is working on plans that help to grow the economies of other countries. For example, in the Middle East and North Africa, the U.S. is encouraging entrepreneurship. **Entrepreneurship** is the starting of new businesses. Entrepreneurship in turn, supports the economic foundations of democracy.

In Afghanistan, for example, the United States has a vision for a "New Silk Road." The original Silk Road was a main transportation route for trade centuries ago. The new plan will promote stability in the region by linking Afghanistan and its neighbors economically. The hope is that programs like this will lead to more stability and freedom for people all over the world.

Thinking About the Article

Practice Vocabulary

▶ **Use the bold type words from the article. Study the way each word is used. Then complete each sentence by writing the correct word or words.**

foreign policy	Taliban	insurgents	economic security
emerging nation	diplomacy	preemption	entrepreneurship

1. _____were a problem in Afghanistan after the

   United States ousted the _____.

2. A country that has _____ is more likely to be politically
   and socially stable than one that does not.

3. The United States' _____ was very affected by the
   events of September 11, 2001.

4. One way to help create economic stability in a country is to promote

   _____.

5. A country that is just beginning to be industrialized is a/an

   _____.

6. The United States quickly abandoned _____ and

   invaded Iraq under a policy of _____.

Understand the Article

▶ **Write your answer to each question.**

7. One could state that the events of September 11, 2001 started a war. What
   is different about this war from typical wars? _____

8. Describe how U.S. foreign policy changed after 9/11.

9. What was the economic impact of the Afghanistan and Iraq Wars?

10. Why do you think that a country that is economically stable is more likely
    to be politically and socially stable?

Apply Your Skills

▶ **Circle the letter of the best answer for each question.**

11. Which is most likely the author's opinion on the Iraq War?

    A. It was useful.

    B. It was important.

    C. It was rushed.

    D. It was unnecessary.

12. Which best describes the relationship between economic security and political stability based on the article?

    A. Economic security causes political stability.

    B. Economic security correlates to political stability.

    C. Economic security and political stability are the same.

    D. Economic security is not related to political stability.

13. Which claim is supported by the article?

    A. Economics plays a large role in conflict.

    B. The War in Afghanistan was not effective.

    C. The World Trade Center had poor security.

    D. The U.S. foreign policy on Iraq was isolation.

Connect with the Article

▶ **Write your answer to each question.**

14. Reread the part of President George W. Bush's address to Congress and the nation on page 65. If you had been watching on television, how do you think you would have reacted to his address?

_____

_____

_____

15. Think about the economic impact of the wars in Afghanistan and Iraq, as well as the human impact. What are your feelings on whether waging each war was the best foreign policy for the United States?

_____

_____

_____

HISTORY AT WORK

SERVICE: SALES ASSOCIATES

SOME CAREERS IN SERVICE

Education Aide prepares activities and assists museum visitors and groups with the activities

Security Guard monitors exhibits and visitor traffic; provides information as needed

Tour Guide leads visitors through museums and historic sites; makes presentations and conducts demonstrations

Museum Library Aide assists patrons in finding requested information, using library facilities, and obtaining desired material

Over the past decade, museum stores and gift shops have become one important way for many museums to help fund their operations. You find them at historic places you visit. The sales associates at these stores are important to the financial success of the stores and the satisfaction of the customers.

Sales associates must be familiar with all the goods for sale in the store. They see that the displays are attractive and well stocked and that objects are placed in appropriate arrangements. They also handle sales, returns, and exchanges.

Because a sales associate assists customers, he or she should know how the goods in the store relate to the focus of the museum or historic place. A sales associate must also have good communication skills and a pleasant personality and appearance. A sales associate may need to write notes to fellow workers or provide written follow up to a customer's request. Strong math and computer skills are also expected for sales and inventory management.

Look at the sidebar of Some Careers in Service.

- Do any of the careers interest you? If so, which ones?

- What information would you like to find out about those careers?

On a separate piece of paper, write some questions that you would like answered. You can find out more information about those careers in the *Occupational Outlook Handbook* at your local library or online.

▶ **Use the material below to answer the questions that follow.**

Coleman is a sales associate in the gift shop at the Smithsonian Institution's Museum of American History in Washington, D.C. He is showing a shopper objects that are on sale in the gift shop.

Coleman: Here we have a copy of an iron from the colonial days. Notice the size of this iron compared to the irons of today. Today's irons are much larger. They are made of plastic and metal; their handles are plastic and the base is metal. This colonial iron is made completely of metal and is about one-third the size of a modern iron. Hot coals were used to heat the colonial iron. The little door at the back of the iron was opened and hot coals were put inside. The door was closed and the coals heated up the metal. Before the iron could be used, a damp cloth was wrapped around the handle so the person ironing wouldn't get burned.

1. Which of the following materials was used to heat the colonial iron?

   A.   electricity

   B.   plastic

   C.   hot coals

   D.   a damp cloth

2. Which of the following statements makes an accurate comparison?

   A.   Colonial irons and modern irons both have plastic handles.

   B.   Modern irons are much heavier than colonial irons.

   C.   Modern irons are smaller than colonial irons.

   D.   Colonial irons were smaller than modern irons.

3. Why would it be important to close the door of the colonial iron before using it?

   A.   to prevent the coals from cooling off too quickly

   B.   to prevent the coals from spilling onto the material

   C.   to help the iron heat up more quickly

   D.   all of the above

4. Many of the objects we use today were invented years ago, such as the colonial iron demonstrated by Coleman. Compare and contrast an object or invention we use today with its predecessor. Use a separate piece of paper to discuss how they are the same and how they are different.

The St. Augustine Colony

Juan Ponce de León, a young Spanish noble, was one of the first Europeans to explore the Americas. He was part of Christopher Columbus's 1493 return voyage. When the Spanish king heard of gold in Puerto Rico, he sent Ponce de León to explore in 1508. Within a year the island was inhabited by settlers, who made the Native Americans dig for gold. The king appointed Ponce de León governor of Puerto Rico.

Legend says that Ponce de León went in search of the "Fountain of Youth." In 1513 he sailed north to a land that he named La Florida. He was the first European to set foot on the North American mainland. During the next several years, Ponce de León tried to colonize La Florida. But at each site Native Americans drove him out.

In 1564 the king of Spain learned that a group of French Protestants had started a colony in northeastern Florida. The king was angry because he believed all of La Florida belonged to Spain. The king sent his most experienced admiral, Pedro Menéndez de Avilés, to destroy the French colony. Menéndez de Avilés and his soldiers surprised the French colonists and killed them all. Then the Spanish built a colony called St. Augustine near the place where their fleet had landed.

By the time the first permanent English colony in America was founded, St. Augustine was already 40 years old. It became an important military base for the Spaniards. The soldiers guarded the Spanish ships carrying gold and silver from Mexico to Spain. They also kept out French and English colonists. St. Augustine now has its place in history as the oldest permanent European settlement in what is now the United States.

▶ **Circle the letter of the best answer for each question.**

1. Why did the king of Spain want to build a colony in La Florida?

    A.   to protect Spain's claim to La Florida

    B.   to help the French build a colony

    C.   to prove to Ponce de León that La Florida had gold

    D.   to beat the English and French to the Americas

2. According to the passage, which of the following events happened first?

    A.   The king of Spain sent Menéndez de Avilés to secure Florida.

    B.   Juan Ponce de León came to the Americas from Spain.

    C.   English settlers established a colony in North America.

    D.   French Protestants established a colony in Florida.

The United States in 1863

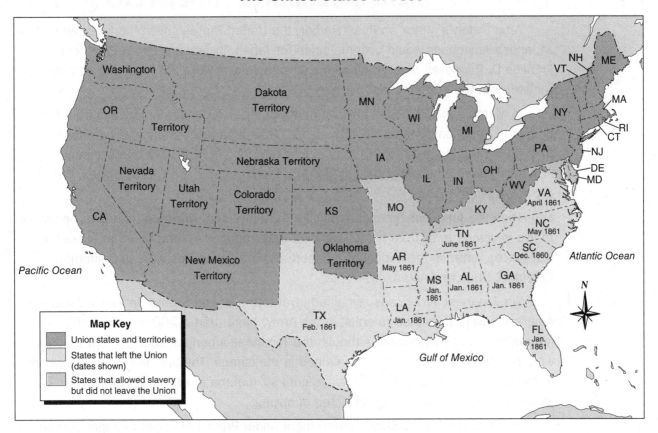

Map Key
- Union states and territories
- States that left the Union (dates shown)
- States that allowed slavery but did not leave the Union

▶ **Use the map to complete each statement correctly.**

3. The first state to leave the Union was _____ .

4. The Emancipation Proclamation freed slaves living in any state fighting the

Union but not in the states of _____ .

5. The states that were subject to Reconstruction to be readmitted to the Union were

_____ .

_____ .

▶ **Circle the letter of the best answer for the question.**

6. Why were states that allowed slavery but did not leave the Union called border states?

A. They all lay along the southern border of the Confederacy.

B. They formed the northern border of the United States.

C. They all separated the rest of the states from the western territories.

D. They separated the Union from the Confederacy.

The Internment of Japanese Americans

After Japan's attack on Pearl Harbor, the United States government feared that Japanese Americans would become spies for Japan. In January 1942, President Franklin D. Roosevelt ordered all **aliens,** or people who were not American citizens, to register with the government.

In March, officials began arrangements to move Japanese Americans from their homes in west coast states. More than 120,000 Japanese Americans were forced to sell their homes and most of their belongings. About 77,000 of these Japanese Americans were American citizens. Many had been born in the United States, but that did not seem to matter.

Then the Japanese-American families were interned. **Interned** means to be forced to live in camps away from home. Families were rounded up and taken to out-of-the-way places, often in the middle of a desert. Internment camps were in California, Colorado, Utah, and Arkansas.

Yet Japanese Americans remained loyal to the United States. In 1943, Japanese Americans were permitted to enlist in the Army. More than 1,200 men from the internment camps signed up. Although the Japanese-American soldiers' war records were outstanding, their families remained in the camps. The last Japanese Americans at the camps were not allowed to leave until six months after the war ended. No Japanese American was ever convicted of spying.

In 1988, the United States government under President Ronald Reagan formally apologized to 60,000 surviving Japanese Americans who had lived in the internment camps. The government gave each survivor $20,000 as **reparations,** or payment for damages.

▶ **Circle the letter of the best answer for each question.**

7. Why were Japanese Americans interned?

    A.   The government wanted Japanese workers in defense industries.

    B.   The government feared that Japanese Americans were responsible for World War II.

    C.   The government feared that Japanese Americans might be spies for Japan.

    D.   The government feared that Japanese Americans would refuse to join the armed forces.

8. Which conclusion does the article support best?

    A.   Japanese Americans were spies for Japan.

    B.   The internment of Japanese Americans was an injustice.

    C.   Japanese Americans didn't mind the internment camps.

    D.   The United States won the war with Japan.

American Workers and Labor Unions

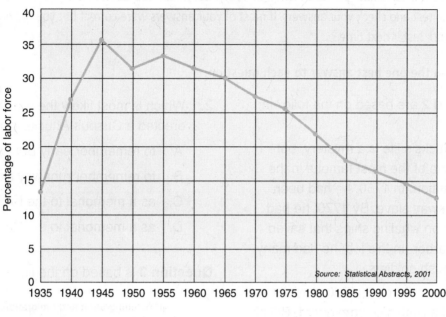

Union Membership in the United States, 1930–1995

Source: Statistical Abstracts, 2001

Year

▶ **Use the graph to write the answers to each question.**

9. Union membership kept increasing until what year?

_____

10. What is the general trend shown on the graph?

_____

11. What might explain the steep rise in membership from 1940 to 1945?

_____

▶ **Circle the letter of the best answer for each question.**

12. Which was the mean percentage of labor force that belonged to unions between 1935 and 2000 using the data shown on the graph?

    A.   about 10%

    B.   about 15%

    C.   about 25%

    D.   about 35%

SOCIAL STUDIES EXTENSION

For the next two weeks, collect the front sections of daily newspapers and read the headlines. Which news items indicate progress for your town or our nation? Which indicate conflict? Which will have lasting impact and make history?

MINI-TEST

This is a 15-minute practice test. After 15 minutes, mark the last number you finished. Then complete the test and check your answers. If most of your answers were correct but you did not finish, try to work faster next time.

▶ **Directions: Choose the one best answer to each question.**

Questions 1 and 2 are based on the following information.

Crispus Attucks's life is a mystery, but his death was one of the most famous in the American Revolution. In 1750, he had been sought as a runaway slave. By 1770, he had become a sailor on whaling ships that sailed out of Boston Harbor. In this job, he had many conflicts with British soldiers.

On the night of March 7, 1770, Attucks and others harassed a British custom guard. British soldiers fired on the crowd. Attucks and several others were killed in what later became known as the Boston Massacre. Thus, Crispus Attucks, a former slave, became the first casualty of the American Revolution. Attucks has been remembered as, "the first to defy; the first to die." A Crispus Attucks monument was erected in Boston Common in 1888.

1. What was the cause of Crispus Attuck's death?
   He was killed because he

   A. was a runaway slave

   B. had become a sailor on a whaling ship

   C. had become a guard at a custom office

   D. was in a confrontation with British soldiers

2. Which is most likely the reason that Boston erected a Crispus Attucks monument?

   A. to remember early Boston

   B. to remember runaway slaves

   C. as a memorial to the British soldiers

   D. as a memorial to the Revolution

Question 3 is based on the line graph below.

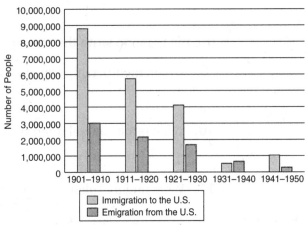

U.S. Immigration and Emigration, 1901–1950

Sources: U.S. Census Bureau; Warran and Kraly, *The Elusive Exodus*, 1985

3. In which years was the number of people immigrating to the United States most similar to the number leaving?

   A. 1901–1910

   B. 1911–1920

   C. 1921–1930

   D. 1931–1940

Questions 4 and 5 refer to the following photograph of unemployed workers during the early 1900s.

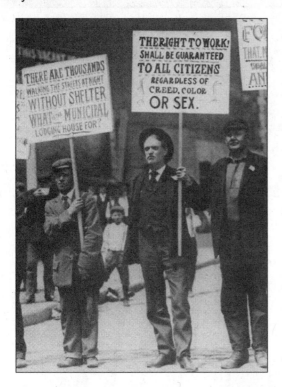

4. What is the main point of the photograph? Unemployed workers

   A. started receiving benefits in the early 1900s

   B. marched for jobs and against discrimination

   C. wanted to stay in municipal shelters

   D. demanded that the military be used against demonstrators.

5. Which point of view does this picture support best?

   A. We must unite to fight for our rights.

   B. The army should give us all jobs.

   C. We need to stay in shelters until we are able to find work.

   D. All able-bodied people should receive unemployment compensation.

Questions 6 and 7 are based on the following information.

The third chief justice of the U.S. Supreme Court, John Marshall, wrote one of the most important Supreme Court decisions in history. In the case *Marbury* v. *Madison* (1803), his decision made the Supreme Court the final authority on which laws are constitutional and which are not. This decision clarified the power of the judicial branch in relation to the executive and legislative branches of government.

6. What influence has *Marbury* v. *Madison* had on the Supreme Court?

   A. The Supreme Court consists of a Chief Justice and associate justices.

   B. The decisions of the Supreme Court are made in writing.

   C. Supreme Court justices are nominated for life terms.

   D. Supreme Court decisions are based on specific sections of the Constitution.

7. Which of the following conclusions is supported by the information?

   A. John Marshall was a minor figure in U.S. history.

   B. *Marbury* v. *Madison* ensured that the judicial branch became an equal partner with the other two branches.

   C. The Supreme Court building in Washington, D.C., should be named after John Marshall.

   D. After John Marshall presented his decision in *Marbury* v. *Madison*, the Supreme Court became the nation's highest court.

Check your answers on pages 234–235.

World history is the story of people and events around our planet. It is the story of ancient times and of current events.

Events throughout the world have had a strong impact on Americans. They continue to influence us today. As Americans, we are neighbors with all nations and peoples. We can benefit from learning about people in other times and places.

Name two events that you think were important to the world's history.

_____

_____

Thinking About Geography and the World

You may not realize how much you already know about geography and the world. Think of what you may have heard or read about events in other parts of the world.

Check the box for each fact that you already know.

☐ Many ancient civilizations developed along major rivers.

☐ Persia, Rome, and China all had large, long-lasting empires.

☐ Europeans began to colonize the Americas about 500 years ago.

☐ The Industrial Revolution began in Europe and changed people's lives around the world.

☐ Mexico was a Spanish colony and became an independent nation in the early 1800s.

☐ The United Nations was established in the mid-1900s after the second world war.

Write two other facts that you know about geography and the world.

_____

_____

Previewing the Unit

In this unit, you will learn:

- how Chinese emperors protected their land from invaders

- how various European inventions changed life around the world

- how Mexico became a modern country

- how the government of South Africa changed over time to become a full democracy

- how the United Nations tries to keep peace in the world

- how the Exon Valdez oil spill affected the environment

- how desertification destroys land

Lesson 10	**The Age of Empires**
Lesson 11	**A Time of Enlightenment**
Lesson 12	**The Rise of Nations**
Lesson 13	**Democracy and Independence**
Lesson 14	**Global Interdependence**
Lesson 15	**Rescuing an Environment**
Lesson 16	**Taking Care of Resources**

THE AGE OF EMPIRES

Vocabulary

empire

civilization

barbarian

peasant

dynasty

Long ago, China was made up of many kingdoms. Qin (pronounced "Chin") was one of the largest kingdoms. The ruler of Qin set out to conquer his neighbors. By 221 B.C., he had united all of China's kingdoms. He took the name of Qin Shi Huangdi—"First Emperor of China."

Some people who lived north of China invaded Shi Huangdi's newly conquered lands because they thought that these kingdoms were without leaders. In response, Shi Huangdi sent his leading general and 300,000 troops to drive out the invaders. He also ordered his army to build a wall to keep out enemies. This was the beginning of the Great Wall of China.

Relate to the Topic

This lesson is about the development of the Great Wall of China during the rule of several Chinese emperors. Imagine an emperor as being like the head of a large company. Why do you think many emperors and business leaders want to make their kingdoms and companies larger?

_____

_____

_____

_____

Reading Strategy

SCANNING A MAP   Maps can give you a lot of information more quickly than words alone. The scale on a map helps you measure distances represented on the map. Scan the map on page 81 and find the scale in the lower right-hand corner. Then answer the questions.

1. What is the map about?

   _____

   Hint: Read the title of the map.

2. What is the distance between Beijing and Jiayuguan?

   _____

   Hint: Use the scale to find the approximate distance.

The Great Wall of China

The Great Wall of China runs from the western city of Jiayuguan to the Yellow Sea. Between these points, the wall zigzags across 2,150 miles. Building this marvel took 1,800 years and millions of laborers.

Beginning the Great Wall

As early as 500 B.C., local Chinese rulers had walls erected to mark their borders and to keep out invaders. This piecemeal wall building went on for about 300 years. Then, Shi Huangdi established his empire. An **empire** is a group of countries or territories governed by one ruler. These early Chinese kingdoms were independent states. But their people shared similar ways and values, such as love for learning. In other words, they had a common **civilization.**

Huns and other groups who wandered Mongolia—the land north of China—followed a different way of life. They valued strength in battle and skill with horses. The Chinese considered them barbarians. A **barbarian** is someone whom others regard as inferior and ignorant.

Shi Huangdi decided to keep barbarians out of China and to mark his empire's northern border with a great wall. He had his army and one-half million **peasants**—poor, uneducated farmers—create this wall from the many earlier walls. Most of the early walls were crude structures, so the workers rebuilt them as well as building the connecting sections. The wall followed the land. It snaked along rivers rather than across them and up hills rather than around them. By the end of Shi Huangdi's 15-year rule, about 1,200 miles of wall had been completed.

The Great Wall of China

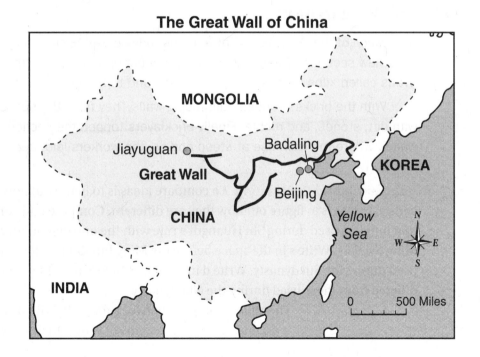

Shi Huangdi's workers put up a closed, wooden framework along the planned route of the wall. Then they packed the space inside the frame with three to four inches of dirt at a time. They pounded each layer of dirt before adding the next layer. Eventually the wall rose more than 20 feet.

Shi Huangdi's wall was only the beginning. In A.D. 446, another emperor drafted 300,000 people to work on the wall. About 100 years later, another emperor forced 1.8 million peasants to continue building the wall. The last work on the Great Wall for several centuries was finished by A.D. 618 under the Sui dynasty. A **dynasty** is a ruling family whose members govern over a long time.

Mongol Rule in China

After the Sui dynasty, the Tang and following dynasties built up the army rather than the Great Wall. Meanwhile, the tribes of Mongolia united under Genghis Khan and conquered lands from Korea to Russia and into India. In 1279, Mongols led by Kublai Khan, the grandson of Genghis, crossed the crumbling wall. They defeated the Chinese army and added China to their empire.

Kublai Khan established the Yuan dynasty, which ruled China for about one hundred years. The Mongols put themselves and foreigners, such as Italian Marco Polo, into high positions. The Chinese resented the way their Mongol rulers tolerated people who did not follow age-old Chinese beliefs.

In the mid 1300s, famine and flooding in China sparked uprisings. A peasant leader and his followers drove the Mongols out and founded the Ming dynasty. To keep the Mongols out, Ming rulers chose to rebuild the wall rather than the army.

The Ming Dynasty

Much of the Great Wall that remains today dates back to the Ming dynasty. To build new sections of wall, workers laid foundations of stone. Other workers set up ovens called kilns to make bricks and tiles and to burn lime for mortar.

With the bricks, workers built facing walls. They filled the space between the walls with dirt, stones, and rubble. Finally bricklayers topped the sections of wall with brick walks. Where the wall rose at steep angles, the workers laid steps.

▶ Comparing and Contrasting To compare ideas is to figure out how they are alike. To contrast ideas is to figure out how they are different. Compare and contrast the method that builders used during Shi Huangdi's rule with the one that builders used during the Ming dynasty. Write s in the space before the Ming building method that is similar to one used during the Sui dynasty. Write d in the space before the Ming building method that differed from those used during the Qin dynasty.

        _____ A.   They filled the space between the walls with dirt.

        _____ B.   Workers topped the sections of wall with brick walks.

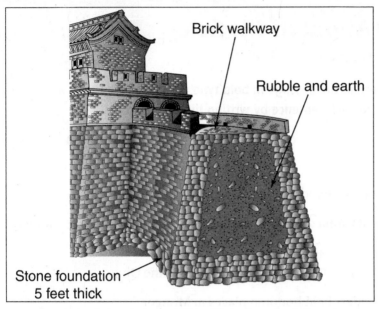

Brick walkway

Rubble and earth

Stone foundation 5 feet thick

Cross-section of the Great Wall built during the Ming dynasty

The wall served as a pathway as well as a barrier. Every 200 yards the builders erected a stairway on the Chinese side of the wall. Soldiers climbed the stairway to the top of the wall, where they could march ten abreast. In this way, they could rush to any part of the wall under attack.

The builders also included about 25,000 watchtowers in the wall. Each tower housed 30 to 50 soldiers. In peacetime, the soldiers kept the wall repaired and oversaw the traders who entered through the wall's gates. During wartime, the soldiers drove off invaders with cannons atop the towers.

The Great Wall proved a good defense for almost 300 years. But in 1644, a Chinese traitor opened a gate in the wall to let in Manchu warriors. They were wanderers like the Mongols and came from the land northeast of China. The Manchus defeated the Ming army and set up the Qing (pronounced "ching") dynasty, which ruled China until 1911.

The best-preserved part of the Great Wall is probably the Badaling section built during the Ming dynasty. From its top, you can still see the mounds where soldiers built fires for sending smoke signals. These signals warned troops miles away of approaching invaders.

Other sections of the wall have not fared as well as Badaling. The government of China has allowed many parts that are out of tourists' reach to decay. Even so, historians today consider the Great Wall a wonder of the world. It affirms, for all to see, a people's ingenuity.

▶ Applying an Idea to a New Context Ideas, such as the Great Wall of China, are often presented in one particular situation, or context. Many peoples in other parts of the world also built walls on their borders or around their cities. Hundreds of years ago, the Hausa people of West Africa built a large wall around Kano, a major business and cultural center. This wall was about 15 miles long and more than 65 feet high. Did the Hausa and the Chinese build walls for the same reason? Circle the letter of a reason that they most likely shared.

    A. to serve as a market site

    B. to protect people from invaders

    C. to set up a marching route for guards

Thinking About the Article

Practice Vocabulary

▶ **The words below are in the passage in bold type. Study the way each word is used. Then complete each sentence by writing the correct word.**

empire	civilization	barbarian
peasants	dynasty	

1. Sui emperors considered a Mongol a(n) _____ .

2. The emperor of China depended on the _____ for food and labor.

3. The last _____ in China was the Qing.

4. Warriors and riders held honored places in Mongol

   _____ .

5. In 1279, Kublai Khan made China part of the Mongol

   _____ .

Understand the Article

▶ **Write the answer to each question.**

6. Why did Shi Huangdi have the Great Wall built?

   _____

   _____

7. How did emperors immediately following the Sui dynasty try to stop invaders?

   _____

   _____

   _____

8. Why did the Chinese resent their Mongol rulers?

   _____

   _____

9. Suppose that five watchtowers along a stretch of the wall hold the following numbers of soldiers: 34, 62, 58, 45, and 45. What is the mean, the median, and the mode of this data set to the nearest whole numbers?

   _____

   _____

Apply Your Skills

▶ **Circle the letter of the best answer for each question.**

10. Which author of this article would be the most credible?

    A.   a Chinese professor who studies the Great Wall

    B.   an American writer who researched online

    C.   a high school teacher of English in China

    D.   a magazine author who writes about landmarks

11. Which of the following is an opinion from the article?

    A.   Soldiers could march on the wall ten abreast.

    B.   Building the Great Wall took 1,800 years.

    C.   The best-preserved part of the wall is the Badaling section.

    D.   Building the Great Wall was better than building an army.

12. Which shows the order in which the major dynasties of China ruled?

    A.   Ming, Tang, Qin, Sui

    B.   Sui, Tang, Ming, Qin

    C.   Tang, Ming, Sui, Qin

    D.   Qin, Sui, Tang, Ming

Connect with the Article

▶ **Write your answer to each question.**

13. The Great Wall can no longer keep invaders out of China. How do you think aircraft helped make the wall an ineffective defense in wartime?

14. Do you consider any structures in the United States as awe-inspiring as the Great Wall of China? Explain your answer.

A TIME OF ENLIGHTENMENT

Vocabulary

century

orchestra

navigator

latitude

longitude

chronometer

pendulum

smallpox

vaccination

immune

The 1700s were an exciting time in Western Europe and North America. Historians call this period the Enlightenment. During the Enlightenment, some thoughtful people began questioning the right of their rulers to govern. They also took a fresh look at nature and the arts.

The biggest influence on the thinkers of the Enlightenment was modern science. The new scientific method held that knowledge came not from following tradition without question but instead from observing and experimenting. One result of all the new observations and experimentation was a flood of inventions.

Relate to the Topic

This lesson is about inventions from the 1700s. It describes advances made in music, timekeeping, and medicine. List two ways your life might be different without music, watches, and modern medical care.

_____

_____

_____

Reading Strategy

USING A TITLE TO PREVIEW   The title, or name, of an article can help you focus your reading. Read the title at the top of page 87. Then answer the questions.

1. What is the main topic of the article? _____

_____

Hint: Decide which is the most important word in the title.

2. How does knowing the topic help you plan your reading of the article?

_____

_____

Hint: What information will you look for as you read?

The Age of Inventions

During the Enlightenment, thinking changed from believing life is guided by God to one of believing all men are free by nature. John Locke was a philosopher who championed a natural rights philosophy. He felt that the rights to enjoy life, liberty, and property, for example, are based in nature, and not in a particular society. This philosophy led people to explore new ideas and inventions for their enjoyment.

The eighteenth **century,** or 1700s, was a fruitful time for inventors. They produced advances in many fields—music, timekeeping, and medicine, to name just a few. Their contributions to history and culture amounted to more than inventions. They made possible richer music, a keener sense of time, and longer lives.

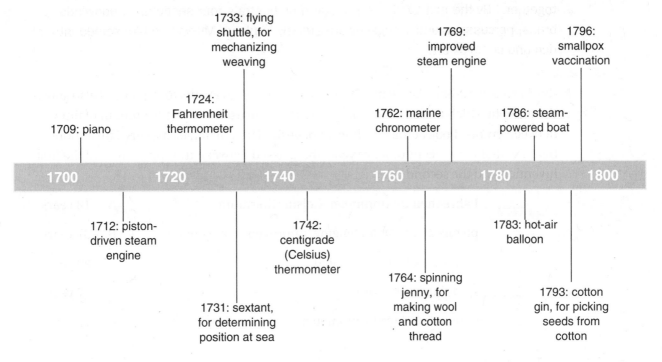

1733: flying shuttle, for mechanizing weaving

1769: improved steam engine

1796: smallpox vaccination

1724: Fahrenheit thermometer

1762: marine chronometer

1786: steam-powered boat

1709: piano

| 1700 | 1720 | 1740 | 1760 | 1780 | 1800 |

1712: piston-driven steam engine

1742: centigrade (Celsius) thermometer

1783: hot-air balloon

1731: sextant, for determining position at sea

1764: spinning jenny, for making wool and cotton thread

1793: cotton gin, for picking seeds from cotton

Reinventing Music

Since the early 1400s, musicians had been making do with a keyboard instrument called a harpsichord. When a player pressed one of the keys, a pick inside the harpsichord popped up and plucked a tight metal string. The string vibrated and made a sound. How lightly or firmly the player touched the key made little difference in tone. All sounds that the harpsichord made were equally loud. Any musician who wanted to play softly or build to a loud finish was unable to do so.

In 1709, Italian Bartolomeo Cristofori replaced the picks in a harpsichord with hammers. Instead of plucking the strings, the hammers hit them with the same force that the fingers struck the keys. Now players could control how softly or loudly a note sounded. Cristofori named the new instrument "harpsichord with softness and loudness." In Italian the words for the last part are *piano e forte*. Over the years, English-speaking people shortened the instrument's name to *pianoforte* or *piano*.

The piano was only one of several new or improved instruments that came out in the eighteenth century. Many instruments achieved a greater range of sound. For example, between 1775 and 1780, French violin maker François Tourte developed the modern shape of the violin bow. Rubbing the bow on an instrument's strings makes sound. Tourte's bow allowed the same violin to make powerful or delicate music.

Great eighteenth-century composers—Franz Joseph Haydn, Wolfgang Amadeus Mozart, and Ludwig van Beethoven—embraced the variety of sounds. A piece of music they wrote might require pianos, violins, drums, and flutes. To play this kind of music, the orchestra emerged.

Once, the word *orchestra* meant only "the space in front of a stage." During the early 1700s, **orchestra** also came to mean "a group of musicians performing music together." By the mid 1700s, the modern orchestra's four sections—woodwinds, brass, percussion, and strings—were already in place. Music had blossomed into a rich and complex art.

▶ Reading a Timeline   A timeline shows when a series of events took place. It also shows the order in which these events happened. It can be used to find the amount of time between events. Look at the timeline on page 87. Then match each pair of inventions below with the correct number of years that passed between the appearance of the first invention and the second one.

_____ Fahrenheit thermometer/Celsius thermometer	A.	18 years
_____ piston-driven steam engine/improved steam engine	B.	31 years
_____ piano/steam-powered boat	C.	29 years
_____ spinning jenny/cotton gin	D.	57 years
_____ sextant/marine chronometer	E.	77 years

Taking Clocks to Sea

In early times, ships sometimes lost their way going long distances at sea. During the 1700s, however, the oceans became the main channels of trade. A **navigator**—the person who charts the position and course of a ship—already knew how to figure out **latitude,** the distance north or south of the equator. He also knew that in one hour, Earth turns 15 degrees of **longitude,** the distance east or west on Earth relative to Greenwich, England. But in 1700, the only way to know ship's longitude was by observing the moon, and a navigator often lacked clear weather at sea.

But if a navigator had a **chronometer,** or very accurate clock, he could easily find the ship's longitude. How? The clock would be set at London time. When the sun shone directly overhead, the time aboard ship was noon. If the clock said that the time in London was 2:00 P.M., then the navigator would know that the ship was 30 degrees west of London.

In 1700, most clocks were run with pendulums. A **pendulum** is a weight that swings back and forth at regular intervals, ticking away the minutes. On a rolling ship, a pendulum clock could not stay accurate because movement would disturb its regularity. A mistake of one minute could mean going 450 miles off course.

The British government offered a prize for the invention of a seagoing chronometer. English carpenter John Harrison wanted the prize. He observed clocks in which springs did the work of pendulums. In the clocks that Harrison made, he added a second spring that kept the first spring moving. In 1762, after 34 years of experimenting, Harrison had a small clock that kept accurate time despite heat, cold, humidity, or the motion of a ship on a 156-day voyage. Harrison's chronometer won the prize. It also gave the world a model for portable and accurate clocks that people called watches. Watches allowed people to always know the time, anywhere they went.

Preventing Disease

At one time, people feared **smallpox** more than any other disease. Smallpox spreads, by way of sneezes, coughs, or items handled by someone with the disease. Smallpox symptoms included a rash that fills with pus. Four out of ten people who came down with the disease died. Those who survived had deep pits in their skin where the rash had been. Some survivors were left blind.

English doctor Edward Jenner observed many milkmaids—women who milked cows for a living—with cowpox. This was a mild form of smallpox passed from cows to humans. Jenner noted that milkmaids who had had cowpox never caught smallpox.

In 1796, Jenner tried an experiment. He injected the pus from a cowpox sore into a healthy boy, who then developed cowpox. Afterward Jenner injected the same boy with pus from a smallpox sore. The disease failed to develop.

Jenner had invented the first practical smallpox **vaccination,** which got its name from the *vaccinia* virus that produces cowpox. He encouraged other doctors to vaccinate against smallpox. Through their success, *vaccination* came to mean "injecting a substance that makes a person **immune,** or safe, from a disease that spreads."

In 1980, the World Health Organization declared smallpox a disease of the past. Today, however, there are fears that terrorists could use smallpox as a weapon. Many countries are making plans to deal with possible new outbreaks of smallpox.

▶ Summarizing When you summarize something, you reduce a large amount of information to a few sentences. These sentences restate only the major points of the information. For example, the sentence that defines vaccination in the last paragraph summarizes Jenner's process. Reread the information under "Preventing Disease." Then summarize it by completing the sentences below.

A. Dr. Edward Jenner observed that _____

B. He experimented by _____

C. The results of the experiment were _____

Check your answers on page 236.

Thinking About the Article

Practice Vocabulary

▶ **The words below are in the passage in bold type. Study the way each word is used. Then complete each sentence by writing the correct word.**

century	orchestra	chronometer
smallpox	vaccination	immune

1. One of the worst diseases of the 1700s was _____.

2. Violins and French horns are instruments in a(n)

   _____ .

3. A(n) _____ helps prevent disease, not cure it.

4. A navigator uses a(n) _____ to figure out the exact position of a ship at sea.

5. The World Health Organization declared smallpox a thing of the past in

   the twentieth _____.

6. Jenner injected a boy with the cowpox virus to make him

   _____ to a worse disease.

Understand the Article

▶ **Write the answer to each question.**

7. How do a harpsichord and piano differ?

   _____

8. How did John Locke's philosophy of natural rights influence the creation of new inventions in the 1800s?

   _____

   _____

9. Why were watches not practical until John Harrison invented his chronometer?

   _____

   _____

10. How did Edward Jenner get the idea that smallpox can be prevented?

    _____

    _____

Apply Your Skills

▶ **Circle the letter of the best answer for each question.**

11. Which of the following claims is not supported by the article?

A. Cowpox is a form of smallpox.

B. Nearly half of the people who got smallpox died.

C. People who had had cowpox did not get smallpox.

D. Terrorists have used smallpox as a weapon.

12. Which words in the section "Reinventing Music" does the author use to show his or her point of view on new music?

A. lightly or firmly

B. powerful or delicate

C. rich and complex art

D. how softly or loudly

13. From whom or what did John Locke believe man received his rights?

A. from God

B. from nature

C. from kings

D. from nations

Connect with the Article

▶ **Write your answer to each question.**

14. Think of a musical instrument you play or like to hear. How is sound produced?

_____

_____

15. Name two diseases for which you would like researchers to find a vaccine and governments to require widespread vaccinations. Explain why you chose these diseases.

_____

_____

_____

LESSON 12

THE RISE OF NATIONS

Vocabulary

conservative

liberal

diplomat

democracy

duties

capital

gross national
    product

gross domestic
    product

strike

union

In 1521, the land that is now Mexico became a part of Spain's large empire in the Americas. Mexico stayed under Spain's rule for 300 years, until a revolution brought independence in 1821. Then one leader after another used force to gain control of the young nation's government.

Mexico's unstable politics kept its economy from developing. Meanwhile, other countries were using new inventions to industrialize. Fifty-five years after independence, Porfirio Díaz took control of Mexico. He modernized the country's economy on the eve of the twentieth century.

Relate to the Topic

This lesson is about how Porfirio Díaz modernized Mexico's economy between 1876 and 1911. His improvements, however, came at a high price for most Mexicans. Think about the expression *Do it for your own good.* Explain why you think that some people would have mixed feelings about that advice.

_____

_____

_____

Reading Strategy

SCANNING A TABLE   Tables can be an excellent way to present information—especially statistics—in social studies material. A **table** is a type of list that organizes information in rows and columns. Look briefly at the table on page 94. Be sure to scan the various labels. Then answer the questions.

1. What is the general topic of the table? _____
    Hint: Read the title at the top of the columns.

2. Name two activities other than agriculture for which figures are given.

    _____

    Hint: Study the labels across the tops of the columns.

Modernizing Mexico

After Mexico became independent, different groups fought for control of the government. In its first 55 years, Mexico had 75 leaders. These leaders were either conservatives or liberals. **Conservatives** wanted little change. They were wealthy landowners whose ancestors had come from Spain. They wanted a government with a strong army to enforce laws. Most Mexicans, however, were of Indian or mixed ancestry. Many were poor farmers. They wanted a government that would act on their behalf. They were called **liberals.**

A Struggling Nation

Porfirio Díaz had both Indian and Spanish ancestry. He had fought on the side of the liberals in a civil war against the conservatives. Many Mexicans considered Díaz a hero and thought he should lead Mexico. After liberal President Benito Juárez died, Díaz and his soldiers drove out the president who followed Juárez.

Díaz took over the Mexican government in 1876. At the time, Mexico's economy was in shambles. One reason was that Mexico had spent more money on the goods it bought than it received for the goods it sold. Also, wealthy Mexicans and foreign investors would not risk their money in a nation without strong leadership. So Mexico had little of the advanced technology seen elsewhere in the world.

Díaz realized that Mexico had a low standing among nations. Few diplomats lived there. A **diplomat** is a person whom a nation's leader chooses to handle relations with another nation. Díaz invited diplomats from the United States, Europe, and Asia to Mexico. He wanted to show them that Mexico had a firm leader in charge. He thought that perhaps their countries then would invest in Mexico's economy.

▶ Identifying Faulty Logic A statement with faulty logic may seem reasonable at first. However, when you think about it, the statement makes little sense. Often such statements contain a hasty generalization. A **hasty generalization** is based on little or no evidence. Words such as *all, none, never,* and *always* may signal hasty generalizations. Review the article above. Then select the statement with faulty logic from the following sentences.

A. After independence, Mexicans spent all their time on politics and none on their economy.

B. Liberal Mexicans outnumbered conservatives, so the liberals sometimes took control of the government from the wealthy.

Díaz Modernizes

Díaz's motto was "Order, Then Progress." His advisors told him to improve the economy first and to put democracy on hold. **Democracy** is a system of government that gives all of its citizens the power to make choices.

Check your answers on page 237.

Díaz sent soldiers to all parts of the country. He added more *rurales* (rural police). Mexico needed the money from **duties,** or taxes collected on goods entering the nation. But smugglers paid no duties. If caught, they suffered heavy penalties.

Next Díaz worked on progress. Land belonging to Indians was put up for sale. When some Indian peoples protested, Díaz's troops enslaved them and made them work for wealthy landowners.

Investors began investing in Mexico's economy. Foreign **capital**—money spent for production or investment—was put to immediate use. It bought modern equipment for textile, paper, and steel mills. It also paid for developing Mexico's natural resources. An American investor bought land and explored for oil. As a result, Mexico became one of the world's largest oil suppliers by the early 1900s.

Figures below show the growth in Mexico's gross national product. The **gross national product** is the total value of everything a nation produces. A country's gross national product indicates the growth and health of its economy. In contrast, the **gross domestic product** of a country is the total value of final goods and services produced within the country's borders. Both are indicators of the health of an economy.

MEXICO'S ECONOMIC GROWTH INDICATORS

Gross National Product*

Year	Mining	Agriculture	Manufacturing	Oil	Transportation	Other Activities	Total
1895	431	2,107	806	none	204	5,315	8,863
1900	541	1,991	1,232	none	237	5,890	9,891
1905	848	2,543	1,475	1	299	7,294	12,460
1910	1,022	2,692	1,663	19	295	7,833	13,524

*in millions of pesos at 1950 prices

Foreign Capital in Mexican Mining and Industry 1896–1907

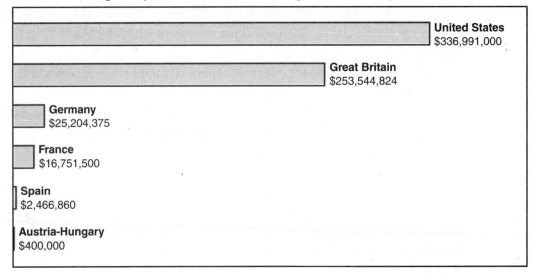

United States $336,991,000

Great Britain $253,544,824

Germany $25,204,375

France $16,751,500

Spain $2,466,860

Austria-Hungary $400,000

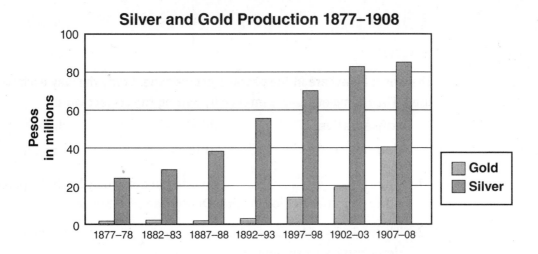

Silver and Gold Production 1877–1908

▶ Drawing Conclusions from Tables and Graphs To draw a conclusion, you must identify which facts are important. Then you decide what they tell you about the topic. One way of presenting facts is a graph, a special kind of drawing that is used to compare information. A table is a kind of list with information organized in columns and rows. Look at the table and graphs on pages 94 and 95. They show facts about Mexico's economic growth under Díaz's leadership. Based on the facts in the table and graphs, which of the following conclusions can you draw?

A. The value of agricultural products outstripped the value of mining products because of foreign investments.

B. Foreign capital and modern equipment helped Mexico uncover its gold and silver.

The Toll on Mexicans

Mexico's economic boom did not help most Mexicans. They worked at difficult and dangerous jobs. Factories stayed open 15 hours a day. Workers, including children, worked the entire time with only two short breaks for meals. Mines were very unsafe. One reported 500 deaths in five years.

Díaz made sure that workers had little power. He made **strikes** illegal. In some industrial towns, joining a **union** was a crime. Without labor unions, workers had no protection against their bosses' abuse.

Mexico's population went from 8.7 million in 1876 to more than 15 million in 1911. With such growth, proper housing was a major problem. Many people lived in rundown shacks. Several families often lived together in very small quarters. These conditions led to increased illnesses and deaths. Between 1895 and 1911, more people died in Mexico City alone than in the entire United States.

By 1910, Díaz had achieved his peaceful and united nation but Mexicans were far from happy. Most had longed for democracy. Instead they experienced violence and growing poverty. The Mexican people would have to face another revolution before they achieved democracy.

Check your answers on page 237.

Thinking About the Article

Practice Vocabulary

▶ **The words below are in the passage in bold type. Study the way each word is used. Then complete each sentence by writing the correct word.**

| conservatives | liberals | diplomat |
| democracy | duties | capital |

1. The _____ invested in Mexico by business people from other countries helped Porfirio Díaz modernize Mexico.

2. The majority of Mexicans were _____ who wanted a democratic government.

3. _____ collected on goods at the American border helped Mexico build up its treasury.

4. Wealthy Mexicans who wanted the strong protection of the military behind the government were called _____ .

5. A _____ from Japan was one of the first from Asia to visit Mexico.

6. Mexicans would go through a second revolution before they achieved _____ .

Understand the Article

▶ **Write the answer to each question.**

7. How would you describe the first 55 years of nationhood for Mexico?

_____
_____
_____

8. Why was Mexico not as technologically advanced as other countries around the world at the same time?

_____
_____
_____

9. Look at the graph on page 95. Does the relationship between the value of gold and silver mined show correlation, causation, or neither? Explain.

_____
_____

Apply Your Skills

▶ **Circle the letter of the best answer for each question.**

10. Based on the graph on page 94, which is an approximate median amount invested in Mexico's industries by foreign countries?

    A.   about $2,000,000

    B.   about $20,000,000

    C.   about $25,000,000

    D.   about $105,000,000

11. Look at the table on page 94. Which of the following conclusions is supported by the economic facts?

    A.   Mining production decreased during Díaz's presidency.

    B.   Manufacturing doubled while Díaz was in office.

    C.   The gross national product tripled under Díaz's leadership.

    D.   Mexico had a growing oil industry in the 1800s.

12. Based on the graph from page 94, which conclusion can you draw about investors in Mexico?

    A.   Americans invested more money than the combined investment from Europeans.

    B.   Germany invested more in Mexico than any other European country.

    C.   Spain invested the least money of all the countries shown.

    D.   Great Britain's investment equaled the combined money from Germany, France, Spain, and Austria-Hungary.

Connect with the Article

▶ **Write your answer to each question.**

13. Today, companies and governments think much more about sustainability, which is the effort to use natural resources responsibly and without using them up. How might Mexico have done things differently when Díaz was in power if sustainability had been the goal?

_____

_____

14. In addition to the toll on its people, what toll do you think Mexico's economic boom in the early 1900s took on the environment? How did the people change the environment? How would we do things differently today?

_____

_____

DEMOCRACY AND INDEPENDENCE

Vocabulary

republic

civil rights

parliament

apartheid

racist

sanctions

Black South Africans will long remember 1994. That was the year in which they were first allowed to participate in government elections in their country.

For decades, laws had stripped them of all political rights and freedoms. Laws also had separated them from white South Africans. Finally the years of oppression and protest had ended. Black and white South Africans faced the challenge of working together to build harmony in their new government.

Relate to the Topic

This lesson is about change in South Africa's long-standing policy of separating blacks and whites. Hostility between the races can lead to crimes committed out of racial hatred. In the United States, some states' laws give stiffer punishments to persons who commit such hate crimes. Do you think that our court system should handle hate crimes differently from other crimes? Explain.

Reading Strategy

PREVIEWING A POLITICAL CARTOON   Some social studies materials contain political cartoons. A **political cartoon** is a special type of cartoon that presents an opinion about a controversial topic. Previewing political cartoons helps you know what information to look for as you read. Look at the cartoon on page 101. Then answer the questions.

1. What shape is the woman's face? _____

_____

Hint: Think of the shapes of the continents.

2. How would you describe her expression?

_____

Hint: Look at what her eyes and mouth are showing.

Against Apartheid

For nearly 600 years, native black Africans and descendants of white Europeans have lived in South Africa. During most of this time, the whites ruled and mistreated the blacks. However, in the 1990s, black South Africans gained political power in their homeland.

The Fight over Land

Thousands of years ago, hunters and food-gatherers called the San made what is now South Africa their home. Their descendants, the Khoikhoi (KOY koy), raised sheep, goats, and cattle. Other black African groups who spoke the Bantu language migrated to the area from the north. They farmed the fertile soil and developed tools that helped improve their harvests. They fashioned some tools from iron.

In the 1400s and 1500s, Europeans searched for trade routes to Asia. One route went around the Cape of Good Hope at the southern tip of Africa. Portuguese sailors stopped on their way to Asia. They traded goods with the Khoikhoi. Later Dutch traders built a colony at the cape where sailors could rest on their long voyages. These Dutch were the first Europeans to settle in southern Africa.

During the 1600s, the mountains and rich valleys on the Cape of Good Hope attracted settlers from other European countries. All the Europeans called themselves Boers, the Dutch word for "farmers." The Boers stole Khoikhoi land and livestock to start farms of their own.

At first, the black Africans viewed the Europeans as mere visitors. The black Africans welcomed the trade, especially when they received iron in return for animal hides. But when they saw the Europeans planned to stay, some Khoikhoi rebelled. In 1659 they attacked the Boers, hoping to gain back herds they had lost. The attempt failed.

The Khoikhoi could not win against the Boers' firearms. In 1713, smallpox, a disease brought from Europe, killed many Boers and nearly all the Khoikhoi. The population decline brought a decline in the Khoikhoi's way of life and culture. Many Khoikhoi became servants of the Boers.

▶ **Recognizing Values** A people's culture influences the values that they hold. Values are what people feel are important, right, and good. People may indicate their values by what they say. Yet people's actions often reveal more about their values than words do. Reread the third and fourth paragraphs under "The Fight Over Land." Then match each beginning with its ending below to form statements about the values of the European settlers and the native Africans.

1. The Boers stole from the Khoikhoi because _____

2. The black Africans welcomed European trade because _____

   A. they valued land.   B. they valued iron for tools.

The White Minority and the Black Majority

European domination of South Africa only began with the Boers. During the 1800s, the British built an empire in Africa. They saw the riches of South Africa much as the Boers had. The Boers, however, refused to share the land that they considered theirs. By 1854 they had carved out two republics, the Transvaal and the Orange Free State. A **republic** is a self-governing territory. The British started colonies in a place called Natal and on the Cape of Good Hope.

British rule angered the Boers who lived on the cape. Some decided to leave. As Boer settlers moved north and east from the cape, they met Bantu-speaking groups, such as the Xhosa (KOH suh), Sotho, and Zulu. The Boers captured black Africans and enslaved them. The white Africans believed that owning slaves was their right even though blacks outnumbered the whites.

Discoveries of gold and diamonds in present-day South Africa led to war between the British and the Boers. The British eventually won the Boer War, which lasted from 1899 to 1902. As a result, the Boer republics became British colonies. In exchange, the British guaranteed positions of power to the white residents, who now called themselves *Afrikaners*. The British also refused to grant the black majority suffrage, or the right to vote.

In 1910, the four South African provinces united under one constitution. Black Africans still could not vote. So they organized a political group devoted to gaining their civil rights. **Civil rights** are peoples' freedoms, including the right to be treated equally with other people. This political group would later be known as the African National Congress (ANC).

Soon after the union, the South African **parliament,** or law-making body, passed laws that caused hardships for black Africans. For example, a law in 1911 reserved high-paying jobs for whites. The law forced even skilled blacks into the lowest-paying jobs. A 1913 land act set aside just ten percent of the country's land for blacks—although blacks made up nearly 80 percent of South Africa's population.

In 1948, the white government passed a formal policy that separated whites from blacks. Called **apartheid,** which means "apartness," the policy described who was "black," who was "white," and who was "colored"—a person of mixed race. Blacks and coloreds had to carry cards showing their race. In the 1950s, black Africans also had to carry small books with their fingerprints, racial background, and other details of their lives. Police demanded to see this book whenever a black African was in a city or in a whites-only area. If the person was not carrying the book, the police could put him or her in jail.

Apartheid caused much pain among black South African families. Most were very poor. Families broke apart when fathers went to jail. The government-run schools paid low salaries to the poorly trained teachers of black students. Officials decided what was taught, and they discouraged important subjects, such as mathematics. When the ANC decided to start its own schools, the government outlawed private schools.

The Long Road to Democracy

The ANC knew it needed to take stronger action against apartheid policies. It joined with other groups to encourage protest among black Africans. During the early 1950s, the police arrested nearly 9,000 blacks for purposefully disobeying apartheid laws. By the 1960s, the ANC promoted even stronger opposition. New young leaders, such as Nelson Mandela, spoke of a government with equality for all Africans. ANC members also began training for an armed uprising. In 1962, when word of the ANC plans reached the government, it arrested Mandela and 17 other leaders.

Other nations became keenly aware that South Africa's government was **racist,** or favored one race over another. News stories began to cover the protests and riots between the police and black South Africans. The Olympic organizers even banned South Africa from the 1968 and 1972 games. In 1976 thousands of black children in Soweto, near Johannesburg, marched to protest their poor schooling. As they sang freedom songs, police used tear gas. When the children threw rocks, the police opened fire and killed 176 people. To show disapproval of South African policies, many nations started sanctions. **Sanctions** are economic or military measures that nations use to pressure another nation to stop violating some international law or human right.

During the 1980s, global economic sanctions hurt South Africa's economy. Cries to release Nelson Mandela, who had been in prison for more than 20 years, grew louder. In 1990 the white government freed Mandela. It began to work toward equal rights for blacks and coloreds. In 1994, South Africa held elections that were open to all races. Seventeen million black voters went to the polls for the first time. As a result of the election, Nelson Mandela became South Africa's president.

South Africa adopted a new constitution, with a detailed bill of rights, in 1996. Three years later, Mandela stepped down. Another black South African, Thabo Mbeki, was elected in his place. Today South Africa struggles with unemployment, a high crime rate, and the growing incidence of AIDS. However, the country's success in ending apartheid provides hope that it will be able to deal with its other challenges.

▶ **Reading a Political Cartoon** A political cartoon expresses an opinion on an issue. The artist uses symbols and exaggerated drawings to express his or her views. Study the cartoon above. Who does the woman represent?

A. black Africans
B. all Africans

Thinking About the Article

Practice Vocabulary

▶ **The words below are in the passage in bold type. Study the way each word is used. Then complete each sentence by writing the correct word.**

republic	civil rights	parliament
apartheid	racist	sanctions

1. The South African _____ began making anti-black laws in the early 1900s.

2. In 1948, the government's abuse of black South Africans' rights became a policy called _____ .

3. Black South Africans wanted the same _____ that white South Africans had.

4. _____ practices in South Africa date back to the Boers who enslaved the black Africans they defeated in battle.

5. South Africa was a colony in the British empire, but in 1961 the colony became a(n) _____ :

6. A nation can use _____ to pressure another government to stop violating a law or human rights.

Understand the Article

▶ **Write the answer to each question.**

7. How has the population of South Africa changed over the last 600 years?

_____

8. How did cultural diversity lead to apartheid?

_____

_____

9. List three ways that apartheid violated the basic freedoms of black South Africans.

_____

_____

10. What is the author's viewpoint on apartheid? Explain.

_____

Apply Your Skills

▶ **Circle the letter of the best answer for each question.**

11. Which of the following actions of ANC members is evidence that they valued learning?

    A.   They planned to fight the government, if necessary.

    B.   They devoted time to working for civil rights.

    C.   They joined other groups to encourage resistance among black Africans.

    D.   They tried to open nongovernment schools for black children.

12. Look again at the cartoon on page 101. What is the cartoonist trying to show about black Africans in Africa?

    A.   They are lazy.

    B.   They are proud.

    C.   They are weary.

    D.   They are careless.

13. Why does the artist draw the woman's face in the shape of Africa?

    A.   to show that whites are wealthier

    B.   to show that whites are intruders

    C.   to show that black Africans are more powerful

    D.   to show that whites have no place in Africa

Connect with the Article

▶ **Write your answer to each question.**

14. How might the number 9,000 be different if the same article was written from the view point of a Boer at the time? Explain.

15. Nelson Mandela became the leader of South Africa after the 1994 election. If you had been elected president of South Africa instead of Mandela, what would your first actions as the head of its government have been?

GLOBAL INTERDEPENDENCE

Vocabulary

charter

neutral

cease-fire

mediator

allies

deadlocked

province

civil war

The year was 1944, and World War II was still raging. Even so, Great Britain, the United States, and China were looking ahead to peacetime. Their delegates met in Washington, D.C., to draw up a plan for a world organization called the United Nations. Its purpose was to stand up to national leaders who bullied their neighbors or their own people, as Germany and Japan had done at the start of the war.

Relate to the Topic

This lesson is about United Nations peacekeeping forces. It describes who they are and what they do in the troubled spots they protect. Think about a recent newspaper or television report about fighting in a distant region of the world. Where was the fighting, and what was it about?

_____

_____

_____

Reading Strategy

USING HEADINGS TO ASK QUESTIONS The headings of an article can help guide your reading. They also can help you review what you have read. Skim the headings in the article that begins on page 105. Then answer the questions.

1. What is one question that you could ask about a group of people?

   _____

   _____

   Hint: You could start a question with the word Who.

2. Write a question that you could ask about a place.

   _____

   _____

   Hint: You could start a question with the word Where.

UN Peacekeeping Forces

By the end of World War II, most leaders had realized that they needed the combined strength of several nations to stand up to powerful enemies. So 51 countries formed the United Nations (UN) in 1945. Their representatives approved its **charter,** or plan, at a meeting in San Francisco.

The UN Charter created a Security Council. The Security Council is responsible for maintaining peace in the world. The United States, Great Britain, Russia, China, and France are permanent members of the Security Council. The General Assembly—delegates from the 191 countries who now belong to the United Nations—elects ten temporary members.

Peacekeepers to the Rescue

The members of the Security Council decide how to handle trouble-making governments, warring countries, or warring groups within a country. The council's actions can range from scolding publicly to sending troops. Troops under UN command are known as peacekeeping forces. The secretary-general, the chief officer of the UN, appoints their commander.

Peacekeeper forces must be **neutral.** In other words, they cannot take sides. So the soldiers come from countries that are not directly involved with the conflict at hand. The soldiers fall into two groups—observers and peacekeepers.

The observers are unarmed officers who visit an area in small numbers simply to watch. Then they report back to the UN. They wear blue helmets or berets. The jeeps and other vehicles that accompany them are white and marked with *UN* in large, dark letters. Observers monitor situations such as an election or a **cease-fire**—a pause in fighting. For example, in the 1990s, the UN sent observers to Nicaragua in Central America to witness the change from civil war to a democratic government.

Flags of UN members flying outside the UN building

Lightly armed soldiers do the actual peacekeeping. They often do not have tanks or heavy weapons. They sometimes do their job by coming between warring parties. Either side must then attack UN soldiers first in order to get to its enemy. The UN soldiers also act as **mediators,** or go-betweens, to settle disagreements between enemies. Both kinds of peacekeeping are often necessary to maintain a cease-fire.

▶ **Understanding a Photo** Pictures often contain as much information as words do. Look at the photo on page 105. It shows flags of UN members. What does this photo suggest about the United Nations?

    A. The UN encourages cooperation between nations.

    B. The UN takes pride in its public appearance.

Early Missions in the Middle East and Africa

On several occasions, UN troops have stepped in to make peace in the Middle East and Africa. One of the earliest instances was the Suez Crisis in 1956. The United States and Great Britain had offered to help pay for the Aswan High Dam project in Egypt. But Egypt's President Gamal Nasser also asked the Soviet Union for money. The Americans and British distrusted the Soviet Union and withdrew their offer. On July 26, 1956, an angry President Nasser responded by claiming that the Egyptian government owned the Suez Canal.

The Suez Canal was an important shipping lane. Until Egypt seized the canal, a company half-owned by the British ran it. So, with the help of its **allies,** France and Israel, Britain tried to retake the canal by force. Israel attacked Egypt from the air on October 29, and British and French troops landed on its Mediterranean shore on November 5.

President Nasser requested help from the UN. Members of the Security Council were **deadlocked**—unable to agree on what to do. So the General Assembly voted to send troops. A cease-fire took effect on November 6, and Great Britain, France, and Israel withdrew from Egypt. Six thousand UN troops guarded the borders after the withdrawal.

On this mission, none of the troops were from Great Britain, France, the United States, or the Soviet Union. For the first time, an international police force took action without a major power involved. Since then, United Nations peacekeepers have gone several more times to the Middle East. To this day, UN observers continue to monitor borders there.

In the 1960s, the Congo crisis brought UN peacekeepers to Africa. The Congo declared independence from Belgian rule in 1960 and renamed itself Zaire. But the new central government could not control the far-flung parts of the country. Katanga and other **provinces**—regions similar to states in the United States—tried to pull out and establish their own countries.

Zaire's Prime Minister Patrice Lumumba requested aid from the UN. In 1962 UN forces arrived to keep order. Despite their presence, Zaire collapsed into **civil war,** and all that the 20,000 UN soldiers could do was to protect civilians, or nonmilitary persons.

In 1988, the UN peacekeeping forces received the Nobel peace prize. This award recognized the growing importance of international forces. In the 1990s, the UN definition of "keeping peace" became broader. Some missions, like the one in Somalia, focused on saving a country's people rather than its government.

Saving Somalis

Siad Barre was the ruler of Somalia. For years his harsh treatment of the people had caused revolts. Several groups of rebels came together in the United Somali Congress (USC) and overthrew Siad in 1991.

Groups in the USC then quarreled about who would take Siad's place. Heavy fighting broke out in a major grain-growing region of the country. The fighting drove out the farmers. Harvests had already fallen off because of a drought that began in 1989. As a result of the drought and the fighting, the country had almost no food.

By spring of 1992, civil war had killed about 30,000 Somalis. However, ten times more people had died from hunger. By June about 3,000 people were dying each day.

Agencies from all over the world flew in food. But the warring groups hijacked the food before the Red Cross and similar nongovernmental organizations (NGOs) could distribute it. So the UN Security Council approved a peacekeeping force to help deliver the food. Over six months, American planes flew 28,000 tons of food to Somalia, and 500 UN peacekeepers from Pakistan arrived to protect it. Still the food could not reach central Somalia, where people needed it most.

Relief to the hungry took many more soldiers. On December 12, 1992, thousands of troops from Canada and France began arriving to protect the trucks that would deliver the food. More soldiers spread out to the relief stations where the food would be distributed to the people. American soldiers and sailors began building and improving roads to the stations.

By February 1993, food and other aid was being distributed in all parts of the country. Famine was no longer a danger, and convoys full of supplies were rolling along on new or improved roads. Cooperation among governments, UN agencies, and NGOs had accomplished a truly humane mission.

▶ Getting Meaning from Context Sometimes you can figure out the meaning of an unfamiliar word from its context, or the sentences around it. Find the word *famine* in the last paragraph and choose the definition that fits the word's context.
   A. a scarcity of food
   B. a lack of rainfall

Check your answers on page 238.

Thinking About the Article

Practice Vocabulary

▶ **The words below are in the passage in bold type. Study the way each word is used. Then complete each sentence by writing the correct word.**

charter	neutral	cease-fire
deadlocked	provinces	mediator

1. The peacekeeping officer acted as a _____ between leaders of Somali groups.

2. The United States was _____ in the Bosnia conflict, and so American troops were included in the UN force sent to Bosnia.

3. The new secretary-general scanned the _____ for a description of his duties.

4. When the Security Council was _____ , the General Assembly approved the use of UN troops in Egypt.

5. The rebels in Katanga and other _____ declared a

    _____ so they could discuss their demands with Zaire's prime minister.

Understand the Article

▶ **Write the answer to each question.**

6. How does a UN observer differ from a UN peacekeeper?

    _____

    _____

    _____

7. How might cultural differences have played a role in why it was difficult for the government of Zaire to control far flung parts of the country?

    _____

    _____

    _____

8. Why did Somalis have so little food in 1992?

    _____

    _____

Apply Your Skills

▶ **Circle the letter of the best answer for each question.**

9. Look again at the photo on page 105. Which of the following is an informed hypothesis based on the photo?

A. The UN takes pride in flying its members flags.

B. The UN is made up of many different nations.

C. The UN has many peacekeeping forces.

D. The flags for the UN Security Council members are the first fifteen flags.

10. Which event came first in the cultural and political conflict in Somalia?

A. American planes flew 28,000 pounds of food to Somalia.

B. The United Somali Congress overthrew Siad.

C. Troops from Canada and France arrived.

D. About 3,000 people were dying each day.

11. Why is it important that the UN peacekeeping soldiers not be from one of the countries where they are keeping peace?

A. They may leave and go home.

B. They may know more information than is allowed.

C. They may have an advantage in combat.

D. They may feel a need to help people of their culture.

Connect with the Article

▶ **Write your answer to each question.**

12. Is this statement a fact or an opinion? "The UN peacekeeping mission to Zaire was a failure." Do you agree or disagree with this statement? Explain your answer.

_____

_____

13. If you were going to be a mediator in a disagreement between two friends, why would it be important that you remain neutral in the dispute?

_____

_____

_____

RESCUING AN ENVIRONMENT

Vocabulary

sound

environment

glacier

iceberg

crude oil

March 24, 1989, was the date of a terrible oil spill in North America. Along the southeastern coast of Alaska, a huge oil tanker ran off course and struck a reef. The tanker's bottom tore open. Almost 11 million gallons of oil spilled into the sea.

Many people rushed to clean up the oil spill. They worked to help save the wildlife along Alaska's coast.

Relate to the Topic

This lesson is about how people rescued Alaska's southern coast after an oil spill. Smaller but similar problems with pollution can affect everyone's surroundings. What could you do to improve a garbage-strewn park in your neighborhood?

_____

_____

_____

_____

Reading Strategy

RELATING TO WHAT YOU KNOW   Understanding facts in informational material is easier if you compare those facts with what you have previously read or experienced. Read the first three paragraphs on page 111. Then answer the questions.

1. Does this description of Alaska's environment match what you already know about it?

   _____

   _____

   Hint: When you hear the word Alaska, what picture comes to mind?

2. What do you already know about the way that oil is transported?

   _____

   _____

   Hint: What have you learned about oil by watching the news?

Oil Spill in Alaska

The oil spill took place in Prince William Sound. A **sound** is a long, wide inlet from the ocean. Prince William Sound, which is off the Gulf of Alaska, has a marine, or sea, environment. An **environment** is all of the living and nonliving things that make up a place's surroundings. People, fish, seaweed, and other animals and plants are the living parts of the environment of Prince William Sound. The nonliving parts are soil, rocks, water, and glaciers that line the coast. A **glacier** is an enormous mass of ice that moves slowly over land.

Every part of an environment is closely tied to all its other parts. Sea otters, for example, depend on fish and birds for food. Seal meat and fish are important to Native Alaskans' diet. Many people who live in the Prince William Sound area fish for a living. Others work in the tourist business. Thousands of tourists visit parks, forests, and wildlife refuges near the sound.

Some people who live along the sound work in the oil industry. They store and ship oil. The Alaskan pipeline carries oil from Alaska's Arctic region to Valdez. This is a port on Prince William Sound. Oil tankers come to Valdez each month to carry Alaskan oil to other parts of the United States.

▶ Using a Glossary or Dictionary When you read the sections in this book, you will come across words in bold type. You can find their meanings in the glossary at the back of this book. You may also come across other words that you do not understand. Look in a dictionary to find the meaning of each word. Then, on the lines below, write the definition that best fits the use of the word in the article.

_____

_____

_____

_____

Disaster in Prince William Sound

On Thursday evening, March 23, 1989, an oil tanker called the *Exxon Valdez* left port and headed for California. Shortly after midnight, the tanker turned sharply to avoid a dangerous iceberg. An **iceberg** is a huge block of floating ice that has broken off from a glacier.

The tanker missed the iceberg but ran over a reef. The smell of untreated oil, called **crude oil,** filled the air. The ship was leaking. By dawn on March 24, a thick oily film, called an oil slick, covered six square miles of the surface of Prince William Sound. By early evening, about ten million gallons of oil had spilled. The oil slick stretched over more than 18 square miles.

Check your answers on page 239.

The slick continued to spread. Wind and water carried the oil farther into the sound. Then a storm hit just four days after the spill, carrying the oil into tiny inlets and coves along the shore. After the storm, the oil slick covered 500 square miles. The oil spill traveled southwest with the ocean currents, polluting more than 1,200 miles of Alaskan coastline.

The spill claimed the lives of 1,000 sea otters. It also killed 100,000 birds, including about 150 bald eagles. People who fished for a living wondered if the oil would harm the salmon, herring, and other fish they depended on.

The Cleanup

No one had ever cleaned up an oil spill as large as this one. So, no one knew exactly what to do. The Exxon Corporation sent about 11,000 workers to help. It owned the *Exxon Valdez*. The company that managed the Alaskan pipeline also took some responsibility for the cleanup. The state of Alaska, the U.S. Coast Guard, and several U.S. government agencies helped, too. But it was not always clear who was in charge.

The cleanup crews tried many ways to remove the spilled oil. Some tried to skim the oil from the water. They transferred it to other ships. The workers needed special equipment, but it was slow to arrive.

Some experts wanted to spray the oil with chemicals. These chemicals act much like a detergent. But the company did not have enough chemicals to treat the whole spill. Besides, state and federal officials were slow to permit the spraying. By the time everybody was ready to act, it was too late. In the end, cleanup crews recovered less than ten percent of the oil.

Exxon Valdez Oil Spill

Meanwhile, workers attacked the spill on the beaches. Some crews tried to blast the oil from rocks. Others sprayed the beaches with hot water and fertilizer. The fertilizer encouraged the growth of bacteria that eat oil.

Some of the cleanup methods worked, while others did more damage than the oil. The hot water killed some wildlife. It also sent oil deep into the gravel beaches, where it was unreachable but still harmful to the environment. The bacteria ate up the oil on some beaches but the fertilizer killed seaweed, a plant important to the region's environment. Workers rescued some of the many fish, birds, and animals. They also protected some fish hatcheries. But, later on, some wildlife died after eating fish or animals that were poisoned by the spill.

▶ **Drawing Conclusions** Recall the last time you listened to someone talk about a problem. Did you make judgments about how the problem started? Or get ideas about how to fix the problem? Or guess how people might react to it? If you did any of these things, you were drawing a conclusion. You based your conclusion on the facts as you understood them.

Reread the paragraphs on pages 112–113 that are under the heading "The Cleanup." From the information presented, what conclusion can you draw about why the oil spill was difficult to clean up? Write your conclusion on the lines below.

_____

_____

The Effects of the Oil Spill

Just after the oil spill, many people believed that wildlife would never return to Prince William Sound. Yet less than a year later, the air and water were clear again. Fish and whales that had survived the spill returned to the sound in the spring as they always had. Plants began to grow again.

The environment had changed, however. By spring of 1991, many groups of sea birds had not recovered from the spill. Scientists said it would take from 20 to 70 years for the birds to build up their numbers to the population levels before the spill. Injuries to other wildlife were just beginning to show. Studies showed that oil still at the bottom of the sound continued to harm the sea life.

In 1994, a federal court jury ordered the Exxon Corporation to pay $5 billion to Alaskans who earned their living by fishing. Native American companies and Alaskan cities also shared this award. In a separate settlement, the United States and Alaskan governments won $900 million. To administer that money, state and federal officials formed the *Exxon Valdez* Oil Spill Trustee Council, with headquarters in Anchorage. This group uses the settlement money to restore natural resources and the activities that depend on these resources, such as commercial fishing and tourism. The council monitors and evaluates restoration activities and meets several times a year to report on the progress of recovery efforts.

Thinking About the Article

Practice Vocabulary

▶ **The words below are in the passage in bold type. Study the way each word is used. Then complete each sentence by writing the correct word.**

sound	**environment**	**glacier**
iceberg	**crude oil**	

1. A(n) _____ is an inlet of the ocean.

2. A nearby body of water has a strong influence on the surroundings in

   a marine _____ .

3. A(n) _____ is formed when snow and ice accumulate
   on land over a long period of time.

4. Tar and gasoline are two products that come from

   _____ .

5. A(n) _____ poses dangers to ocean liners and other
   ships traveling in northern waters.

Understand the Article

▶ **Write the answer to each question.**

6. Look at the map on page 112. The spill happened in Prince William Sound.
   What can you tell about the ocean currents near the oil spill based on the
   map? Explain.

   _____

   _____

   _____

7. How does the author's point of view change within the article when he or
   she discusses the state of wildlife in the area after the oil spill?

   _____

   _____

8. Use the map on page 112. What feature of a sound makes it a particularly
   bad location for an oil spill?

   _____

   _____

Apply Your Skills

▶ **Circle the letter of the best answer for each question.**

9. Which of these events happened last?

   A. Exxon Mobil paid $5 billion to Alaskan fisherman.

   B. The Exxon Valdez hit a reef.

   C. Experts wanted to spray the oil with chemicals.

   D. Some wildlife ate contaminated fish and died.

10. The spring after the oil spill, plants sprouted, whales returned, and salmon catches were high. Based on this information and what you read in the article, which of the following could be the author's point of view?

   A. Every part of the cleanup was a success.

   B. The cleanup harmed more living things than it helped.

   C. The water in the sound could no longer support life.

   D. The cleanup helped some living things in the environment.

Connect with the Article

▶ **Write your answer to each question.**

11. Locate the wildlife refuges on the map on page 112. What problems might workers at hotels near these refuges have faced during the rest of 1989? Explain your answer.

   _____

   _____

   _____

12. The year after the oil spill, Congress created an oil-spill cleanup fund as a result of the *Exxon Valdez* accident. The money for the fund comes from taxes on crude oil. Do you think this tax affects the price you pay for oil products, such as gasoline? Explain your answer.

   _____

   _____

   _____

   _____

LESSON 16

TAKING CARE OF RESOURCES

Vocabulary

topsoil

desertification

drought

overgrazing

displace

ecotourism

When you choose your activities, you may ask yourself, "Do I have enough money for this?" or "How much time will it take?" Money and time are two resources that are important to many people.

A resource is anything that people can use to satisfy their needs. Natural resources are essential materials supplied by nature. They include water, land on which plants can grow, and minerals. Natural resources support all of our activities. Without natural resources, life would be impossible. Therefore, preserving natural resources is a matter of vital importance to everyone.

Relate to the Topic

This lesson is about a global threat to productive land. Think back over the past 24 hours. List some things you ate that grew on or fed from the land.

_____

Why is it important to preserve productive land? _____

_____

_____

Reading Strategy

PREVIEWING A BAR GRAPH   Looking ahead at illustrations, such as bar graphs, can help guide your reading. Look at the bar graph on page 118. Consider why this information might be given. Then answer the questions.

1. What is one word that you expect the lesson to explain?

   _____

   Hint: Study the title of the graph.

2. What three types of land usage do you expect you will learn about?

   _____

   _____

   _____

   Hint: Look at the legend to the graph.

116   *Check your answers on page 240.*   UNIT 2 · GEOGRAPHY AND THE WORLD

Preserving Productive Land

With the gales came the dust. Sometimes it was so thick that it completely hid the sun. . . . At other times a cloud is seen to be approaching from a distance of many miles. Already it has the banked appearance of a cumulus cloud, but it is black instead of white, and it hangs low, seeming to hug the earth. . . . Birds fly in terror before the storm, and only those that are strong of wing may escape.

Where did these storms take place? In the African Sahara? Actually, this description came from a Kansas wheat farmer. He is talking about the Dust Bowl, a name given to parts of Texas, Oklahoma, Kansas, New Mexico, and Colorado in the 1930s. Winds raging across the Dust Bowl blew away the **topsoil**—the surface soil usually anchored down by plants. "Black blizzards"

closed down roads and schools in many parts of the country. Some people even got sick and died from inhaling the dust.

The Dust Bowl was an example of **desertification,** or the turning of productive land into desert. But desertification was not a problem only of mid-twentieth-century America. According to the United Nations, in recent years desertification has affected more than a billion people in more than 110 countries.

Causes and Effects of Desertification

Although desertification is a complex process, two main factors contribute to it. One factor is **drought**—a long period of unusually dry weather in a region that normally receives rain. Drought is a natural factor in desertification. It results in not only lack of rain, but also the drying out of soil. Some droughts last for years. In most cases, however, droughts end. The rain returns, and the land becomes productive again—especially when people have taken care of it.

The other main factor in desertification is abuse of the land by people. One kind of abuse is **overgrazing.** This is the practice of letting too many animals feed on the grasses or of letting animals feed in one part of an area for too long. Cutting down too many trees and farming the land too heavily are other kinds of abuse. These are common practices in places where people are poor and depend on agriculture for their living. Abuse of the land ruins the ability of plants to hold topsoil in place.

Either drought or overgrazing can cause desertification. When both occur, the process speeds up. This is what happened in the Dust Bowl, when decades of overfarming were followed by drought. Thousands of family farms in the Dust Bowl and in nearby regions were ruined as a result.

Blowing dust troubles parts of the world that suffer from desertification. In addition, an increased amount of dust in the air makes it harder for raindrops to form, and lack of rain makes the situation even worse. Finally, dust can travel far enough to damage plants in areas that are not subject to either drought or abuse.

In such conditions, many people are **displaced,** or forced to leave their homes, because of the lack of food. Displaced people create a drain on resources wherever they settle.

Since the Dust Bowl, there have been other extreme cases of desertification. A disaster in the Sahel, a region of western Africa, focused the world's attention on the problem. The Sahel lies between the Sahara to the north and the savannah (tropical/subtropical grasslands) to the south. On average, less than eight inches of rain falls on the Sahel each year. Despite the dry conditions, people raised crops and herds there—often to the point of abusing the land. Between 1968 and 1974, the Sahel suffered a terrible drought. More than 200,000 people and millions of animals starved to death. Another drought brought more suffering to the region in the 1980s.

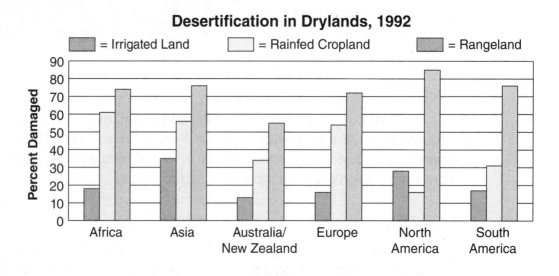

Desertification in Drylands, 1992

▶ **Reading a Triple Bar Graph** Some bar graphs are used to compare information. The triple bar graph above is based on a 1992 study of the world's drylands—regions that can be productive even with little rainfall. The bar graph shows the percentage of drylands in various regions that are estimated to have been damaged by desertification. Use the graph's key to compare the bars.

1. Where has there been more damage to irrigated cropland than to rainfed cropland?
   A. in Asia
   B. in North America

2. Which continents have suffered similar percentages of damage to rainfed cropland?
   A. Australia and South America
   B. South America and Europe

Beating Back the Desert

The Sahel disaster prompted scientists to examine desertification in depth. Based on the information shown in the bar graph on the previous page, they concluded that desertification is a global problem. But it is a problem with solutions. Some methods of preserving land from desertification use state-of-the-art technology. For example, satellite pictures help scientists look for signs of desertification around the world. Many other techniques are more traditional. The United Nations has set up anti-desertification programs in many countries. It does much of its work at the local level, using methods that already are familiar to people or that can be taught easily.

For example, the United Nations encouraged farmers in Brazil to return to a traditional technique called "zero tillage." Using this technique, farmers do not plow their land, but drill seeds through existing plant cover. Zero tillage not only has reduced the loss of soil but has also produced larger corn and soybean harvests. The people of Zhangeldy, in Kazakhstan, also have worked with the UN to combat desertification. They have changed the way that they graze their sheep in order to help prevent overgrazing. With the help of the UN and the Zambia Alliance of Women, women in the community of Shantumbu, Zambia, have been exploring different ways of preserving and healing their damaged drylands. For example, instead of trying to raise crops there, they have turned to raising chickens and pigs for food and income. They are reducing their production of charcoal, which they formerly used for fuel and sold to people in nearby urban areas. Charcoal requires cutting down and burning trees. By reducing charcoal production, the people of Shantumbu are helping to save their forests. They are also promoting ecotourism in the region. **Ecotourism** is travel to areas of natural or ecological interest. The people of Shantumbu can earn money through ecotourism while preserving their local environment.

▶ **Recognizing Unstated Assumptions** Information that you read is usually based on certain **assumptions,** or beliefs. For example, a writer discussing jogging may assume that his or her readers are interested in improving their health. Sometimes writers explain such assumptions. Other times the assumptions are left unstated. In the first paragraph on this page, what is an unstated assumption about change at the local level?
    A.   People who live in an area have the greatest motivation to improve that area.
    B.   Most people are suspicious of high-tech answers to local problems.

Governments can fight desertification on a national level. For example, China has experienced increasing sandstorms because of desertification. In 2002, the Chinese government announced a tree-planting program that would convert cropland to forests. If the program is successful, it should limit desertification dramatically. To succeed, however, the program needs funding of more than $1 billion a year as well as the support of farmers whose land will be taken. At both the national and local levels, stopping desertification is important—but it is not necessarily easy.

Thinking About the Article

Practice Vocabulary

▶ **The words below are in the passage in bold type. Study the way each word is used. Then complete each sentence by writing the correct word.**

topsoil	desertification	drought
displaced	overgrazing	ecotourism

1. When _____ people find a place to settle, they face economic and social challenges in their new homes.

2. Herders who practice _____ can ruin the very pastures they need.

3. During the Dust Bowl, winds blew exposed _____ into "black blizzards" that disrupted people's lives.

4. Some ways of combating _____ include planting trees and adopting zero-tillage farming.

5. _____ can build the economy of a poor area and educate visitors about the environment.

6. Land that has suffered from a period of _____ can become productive again when rains return.

Understand the Article

▶ **Write the answer to each question.**

7. Why are rural areas more at risk of desertification than urban areas?

_____

_____

8. Look at the graph on page 118. Explain how the percentage of land that is damaged relates to the type of land. Is this an example of causation or correlation? Explain.

_____

_____

_____

9. Name something that Brazilian farmers have done to preserve the land.

_____

_____

_____

Apply Your Skills

▶ **Circle the letter of the best answer for each question.**

10. Look at the bar graph on page 118. Which of the following statements about desertification does the information in the bar graph support?

    A.   Desertification has damaged more land in Australia than in Europe.

    B.   Range land has been managed and preserved best in Asia.

    C.   Irrigated land has suffered more damage than rainfed cropland.

    D.   Range land has suffered more damage than cropland.

11. How does drought differ from desertification?

    A.   Desertification refers to land; drought refers to the weather.

    B.   Both drought and desertification can ruin productive land.

    C.   Unlike desertification, drought does not affect the topsoil.

    D.   Land can be reclaimed from drought, but not from desertification.

12. In which area would you expect to find the most desertification?

    A.   in an urban area that is heavily populated

    B.   in a rural area with many farms with livestock

    C.   in an urban area with lots of park space

    D.   in a rural area that is sparsely populated

Connect with the Article

▶ **Write your answer to each question.**

13. What connection do you see between poverty, population density, and land abuse?

_____

_____

14. If you were trying to make the tree-planting program in China succeed, how would you gain the support of farmers who do not want to lose their cropland?

_____

_____

_____

GEOGRAPHY AT WORK

TRANSPORTATION:
TICKET AGENT

Many people love to travel and to see new places or visit old favorites. Other people travel for business or personal reasons. Whether it's travel to a local or faraway spot, ticket agents help travelers get to their destinations on trains, subways, or elevated rail cars. Ticket agents work for railroads or public transit systems. Because they have contact with customers, they should enjoy working with people.

Ticket agents help customers plan departure and arrival times, determine how long a trip will take, book reservations, and buy the tickets. Agents need to have good geography skills. They need to read maps, use tables and charts, and work with fare schedules. They must have a good understanding of directions and know where places are. Because they help customers set travel schedules, ticket agents must have good time measurement and arithmetic skills.

Look at the sidebar showing some of the careers in transportation.

- Do any of the careers interest you? If so, which ones?

- What information would you need to find out more about those careers? On a separate piece of paper, write some questions that you would like answered. You can find out more information about those careers in the *Occupational Outlook Handbook* at your local library or online.

SOME CAREERS IN TRANSPORTATION

Transportation Ticket Agent
makes reservations, sells tickets, and answers customers' questions

Station Agent
assists travelers with special needs

Travel Clerk
plans routes, calculates mileage, and answers questions

Passenger Rate Clerk
sells tickets, plans special or chartered trips, works with customers

© Houghton Mifflin Harcourt • Image Credits: ©Corbis

Rail ticket agents help customers plan their trips and make reservations. **Use the timetable and map below to fill in the spaces in the conversation that follows.**

Train	Washington, D.C. Departure Time	Baltimore Arrival/Departure Times	Philadelphia Arrival/Departure Times	New York Arrival/Departure Times
18	5:30 A.M.	6:15 A.M./6:20 A.M.	7:34 A.M./7:39 A.M.	8:59 A.M.
126	6:15 A.M.	7:00 A.M./7:05 A.M.	8:19 A.M./8:24 A.M.	9:44 A.M.
150	9:00 A.M.	9:45 A.M./9:50 A.M.	11:04 A.M./11:09 A.M.	12:29 P.M.
200	1:56 P.M.	3:41 P.M./3:46 P.M.	4:50 P.M./4:55 P.M.	6:15 P.M.

Eastern Rail Line Timetable—Route: Washington, D.C., to New York, NY

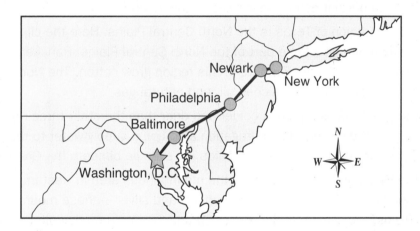

RAIL AGENT: "Good morning. This is the Eastern Rail Line. May I help you?"

CUSTOMER: "Yes. Do you have any trains leaving from the Washington, D.C., area that will get me into New York City by 12:30 p.m.?"

RAIL AGENT: "We have _____ trains that arrive before 12:30 p.m. The train numbers are: _____ ; _____ ; and _____ ."

CUSTOMER: "I have an appointment at 12:45 p.m. in New York. Which train should I take?"

RAIL AGENT: "There is a train that arrives at _____ , but that will only leave you 16 minutes to get to your meeting. I recommend you take train number 126. It arrives in New York at _____ . It will give you plenty of time to get to your meeting."

CUSTOMER: "What is your first stop north of Washington, D.C.?"

RAIL AGENT: "_____ is the first stop north of Washington, D.C."

CUSTOMER: "That stop is closer to my house; I will catch the train there. Thank you. I'd like to buy my ticket now."

RAIL AGENT: "I will be happy to help you."

The Geographic Regions of Texas

Texas is so large that geographers divide it into four regions. Each region has different resources. Those resources help make Texas one of the richest states in the United States.

One region of Texas is called the Gulf Coastal Plain. It covers eastern and southern Texas. The climate in this region is warm and wet. Long ago forests covered the Gulf Coastal Plain. Today, much of the land has been cleared for farming and ranching. Farmers grow cotton, vegetables, rice, and fruit. Oil and natural gas are among the important natural resources of this region.

Another region of Texas is the North Central Plains. Here the climate is drier. Grasslands make up a large part of the North Central Plains. Ranchers graze cattle and sheep on the grasslands. Farmers in this region grow cotton. The North Central Plains are rich in resources such as coal, oil, and natural gas.

The Great Plains region is colder and drier than the other three regions. Farmers must irrigate their wheat fields. Irrigation also helps supply water to the ranchers of this region. Some of the richest oil fields in Texas lie beneath the Great Plains.

The Basin and Range region is the mountainous area in western Texas. Miners have found resources such as gold, copper, and silver in these mountains. Like the Great Plains, the climate is dry. Ranching and farming are possible only through the use of irrigation.

▶ **Circle the letter of the best answer.**

1. How do the farmers and ranchers of Texas use irrigation?

   A. as a way to find rich oil fields

   B. as a way to find natural gas deposits

   C. to get water for their crops and animals

   D. to get water from other regions

2. Someone who wants to go into ranching in Texas should settle in the North Central Plains. Which information best supports this conclusion?

   A. Grassland covers much of the North Central Plains.

   B. The North Central Plains are drier than the Gulf Coastal Plain.

   C. The soil of the North Central Plains is not good for raising crops.

   D. Coal and oil are two resources of the North Central Plains.

Top Ten Cattle-Raising and Oil-Producing States

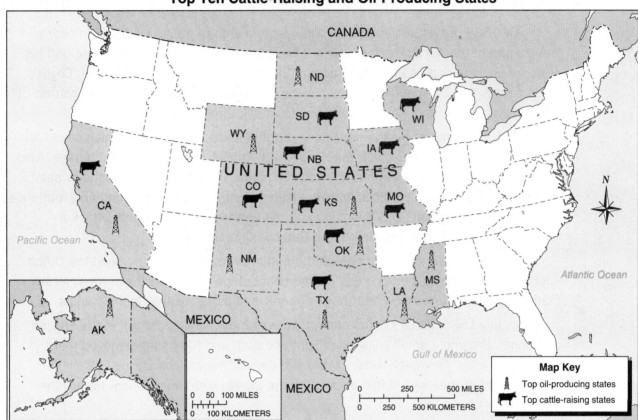

▶ **Use the map to answer each question.**

3. How can you tell which states lead in cattle production?

_____

4. In addition to New Mexico, which states lead in oil production but not in cattle production?

_____

5. Which of the following can be determined from the map?

A. how much oil is produced in the top oil-producing states

B. how long Alaska has been one of the top oil-producing states

C. how many states are top producers of both oil and cattle

D. why the states that lead in both categories border each other

SOCIAL STUDIES EXTENSION Borrow a video about taking care of resources and preserving the environment from your local library. As you watch the video, list ways you can help take care of the environment. Write down at least one new fact about resources that you learn from the video.

Go on to the next page.

The Spanish Empire Tumbles

By 1588, Spain had built the world's largest empire. It included land in nearly every part of the world. But this was not enough for Spain's King Philip II. He had his eye on England and its Protestant queen, Elizabeth I. Under Elizabeth's rule, English sea pirates had been raiding Spanish ships and stealing the treasures they carried from Spain's colonies. So Philip planned to attack the island nation.

The Spanish king built a magnificent fleet of ships, which the Spanish called an **armada.** Many of its 150 ships were huge, with enough space for mules, horses, food, weapons, and hundreds of soldiers. Each ship bore the name of an apostle or saint. To command the armada, Philip chose a high-ranking nobleman who had no experience at sea. The more than 25,000 soldiers on the armada considered this attack a mission to bring England back into the Catholic Church.

England's navy could not defend the nation by itself. Elizabeth asked the Dutch for help. She also called upon English merchant ships to join the Royal Navy. Nearly 200 ships met the armada, but they were only half as big as the Spanish ships.

In July 1588, fierce storms and rough seas made sailing difficult in the English Channel. England's small ships were light and fast, and their sailors moved them expertly through the rough waters. After two days of heavy fighting, the English set fire to eight of their own ships and sent them, loaded with ammunition, toward the armada.

The Spanish Empire 1588

Spanish Empire

The Spanish ships headed north to dodge the attack, but even more English ships chased them. Wild storms wrecked 17 Spanish ships along Ireland's coast. Only a few hundred Spaniards returned home. England had defeated the grand Spanish armada.

Spain's empire was never the same. Its power seemed to sink with its ships. England would become the next great power in Europe.

▶ **Write or circle the answer to each question.**

6. Reread the first two paragraphs of the article on page 126. From the context, what does *armada* mean?

    A. naval commander

    B. Spanish empire

    C. raiding sea pirates

    D. fleet of ships

7. Which part of Philip's plan to attack England is the <u>best</u> example of faulty logic?

    A. He told his soldiers they were winning England back into the Catholic Church.

    B. He named a high ranking but inexperienced nobleman as fleet commander.

    C. He named the ships after apostles and saints.

    D. He brought 25,000 soldiers.

8. What was faulty about Philip's overall plan?

    _____

    _____

    _____

▶ **Look at the map on page 126. Then answer the question.**

9. Why do you think so many areas under Spanish control were along coastlines?

    _____

    _____

SOCIAL STUDIES EXTENSION

Think about a person with whom you often disagree. Choose an issue over which you have disagreed. List points you made in the disagreement, and then list the other person's points. Compare and contrast them. What values do you share? What values are yours alone? What opposite values does the other person hold? What seems to be the reason that you disagree?

MINI-TEST

This is a 15-minute practice test. After 15 minutes, mark the last number you finished. Then complete the test and check your answers. If most of your answers were correct but you did not finish, try to work faster next time.

▶ **Directions: Choose the one best answer to each question.**

Question 1 refers to the following timeline.

Latin American Independence

1. What can you conclude about Latin American independence?

    A. The countries that won independence in the 1800s all broke free of Spain.

    B. Most of the movement's leaders were born in Latin America, not in Europe.

    C. Almost all of these countries became independent within a fifteen-year period.

    D. The independence movement took place only in South America.

Questions 2 and 3 refer to the following information.

One of the major themes of geography is migration. Migration occurs when individuals or groups of people move from one place to another and resettle. Migration has two types of causes: push factors and pull factors.

Push factors force people to move. Drought, famine, and natural disaster are push factors. Other push factors are unemployment, war, and overpopulation.

Pull factors encourage people to move, but moving is a choice. When pull factors are at work, a new location seems to offer people better housing, better job opportunities, or an overall better standard of living.

2. Which of the following is the best conclusion about the nature of push factors?

    When push factors exist,

    A. people are attracted to a different place

    B. people are happy about moving

    C. drought and famine kill many people

    D. moving is a matter of survival

3. Which of the following is an example of a pull factor?

    A. Kurds leaving Iraq during a civil war in the 1990s

    B. Jews escaping from anti-Semitism in Nazi Germany in the 1930s

    C. Irish families leaving Ireland during the potato famine in the 1840s

    D. Americans moving west to settle their own farms during the 1800s

Question 4 refers to the following circle graph.

Volume of Water in the Great Lakes

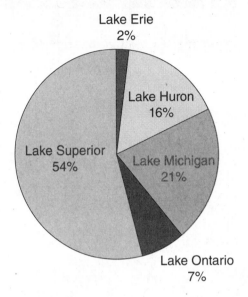

Lake Erie
2%

Lake Huron
16%

Lake Superior
54%

Lake Michigan
21%

Lake Ontario
7%

4. In terms of volume, Lake Superior is larger than all the other Great Lakes combined. Based on the graph, which of the following statements is both accurate and adequate to support this conclusion?
Lake Superior

A. is smaller than Lake Michigan

B. is larger than Lake Erie

C. is larger than Lake Huron and Lake Ontario

D. has 54% of the total volume of the Great Lakes

Questions 5 and 6 refer to the following information.

In the early 1950s, six European nations agreed to cooperate on a number of economic matters. Their association was eventually named the European Economic Community (EEC) and is also referred to as the Common Market.

As more countries joined the EEC, the association began to consider other goals in addition to purely economic ones. In 1993, the organization became the European Union (EU). Member nations agreed to cooperate on immigration, law enforcement, and foreign policy issues. By 2013, the EU had 28 members, and 7 southern and eastern European countries were applying for membership.

5. Which question would a good summary of this passage help answer?

A. What does *Common Market* mean?

B. Which treaty established the EU?

C. How did the EU develop into more than an economic association?

D. Why wasn't England an original member of the EU?

6. Which statement about the European Union is a hasty generalization?

A. European nations make up the membership.

B. Former communist countries may become members.

C. Membership in the EU is likely to increase in the coming years.

D. Members never disagree about policy.

Check your answers on page 241.

Civics is the branch of political science that deals with the rights and duties of citizens. **Government** refers to the system of laws and the political bodies that make it possible for a nation, a state, or a community to function. As a citizen or a resident of the United States, civics and government affect your daily life. Learning about civics and government can help you understand how our country operates.

When did you last vote in an election?

_____

Write two ways state and local government affect your daily life.

_____

_____

Thinking About Civics and Government

You may not realize how much you already know about civics and government. Think of news reports that you have seen or heard. What did they tell you about the workings of your community and the nation?

Check the box for each fact that you already know.

☐ The U.S. system of government is a representative democracy based on the Constitution.

☐ The Bill of Rights guarantees Americans freedom of speech.

☐ The national government is divided into three branches: the executive branch, the legislative branch, and the judicial branch.

☐ The Senate and the House of Representatives are the legislative branch of the national government.

☐ In the United States, you must be at least eighteen years old to vote.

☐ Taxes pay for services that the government provides.

Write two other facts that you know about civics and government.

_____

_____

Previewing the Unit

In this unit, you will learn:

- how local governments deal with community problems

- how the concept of checks and balances is part of our government

- how the government protects the rights of citizens

- what responsibilities citizens have

- how Americans choose their leaders

- how a political campaign is conducted

- how the government gets and uses money for the benefit of the people

Lesson 17	**State and Local Governments**
Lesson 18	**The Constitution of the United States**
Lesson 19	**Rights and Responsibilities**
Lesson 20	**Elections**
Lesson 21	**Paying for Government**
Lesson 22	**Public Policy**

STATE AND LOCAL GOVERNMENTS

Vocabulary

Constitution

federal government

ordinance

hazardous waste

landfill

groundwater

aquifer

recycling

composting

After the Revolutionary War, the loyalty of many Americans was mainly to the state in which they lived. Creating a nation of these separate states led to many questions. What form should the national government take? What powers would the national government have over its citizens? What matters could state and local governments decide for themselves?

The answers to these questions were not easily decided. Some disputes about the powers of the national, state, and local governments arise even today. For the most part, however, government works best when federal, state, and local officials cooperate for the good of all Americans.

Relate to the Topic

This lesson is about ways that state and local governments get rid of trash. Do you recycle cans, plastic, glass, newspapers, or paper? Why or why not?

_____

_____

_____

_____

Reading Strategy

PREVIEWING A POLITICAL CARTOON   A political cartoon can help you better understand ideas. Not only can a political cartoon give information about a topic, it also expresses an opinion about that topic. Look at the cartoon on page 134. Then answer the questions.

1. Based on the cartoon, what do you think the lesson will be about?

_____

Hint: Which words and art details catch your attention first?

2. Who does the man represent?

_____

Hint: What is the man doing?

Taking Care of Everyday Needs

The **Constitution** is the basic law for American citizens. It describes the parts of the government and spells out the powers that belong to each part. These powers are shared between smaller, regional governments and a central, national government. The national government is in Washington, D.C. It is called the **federal government.** The regional governments are all over the nation. They are in states, cities, towns, counties, and villages and are called state and local governments.

The Constitution lists which powers the federal government has and which powers it cannot have. The Constitution also lists powers that state governments have and cannot have. However, many of the powers of state and local governments are not listed in the Constitution. If the Constitution does not ban the states from having a certain power, and it does not give the same power *only* to the federal government, then that power belongs to the states. States, for example, decide how old you must be to get a driver's license. In addition, some powers are shared between the federal government and state and local governments. For example, they may all collect taxes, build roads, borrow money, and make and enforce laws.

Handling Trash

Many powers of state and local governments deal with the basic services people need every day. Cities and counties, for example, pave streets, treat and supply water, manage law enforcement and fire protection, and collect trash. Today, local governments face a trash crisis. Since 1960, the amount of trash people produce has increased dramatically. The Environmental Protection Agency estimates that Americans throw away 250 million tons of trash each year.

Local governments have four choices regarding trash. They can burn it, bury it, compost it, or recycle it. But first they must sort it. Glass, metal, and other solid materials are separated from garbage, which decays over time. Most local governments have **ordinances,** or laws, that require people to separate hazardous wastes from the rest of their trash. **Hazardous wastes** are those items that harm the environment. They include old batteries, motor oil, and certain kinds of paint.

Some counties and towns have furnaces that burn trash. It is burned under carefully controlled conditions, leaving only ash. The ash is then buried.

Most trash is not burned but buried in landfills. A **landfill** is land that is reserved for trash. It is often in areas away from neighborhoods. Trash is buried in the landfill between thin layers of soil. The United States had 8,000 landfills in 1988. Today more than 6,000 of them are closed. Many were older landfills that closed because they were full. Other older landfills closed because they became dangerous. As garbage decays, it forms poisons that can seep into the soil. The poisons pollute **groundwater,** which is an underground source of water. Groundwater feeds wells, springs, ponds, and **aquifers.** About half of the country's drinking water comes from groundwater.

Taking Responsibility

In many states, state and local government officials have worked together to solve their trash problems. They looked at all their options. As a result, they have passed laws that encourage recycling.

Recycling is reusing trash for the same or new purposes. To be used again, most recyclable trash must be processed into a new form. Some places require people to separate recyclable materials, such as aluminum, from their trash. Towns may get people to recycle by establishing "pay-as-you-throw" programs—charging people for trash pickup by the volume or weight of their garbage. The more people throw out, the more they pay. Communities with these programs have seen a decrease in the amount of trash and an increase in recycling.

by John Larter

▶ **Reading a Political Cartoon** A political cartoon expresses an opinion on an issue. The cartoonist uses exaggerated drawings and symbols to express his or her views. It is important to know what the symbols mean and understand why they are used. What idea is the cartoonist expressing in the cartoon?

    A. Society must find better ways to dispose of trash.

    B. Society produces more trash than it can handle.

Some communities practice composting. **Composting** is letting plants and food waste decay on their own. These materials are then turned into rich soil. Many communities have set up leaf-and-yard-waste compost centers. Some communities are beginning to offer curb-side pickup of food waste as well.

Some states have laws that set requirements for new landfills. Towns and cities can no longer build their landfills near aquifers or lakes. The new landfills are also designed to be safer. The pits are lined with layers of sand, plastic, and clay. These linings prevent poisons, which are formed as trash decays, from oozing into the ground outside the pits. Also, pumps remove dangerous liquids from decaying trash. Many communities are cleaning up old landfills. When landfills are full, some local governments recycle the land and build golf courses and parks there.

Most landfills in the eastern half of the United States are full or will be within a few years. These states are more densely populated. A place that is densely populated has many people living within a square mile. Most land in these states is already in use leaving no more land available for new landfills.

Zero Waste

Recycling has been increasing since the 1980s, and today nearly 35 percent of all waste is recycled nationwide. However, local governments are recycling only a fraction of their trash because of the high cost of recycling. Even though new technology has helped lower the costs of recycling and burning trash, landfills are still the cheapest form of trash disposal. In general, it costs approximately twice as much to burn trash as to bury it and approximately three times as much to recycle it.

Some trash experts suggest that manufacturers should work harder to design their products with trash disposal in mind. These experts want companies to create ways for customers to reuse, recycle, or compost products and packaging. They hope to see the day when "zero waste"—in which all materials are either reused or returned safely to the environment—becomes not only a goal but also a reality.

Municipal Solid Waste (MSW) Recycling Rates by Year

1960	1965	1970	1975	1980	1985	1990	1995	2000	2005	2011
6.4%	6.2%	6.6%	7.3%	9.6%	10.1%	16.0%	25.7%	28.5%	31.4%	34.7%

Source: Environmental Protection Agency

▶ Finding the Implied Main Idea   The topic sentence of a paragraph tells the main idea of the paragraph. Sometimes a paragraph has no topic sentence. So the main idea is not stated, but it is implied. The reader must determine the main idea from the details in the paragraph. Reread the first paragraph under the heading "Zero Waste." Which sentence best describes the main idea of the paragraph?
   A. Recycling is an expensive way for local governments to dispose of trash.
   B. More local governments are recycling trash than ever before.

Thinking About the Article

Practice Vocabulary

▶ The words below are in the passage in bold type. Study the way each word is used. Then complete each sentence by writing the correct word.

Constitution	federal government	hazardous wastes
landfill	groundwater	recycling

1. A _____ is likely to be located away from densely populated areas.

2. The Constitution lists powers that the state government and the _____ can and cannot have.

3. Some states have fewer than a dozen curbside programs for _____; other states have hundreds of such programs.

4. Old landfills may leak poisons into the _____, polluting water supplies.

5. The _____ lists the powers of the federal government.

6. _____ include old batteries, motor oil, and certain kinds of paint.

Understand the Article

▶ Write the answer to each question.

7. Why do American citizens pay many different types of taxes?

_____

8. Do you think the author recycles and composts? What language from the article supports your conclusion?

_____

9. Look at the table on page 135. Suppose you graphed the year on the x-axis and the recycling rate on the y-axis. What trend would be shown on the graph?

_____

10. What has to happen before local governments can dispose of trash by burning, burying, composting, or recycling it?

_____

Apply Your Skills

▶ **Circle the letter of the best answer for each question.**

11. Look at the cartoon on page 134. Which opinion does it express?

A. People are too lazy to recycle.

B. People should generate less trash.

C. Peoples' trash smells.

D. We need more landfills.

12. Reread the second paragraph under the heading "Taking Responsibility" on page 134. Which sentence states the paragraph's implied main idea?

A. Most Americans refuse to recycle.

B. Individuals and all levels of government must deal with the trash crisis.

C. Recycling is the answer to the trash crisis.

D. Local governments have set up different ways to get people to recycle.

13. Based on the idea of shared powers, which of the following are both the federal government and state governments allowed to do?

A. declare war

B. print money

C. take out a loan

D. authorize drivers' licenses

Connect with the Article

▶ **Write your answer to each question.**

14. Use the table on page 135. What is the mean recycling rate for 1960 to 2011? What is the median of the data? Round each percentage to the nearest whole number. What is the mode of the data?

----

15. What are you doing now to help your community dispose of trash? What more could you do?

THE CONSTITUTION OF THE UNITED STATES

Vocabulary

legislative branch

executive branch

judicial branch

separation of powers

Constitutionalism

checks and balances

veto

bill

override

impeach

appeal

judicial review

federal deficit

In 1748, French writer Baron de Montesquieu wrote a book praising Great Britain's government. In the book, he explained that the British balanced the power of government among three branches. Parliament made the laws. The courts interpreted the laws. And the monarch and his or her ministers carried out the laws. Under such a system, Montesquieu wrote, "power should be a check to power."

Montesquieu's ideas became popular in Britain's American colonies. Many Americans agreed that government should be divided into branches. Later, they used Montesquieu's ideas when they wrote the Constitution.

Relate to the Topic

This lesson is about the way that the Constitution divides the government's power among three branches. Recall the last time you heard that Congress, the President, or the Supreme Court had taken action. What was the action, which branch of government took this action, and what did you think of it?

_____

_____

_____

Reading Strategy

SKIMMING A DIAGRAM   Diagrams can be an excellent way to present detailed information in social studies materials. Turn to page 140 and look at the diagram. Then answer the questions.

1. What is the main topic of the diagram?

_____

Hint: Look at the title.

2. How does the diagram relate to the topic of the lesson?

_____

_____

Hint: What words are in both the diagram title and the lesson headings?

Separation of Powers

Some powers are given only to the federal government. These include powers like the power to print money, make treaties, declare war, and create post offices. These powers are shared among the three branches of the federal government. Each branch has a specific job. The **legislative branch** makes laws. The **executive branch** carries out laws. The **judicial branch** decides what the laws mean. The Constitution spells out each branch's powers. The three branches work together to govern the nation.

Because each branch has one key job of government, no one branch can become too powerful. This idea is called **separation of powers.** The writers of the Constitution also gave each branch ways to make sure the other two branches do not act beyond their power. The idea that a government can and should be limited in its powers is known as **Constitutionalism.** Each branch has a certain amount of authority over the other branches. This balances the power among them and is called **checks and balances.** The government operates by majority rule—it does what most of the people want. At the same time, the limits on the government make sure that minority rights are not overlooked.

Checks and Balances in the Executive and Legislative Branches

The President and Vice President lead the executive branch of the federal government. They make sure that the laws Congress passes are carried out. This branch is the only one in charge of enforcing laws. It has many departments to help. For example, the Labor Department enforces laws about workers, and the Interior Department carries out laws that deal with the use of the nation's natural resources.

The executive branch has powers that check the legislative branch. For example, the President may **veto,** or reject, bills. A **bill** is a proposed law.

The executive branch also has a power that checks the judicial branch. The President appoints Supreme Court justices and other federal judges.

Congress is the legislative branch and is made up of two houses, the House of Representatives and the Senate. Together both houses of Congress are in charge of making laws. American voters elect the members of each house. This is an example of how the U.S. government follows the concept of popular sovereignty—the idea that the government is created by and for the people.

The legislative branch has powers that check the executive branch. Although the President may veto a bill, the Constitution allows Congress to vote on the bill again. If two-thirds of both houses vote in favor of the bill, it becomes law. This action is called an **override** of the veto. The Constitution also gives Congress the power to approve government spending. To check the President, Congress can deny funds to pay for the President's favorite programs. The legislative branch can check the judicial branch, too. It must approve the President's appointments and has the power to impeach judges. To **impeach** means to accuse someone of misconduct and remove the person from office.

▶ Reading a Diagram A **diagram** shows how a system works. Look at the diagram below. Follow the arrows from each branch of government and read what checks it has over the other branches. Which branch determines if a law is constitutional?

     A. legislative branch   B. executive branch   C. judicial branch

The System of Checks and Balances

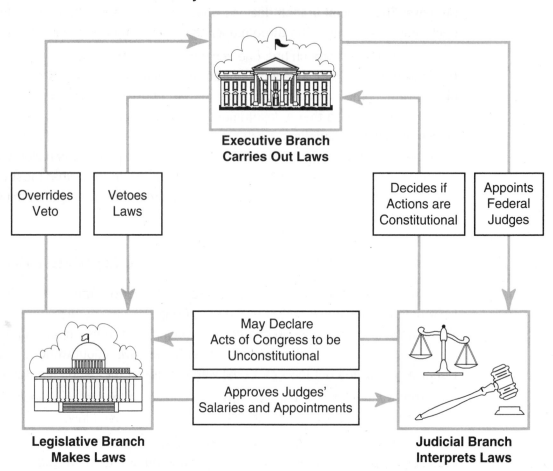

Executive Branch
Carries Out Laws

Overrides Veto

Vetoes Laws

Decides if Actions are Constitutional

Appoints Federal Judges

May Declare Acts of Congress to be Unconstitutional

Approves Judges' Salaries and Appointments

Legislative Branch
Makes Laws

Judicial Branch
Interprets Laws

Checks by the Judicial Branch

The judicial branch of the federal government makes certain that the government follows the Constitution. At the head of the judicial branch is the Supreme Court. It has many lower courts to help it. If citizens object to a decision made in a federal court, they can **appeal,** or bring the case to another federal court called the appeals court. If citizens are unsatisfied with the appeals court's ruling, they can go to the Supreme Court.

The judicial branch checks both the legislative and executive branches in a similar way. It uses its power of **judicial review.** This means the Supreme Court and lower federal courts can determine whether a law passed by Congress follows the Constitution. If the Court rules that a law is unconstitutional, the executive branch stops enforcing the law.

A Case Study in Checks and Balances

Government officials are sometimes frustrated with checks and balances. The following example is a case in which the judiciary checked both the executive and legislative branches. It shows the system of checks and balances in action.

In 1997, Congress passed the line-item veto law. Before this law, the President could reject only an entire spending bill or tax bill. The President could not accept some parts of the bill and reject others. The line-item veto law allowed the President to veto only specific parts of a bill.

Surprisingly, Congress was in favor of this law, which gave the President more power. Lawmakers thought the law would be a good way to control wasteful spending. They hoped it would encourage presidents to lower the huge **federal deficit.** This is the amount of money the government has to borrow each year. Congress knew that governors in 44 of the 50 states had line-item veto power. Governors who had used this power had some success in limiting spending in their state budgets.

Other people thought that giving the President a line-item veto was a bad idea. They said that the Constitution gave the power to control spending to Congress, not to the President. They believed the line-item veto weakened the separation of powers between these two branches of government.

When the new law took effect, President Bill Clinton praised it as "a powerful tool to protect taxpayers." Many presidents before him had wanted more power to curb government spending. Members of the executive branch saw the passage of the law as their victory.

In 1998, the Supreme Court ruled that the line-item veto law was unconstitutional. In the written decision, the justices quoted George Washington, who wrote that a president cannot change the text of a bill by Congress. In addition, the Constitution allows a president to veto a bill, but it does not say if the President can veto only parts of it. The Court decided that Congress could not give this power to the executive branch.

President Clinton was unhappy about the Supreme Court's decision. "The decision is a defeat for all Americans," he said. "It deprives the President of a valuable tool for eliminating waste in the federal budget."

Senators who favored the line-item veto were also unhappy with the decision. Usually Congress combines many kinds of spending in one bill. These unhappy senators threatened to include only one type of spending in each bill. If lawmakers used this method, the President would have to sign or veto thousands of spending bills each year.

▶ Distinguishing Fact from Opinion A **fact** states something that can be proved. An **opinion** expresses what a person or group thinks or believes. Which statement is a fact?

    A. The Constitution's writers gave the executive branch the power to veto bills.

    B. The judicial branch is the most powerful branch of government.

Thinking About the Article

Practice Vocabulary

▶ **The words below are in the passage in bold type. Study the way each word is used. Then complete each sentence by writing the correct word.**

legislative branch	**executive branch**	**judicial branch**
checks and balances	**separation of powers**	**Constitutionalism**

1. Determining whether the federal government acts according to the Constitution is the main job of the _____.

2. The idea of _____ ensures that no one branch of the federal government becomes too powerful.

3. The _____ includes departments, like Labor and Interior, that help enforce laws.

4. The idea that a government can and should limit its powers is

   _____.

5. The Constitution gave the _____ control over government spending.

6. Each branch of the federal government limits the powers of

   the other branches through a system of _____.

Understand the Article

▶ **Write the answer to each question.**

7. What is an example of a power given only to the federal government and not belonging to state governments?

   _____

8. To whom does the concept of popular sovereignty give the power to govern?

   _____

9. Why did the President favor the line-item veto?

   _____

10. What happened after the line item veto bill became a law?

    _____

Apply Your Skills

▶ **Circle the letter of the best answer for each question.**

11. Look at the checks and balances diagram on page 140. Which fact is supported by the information in the diagram?

    A.   The legislative branch is the most powerful because Congress makes laws.

    B.   Each branch of government checks the power of the other branches.

    C.   The veto power gives the President great power over Congress.

    D.   The Supreme Court has lower federal courts to help it interpret laws.

12. A role of the President of the United States is to

    A.   veto laws.

    B.   interpret laws.

    C.   make laws.

    D.   amend laws.

13. Which fact supports the hypothesis that the line-item veto law would have saved the government money?

    A.   Nearly all of the governors of states had line-item veto power.

    B.   Some governors with line-item veto power had success in limiting spending.

    C.   The line-item veto law weakened the separation of powers between the President and Congress.

    D.   The line-item veto law encouraged presidents to lower the federal deficit.

Connect with the Article

▶ **Write your answer to each question.**

14. How is the idea of separation of powers different from the idea of checks and balances?

_____

_____

15. The phrase "majority rule and minority rights" can be used when describing the federal government. Why and how do these two concepts fit together in a democracy?

_____

_____

RIGHTS AND RESPONSIBILITIES

Vocabulary

amendment

Bill of Rights

justice

due process

warrant

indict

rule of law

What do you think Andrew Jackson, the seventh President of the United States, meant by this statement? "Every good citizen makes his country's honor his own, and cherishes it not only as precious but as sacred. He is willing to risk his life in its defense and is conscious that he gains protection while he gives it."

Jackson's words speak of the double nature of citizenship. As citizens, we appreciate what our country gives us. We also respond by giving of our time and talents to our country.

Relate to the Topic

This lesson is about some of the basic rights and freedoms that Americans enjoy—and what is expected of Americans in return. What do you think you should expect of your country? What should it expect of you?

_____

_____

_____

Reading Strategy

RELATING TO WHAT YOU KNOW To make sense of informational reading, compare the facts with what you have read or experienced. Read the first paragraph under the heading "Guarantees of Freedom and Justice" on page 145. Then answer the questions.

1. What do you already know about the First Amendment?

_____

_____

Hint: When or where might you have heard the term First Amendment?

2. When have you experienced the freedoms that the paragraph names?

_____

_____

Hint: Think about the amendment's focus on communication.

Making Freedom Work

After the Constitution was written in 1787, several states were reluctant to approve it. They wanted the document to say that the federal government would protect certain rights of citizens. With these rights Americans would truly be free.

Many of the Constitution's framers saw no need for such a list. Most state constitutions already gave these rights to their citizens. Some of the states, however, pressured the government. In 1789, in the first session of Congress, James Madison of Virginia introduced 17 amendments to the Constitution. An **amendment** is an addition or change.

According to the Constitution, an amendment can be proposed by Congress or the states. Each must have a two-thirds majority vote to propose an amendment. The proposed amendment is sent to the state governors, who forward it to their state legislatures. If three-fourths of the state legislatures ratify it, it becomes an amendment to the Constitution.

The first amendments included the list of rights that many people had wanted to see in the Constitution. By 1791, the states had approved ten of the amendments that Madison had suggested. These first ten amendments to the Constitution are called the **Bill of Rights.**

Guarantees of Freedom and Justice

The Bill of Rights protects the freedom of Americans. The First Amendment is the main guarantee of personal freedoms. This amendment protects the individual right of Americans to speak and write about their beliefs and opinions. It also allows them to gather and associate with people of their choice and to worship, or not worship, freely.

Several of the other amendments in the Bill of Rights guarantee **justice,** or fair and equal treatment under the law. These amendments grant due process to a person who is accused of a crime. **Due process** is the set of steps that law enforcement personnel and the courts must follow to protect the rights of the accused. It includes the right to be represented by a lawyer (Sixth Amendment) and the right to a trial by jury (Seventh Amendment).

Three other amendments in the Bill of Rights describe additional individual rights and protections related to due process. The Fourth Amendment prohibits police and other government agents from searching a person's body, house, car, or other belongings without good reason. Law enforcement personnel must obtain a **warrant**—a legal permit from a court, before they can conduct a search. According to the Fifth Amendment, a person cannot be tried for a crime unless **indicted,** or formally charged. This amendment also says that a person cannot be tried twice for the same crime and cannot be forced to testify against himself or herself. According to the Eighth Amendment, a person who is found guilty of a crime cannot be punished in a cruel or unusual way.

After September 11, 2001, Congress passed the Patriot Act. Some people thought it overstepped the rights of Americans.

The protections that we have as Americans are important, but they are also open to interpretation. The Supreme Court often is asked to decide whether the rights guaranteed by the Bill of Rights apply to specific situations.

Other matters regarding American rights are part of our public debate. For example, the Second Amendment names "the right of the people to keep and bear arms" as key to "a well-regulated militia." Should citizens who are not in the military be allowed to own guns? Should a person need a permit to own a gun? People on opposing sides of the issue interpret the Second Amendment differently.

There are limits on the guarantees provided in the Bill of Rights. For instance, the First Amendment gives people the right to hold parades. In practice, however, they must get a permit before they can parade on city streets. Similarly, a person cannot use freedom of speech to yell "fire" in a theater just to see what happens.

Perhaps at no time are limits on rights and freedoms of greater concern than during war or other national emergency. Many Americans are willing to make some sacrifices for the sake of national security. Still, they are cautious. They know that if they allow some rights and freedoms to be compromised in a time of crisis, it may not be easy to get them back when the crisis has passed.

▶ **Interpreting Political Cartoons** An artist who creates a political cartoon uses symbols and words to express an opinion. A political cartoon may not need many words to express an opinion. Which opinion is expressed in the cartoon above?

    A. The desire for national security may put the Bill of Rights in danger.

    B. The Bill of Rights is dangerous and out of date.

With Rights Come Responsibilities

Guaranteed rights are part of our American heritage. Another part of that heritage is the responsibility to support the United States. Just how can we do that?

One answer is by participating in government. Before elections, for example, responsible citizens inform themselves about the issues and candidates. Some people work on candidates' campaigns or help educate the public about issues that they consider important. They may even run for public office themselves. Then, on election day, they vote.

Another responsibility is to follow the rule of law. **Rule of law** is the idea that everyone must follow the laws and that the laws must be fair and equal. By following the rule of law, citizens are helping to make their community safe. Another way that American citizens act responsibly is by working to make their communities the best they can be. People who organize groups to clean up a park or who set up neighborhood watch groups to help the police keep the street safe are acting as responsible citizens. So are people who volunteer their time at libraries, senior centers, and charitable organizations.

Some of the residents of Hartford, Connecticut, showed how volunteers can improve their communities. A group of people in the West End felt that their neighborhood needed a community center. The people organized and began to plan. They knew that they would need popular support to make the West End Community Center a reality. Members of the West End Community Center Board took their case to the community. They signed up volunteer workers. They talked to businesses about supporting the center. When the city council was ready to decide about the center, the board printed the flyer below in both English and Spanish and distributed it to people in the neighborhood.

West End Community Center

This is it! If you want a Community Center, come down to City Hall and tell City Council.

Monday, March 11 at 7:30PM
at City Hall, 550 Main Street
Public Hearing for the City Council.

The City Council will be deciding whether to give the West End money to buy 461 Farmington Avenue (Mark E. Salomone building, big white building with the columns next to Subway)

If you want to see the plans before Monday, Call or come to the West End Community Center Board meeting on Friday, March 8 at 6PM at Shepherd Park, 170 Sisson Avenue

---

The West End Community Center Board's campaign worked. The city council approved $450,000 for the project. Soon after, the Board began the process of buying a building and raising funds to support the operation of the center.

▶ **Understanding Persuasive Information** Writing that is **persuasive** encourages you to have a certain opinion or to take a certain action. Reread the information in the flyer above. What is the flyer trying to persuade people to think or do?

    A. to believe that a community center would be good for the West End

    B. to speak in support of the community center at the public hearing

Thinking About the Article

Practice Vocabulary

▶ **The words below are in the passage in bold type. Study the way each word is used. Then complete each sentence by writing the correct word.**

amendment	Bill of Rights	justice
due process	warrant	rule of law

1. The _____ guarantees individual rights such as freedom of religion to Americans.

2. A police officer cannot search your home without first obtaining a(n) _____.

3. _____ exists when people receive fair and equal treatment under the law.

4. A(n) _____ is an addition or other change to an existing legal document.

5. _____ is the set of steps that the police and court officials follow to protect the rights of people accused of crimes.

6. The idea that laws must be fair and equal and followed by everyone is known as _____.

Understand the Article

▶ **Write the answer to each question.**

7. What are two individual rights guaranteed in the First Amendment?

   _____

   _____

8. Why is rule of law important?

   _____

   _____

9. How might the author have written differently about the Second Amendment if he or she had lived in the 1790s?

   _____

   _____

   _____

Apply Your Skills

▶ **Circle the letter of the best answer for each question.**

10. Look at the cartoon on page 146. Which statement best summarizes the cartoon's main idea?

   A.   Some people hate the Constitution of the United States.

   B.   Attacking guaranteed rights is as much a danger as terrorism.

   C.   The President should be able to amend the Constitution.

   D.   The Bill of Rights requires people to get a permit for holding a parade.

11. Who may propose an amendment to the Constitution?

   A.   the President

   B.   Congress

   C.   state governors

   D.   the Supreme Court

12. Look again at the flyer on page 147. How is this flyer most likely different from a notice posted by the city council about the community center?

   A.   It is less helpful than a notice.

   B.   It is more legal than a notice.

   C.   It is less informative than a notice.

   D.   It is more persuasive than a notice.

Connect with the Article

▶ **Write your answer to each question.**

13. Why is due process important to Americans?

_____

_____

_____

14. Think about your community. How could you help make it a better place?

_____

_____

_____

ELECTIONS

Vocabulary

politics

political party

nominate

candidate

campaign

primary election

general election

media

political action
 committee

soft money

Each year American voters go to the polls and choose their representatives in government. Every four years Americans elect the President of the United States. Every two years they elect members in the House of Representatives and one-third of the U.S. Senate. Voters also choose state governors, city mayors, local judges and sheriffs, and many other government leaders.

People vote for or against issues as well as candidates on election day. They may vote to approve the local school budget or a new tax for enlarging the public library. By voting, people directly decide important matters of government.

Relate to the Topic

This lesson is about the election process and what it takes to run for political office. When was the last election held in your community? Write something that was decided in that election.

_____

_____

_____

Reading Strategy

SKIMMING BOLDFACED WORDS   You can get an overview of an article by skimming it and looking for boldfaced words—words that appear in dark type. These are words of special importance to the topic. Skim the article that begins on page 151. Look for boldfaced words. Then answer the questions below.

1. List two boldfaced words in the lesson that refer to groups of people.

_____

Hint: Look for nouns, not verbs.

2. What do the boldfaced words you listed have in common?

_____

Hint: Think about the overall topic of the lesson.

The Election Process

The right to vote is one of the most important rights of a citizen. It is a right that many groups of Americans have worked hard to win. Only white men who owned land could vote in the early 1800s. Women could not vote in national elections until 1920. Native Americans did not vote until 1924. African Americans could not vote in some Southern states until the 1960s. And young people did not gain the right to vote until 1971.

American Voters

Americans must meet certain requirements to vote. Voters must be citizens and at least 18 years old. Most Americans are citizens because they were born in the United States. Others came to this country, studied English and U.S. history, passed a test, and became citizens. Voters also must have lived in a state a certain length of time before they can vote. Most states require people to live there at least 30 days before they are eligible to vote. Other state laws also bar certain people from voting. No state allows people who are in a mental institution to vote. Most states will not allow people convicted of serious crimes to vote. Some states disqualify homeless persons.

Voters learn about **politics,** or the ideas and actions of government, at a very young age. As children, they hear their parents talk about issues and leaders. In time the children form opinions. About two of every three Americans have the same political beliefs as their parents. Often they express these beliefs by joining a political party. A **political party** is a group that **nominates,** or chooses, candidates. A **candidate** is a person who runs for public office. People in the same political party often share the same views on one or more issues. If their party's candidate wins the election, the members of the party assume that the candidate will promote their political goals.

The Democratic and Republican parties are the major American political parties. Almost every election has candidates from one or both of these parties. Other political parties have fewer members. These parties often have too little support to run candidates for every political office.

▶ Supporting Conclusions To draw a conclusion, you must identify which facts about a subject are important. Then you judge or decide what the facts tell you about the subject. The judgment you make after examining facts is called a conclusion. The facts on the subject should support your conclusion.

Reread the first paragraph under the heading "American Voters." One conclusion you might draw is that not all voters are American born. Which fact in the paragraph supports that conclusion?

    A.   Most states require people to live there at least thirty days before they can vote.

    B.   Others came to this country, studied English and U.S. history, passed a test, and became citizens

Persuading the Voters

Before an election, a candidate takes part in a series of events called a **campaign.** The goal of the campaign is to persuade people to vote for the candidate. If several members of a political party want to run for the same office, the party chooses its candidate by committee, convention, or a **primary election.** This is an election in which voters choose the party's candidate for the office.

In a presidential election year, many states hold primary elections in the spring. In the summer the delegates, who were selected in the primary, attend the party's national convention. There they nominate the party's candidate for President in the **general election** in the fall. Because of this process, a presidential campaign can last for many months. Candidates must first campaign within their party to get the nomination. Then, if they are successful at the national convention, they must campaign for all the voters' support in the general election.

Many Americans learn about election candidates and issues from the media. The **media** include radio, television, newspapers, and magazines. Reporters present news stories and other information about a campaign. The people who run a campaign also use the media. They run ads to persuade people to vote a certain way. Television has become the key means of gaining support for candidates. To be successful, candidates must get their point across in television ads and compete for the American voters' attention.

Members of the media cover political candidates closely.

Political ad writers use the same methods to win votes that advertisers use to sell products. In recent years many political ad writers have taken a negative approach. They want their candidate's opponents to look like poor choices. Their ads often reveal only some of the facts and may mislead voters.

Advertising is not the only way television presents political information. News programs analyze campaign issues and candidates. Candidates participate in televised debates. Some appear as guests on talk shows. Elections even provide rich material for television comedians. Young people, in particular, often learn about politics while laughing at televised skits and stand-up routines.

▶ **Distinguishing Fact from Opinion** Political ads mix opinions with facts. They do this in order to help the candidate put forth the best image he or she can.

Circle the letter of the opinion below.
A. Our candidate is the best person to speak for our state's concerns.
B. Our candidate has supported children's rights in her work as a defense attorney.
C. Our candidate has worked in the governor's office for 10 years.

Financing Campaigns

Campaigns today are expensive. Running a TV ad just once can cost hundreds of thousands of dollars.

Raising money has become an important task of political parties. Some money comes from individuals. However, most of it comes from **political action committees** (PACs). Special interest groups, such as the American Association of Retired Persons and the National Rifle Association, set up PACs. The PACs give money to candidates who share their political beliefs about certain issues. PACs also do a good job of getting members of special interest groups to vote. Election experts know that PACs can help a candidate win. PACs also may help defeat candidates who oppose their views.

In the 1970s, Americans became concerned about the high cost of running for office. Many worried that the people were losing political power to wealthy persons and PACs whose donations candidates needed to get elected. So, in 1974, congress passed a law limiting the amount of money a person or a PAC could give to a candidate.

The PACs soon found a loophole in the law. It placed no limits on **soft money—** donations made to a state or local political party instead of to a specific candidate. The party could then legally turn this money over to the candidate. Congress finally closed this loophole in 2002 by passing the Bipartisan Campaign Reform Act. This law severely limits the collection and use of soft money. However, in 2010, the U.S. Supreme Court ruled that parts of the Bipartisan Campaign Reform Act are unconstitutional. This decision protects corporations and labor unions from being restricted in making donations to political parties or candidates.

Thinking About the Article

Practice Vocabulary

▶ **The words below are in the passage in bold type. Study the way each word is used. Then complete each sentence by writing the correct word.**

politics	political party	campaign	primary election
general election	media	political action committees	

1. Television advertising is an important way that candidates communicate with voters during a _____.

2. Candidates use all kinds of _____ to communicate with the American voters.

3. Special interest groups called _____ support candidates who promote political beliefs similar to their own.

4. The family is a major influence on Americans' attitudes toward

    _____.

5. The Democratic candidate who wins the _____ in the spring runs against the Republican candidate in November.

6. Democrats belong to the same _____.

7. In the United States, a _____ is held in November.

Understand the Article

▶ **Write the answer to each question.**

8. What three qualifications must an American meet to vote?

    _____

    _____

9. What information from the article indicates that the author believes everyone should exercise their right to vote?

    _____

    _____

10. What is one reason people join political parties?

    _____

    _____

Apply Your Skills

▶ **Circle the letter of the best answer for each question.**

11. Which of the following examples best supports the conclusion that the media sometimes take sides in political campaigns?

    A. A newspaper article describes both sides of a campaign issue.

    B. A television network broadcasts a debate between candidates.

    C. A radio announcer points out factual errors in political ads.

    D. A magazine includes information about only one candidate for senator.

12. Why is a special interest group most likely to form a PAC?

    A. to give money to the candidates who need it the most

    B. to support candidates who share the group's views

    C. to run political ads that present all views on the issues

    D. to encourage people to stay home instead of voting

13. Which of the following statements is a fact, rather than an opinion, about financing political campaigns?

    A. The high cost of running for political office is a major problem in American politics.

    B. Setting up a PAC is the fairest and most effective way to raise money for political campaigns.

    C. It is unfair that wealthy candidates have an advantage over less wealthy candidates in financing political campaigns.

    D. The high cost of political campaigns has raised concerns among many Americans.

Connect with the Article

▶ **Write your answer to each question.**

14. What are your thoughts on interest groups? Should they be allowed to contribute to campaigns? Explain.

15. Most campaign finance laws have failed to hold down the cost of presidential campaigns. What two changes would you make if you were in charge of campaign spending?

PAYING FOR GOVERNMENT

Vocabulary

revenue

income tax

progressive tax

flat tax

sales tax

property tax

excise tax

entitlement

budget

Before the Revolutionary War, Great Britain demanded payment of all sorts of taxes from the American colonists. The colonists were furious that they were required to pay taxes levied by the British Parliament, in which they had no voice. "No taxation without representation" became a rallying cry of the war.

After the war, the new leaders of the country gave Americans a strong voice in government. But they asked themselves if all Americans should decide about taxes spent in only one part of the country. The leaders agreed that people who lived in different parts of the country should decide on their own taxes. Thus, each level of government—national, state, and local—shares the power to tax.

Relate to the Topic

What taxes are you aware of paying now? What taxes do you expect to pay in the future?

_____

_____

_____

Reading Strategy

PREVIEWING GRAPHS   Graphs can present statistical information well—sometimes more clearly than words can. Turn to the circle graphs on page 158. Think about how they can help you prepare to read the lesson. Then answer the questions.

1. How are the two graphs related? _____

_____

Hint: Read the title and headings for both graphs.

2. Based on the graphs, what do you think the lesson will discuss?

_____

Hint: Think about why the graphs might be shown.

Where Do Our Taxes Go?

You probably pay taxes each and every day. For example, the total amount you pay for most items is higher than the posted price because you also pay sales tax. Also, the amount of your paycheck is less than you earned because you pay income tax.

What are taxes, and who decides how much you have to pay? In general, a tax is a contribution that a government requires you to make. Governments use tax **revenue,** or money collected as income, to pay for their cost of operating and to provide services for their citizens.

Since ancient times, governments have collected taxes of various kinds. Today, people use money to pay taxes, but that has not always been the case. In earlier times, for example, some people paid taxes by giving their government part of their harvest or by working on government projects.

How We Pay Taxes

The power to tax is shared by the federal, state, and local governments. **Income taxes**—taxes on earnings—are an important source of government revenues in the United States. Individuals pay personal income taxes, and businesses pay corporate income taxes. The federal government collects the largest share of the personal income taxes levied—some $1.1 trillion in 2012. However, the majority of Americans also pay state income taxes. In some places, people pay local income taxes as well.

How income tax should be calculated is a matter of debate. The federal income tax system is a **progressive tax.** This means that the more money a person earns, the higher the tax rate. In other words, the tax takes a larger percentage of the income of wealthy people than of less-wealthy people. That seems fair to many people. However, some people think that a flat tax is more just. Under a **flat tax,** everyone pays the same percentage regardless of income. Some states levy income taxes at a flat rate.

Most workers pay income tax with each paycheck they receive. A certain amount is automatically deducted from their pay. That way, they do not have to pay their taxes in one large lump sum, and the government receives a flow of revenue throughout the year. Social Security and Medicare taxes are also deducted from most workers' paychecks. These taxes help pay for pensions and healthcare for retired workers.

Another major source of tax revenue is **sales taxes,** or taxes on purchases. Sales taxes are levied in most states, with the individual state governments setting the rate. Local governments may tack on an additional sales tax, or they may choose not to tax certain items. For example, in many places, some food purchases are not taxed.

Property taxes, or taxes on the value of what one owns, are a third source of tax revenue. Real estate—land and the buildings on it—is the main source of property taxes. Property taxes also include taxes on automobiles and business equipment. Most property taxes are state or local taxes.

Excise taxes are taxes on specific items, especially items that the federal, state, and/or local government wants to control. Taxes on cigarettes, alcohol, and gasoline are among the most common excise taxes. If you look at a telephone bill, you will notice that excise taxes are also placed on telephone service.

How Tax Revenue Is Used

How does the government spend your money? The answer depends on whether you are talking about the federal government, the state government, or the local government. The federal government's single largest expense is Social Security. Other major expenses are Medicare, Medicaid (a cost that is shared with state governments), and national defense.

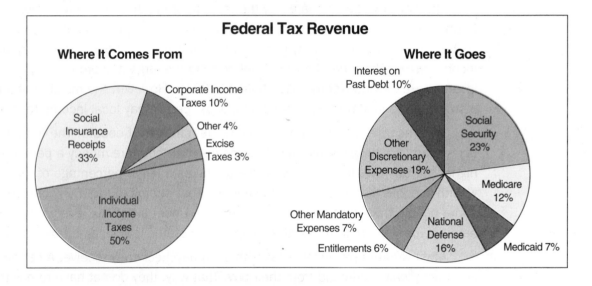

▶ Using Two Circle Graphs A **circle graph** is good for showing parts of a whole. You can learn much by studying two related circle graphs. Study the circle graphs above. Then answer the questions.

1. From which source did the federal government get ten percent of its revenue?
   A. corporate income taxes
   B. excise taxes

2. For which expense did the federal government spend ten percent of its revenue?
   A. Medicare
   B. interest payments

The federal government funds many **entitlements,** or programs for people who meet certain requirements. Federal entitlements include the food stamp program and pensions for armed forces veterans. Other expenses include aid to foreign countries and interest payments on money the government has borrowed.

A chief expense of state governments is education. Education accounts for more than one-third of the money that many states spend each year. The justice and prison systems take a major share of state funds as well. So do a variety of healthcare and social programs known as health and human services.

The largest expense of most local governments is public safety, the services that protect people and property. Police and fire departments are included in this category. Among other expenses are community services, which may include snow removal and a local library system, and capital improvements such as upgrades to the community's streets, parks, and utilities.

At each level of government, the amount to be spent is determined by a **budget,** or spending plan. Unexpected events can create budget problems. Unusually heavy snows, for example, may require a city to spend more on plowing snow than budgeted. Less tax revenue may be collected when a weak economy cuts into the earnings of individuals and businesses.

A weak economy caused serious budget problems in California. That state is home to many businesses that develop computers, computer software, and other technological products. Throughout the 1990s, these businesses were extremely successful. They produced a great deal of tax revenue for the state. In turn, the state increased its spending. More money flowed to California's schools, for example. State employees received raises, and state parks lowered entrance fees.

Then, the economy suddenly changed. Many high-tech businesses closed. Others had to lay off employees and limit production. As a result, California saw the largest drop in revenue since the Great Depression of the 1930s. In 2002, the state faced a gap between revenue and expenses of more than $23 billion. To help make up the difference, the state increased the sales tax and delayed some planned spending. Did these changes work? Many economists were cautious. They said that it would take years of careful money management and an improving economy to put California's state finances back on track. Unfortunately, the recession in 2008 and 2009 deterred progress, but California expects to have a debt of less than $5 million by 2016.

▶ Recognizing the Adequacy of Facts As you read informational materials, consider the **adequacy** of the facts—that is, whether there is enough information to prove a point. Reread the next-to-last paragraph above about California. For which statement does that paragraph provide adequate facts?

    A. In the 1980s, state employees were appealing to the government for pay raises.

    B. In the 1990s, the state government expected good economic times to continue.

Thinking About the Article

Practice Vocabulary

▶ **The words below are in the passage in bold type. Study the way each word is used. Then complete each sentence by writing the correct word.**

revenue	income taxes	budgets
property taxes	excise taxes	entitlements

1. _____ are the type of taxes most commonly collected by both the state and federal governments under the shared power of the states and federal government to collect taxes.

2. _____ provide services to people who meet certain requirements, such as veterans.

3. All levels of government create spending plans called

    _____ .

4. Governments use _____ from taxes to provide necessary services, such as social security and medicare.

5. The government can control certain items to some extent by collecting

    _____ .

6. _____ are usually only collected by state and local governments even though the federal government has the power to collect them.

Understand the Article

▶ **Write the answer to each question.**

7. Why do governments collect taxes?

    ....

    ....

    ....

    ....

8. Do the graphs on page 158 show either causation or correlation? Explain.

    ....

    ....

    ....

Apply Your Skills

▶ **Circle the letter of the best answer for each question.**

9. Look at the circle graphs on page 158. From highest to lowest, what are the federal government's three greatest sources of tax revenue?

    A. excise taxes, social security/social insurance taxes, corporate income taxes

    B. personal income taxes, social security/social insurance taxes, corporate income taxes

    C. corporate income taxes, excise taxes, personal income taxes

    D. social security/social insurance taxes, excise taxes, corporate income taxes

10. Which of the following people would be the most credible and knowledgeable person to author this article?

    A. a tax lawyer

    B. a representative in Congress

    C. the governor of a state

    D. a history teacher

11. Reread the information under "How We Pay Taxes" on pages 157 and 158. Which statement does the information support?

    A. State and local governments have the highest tax rates.

    B. Individual states decide which kinds of taxes to levy.

    C. Without property taxes, there would be no entitlement programs.

    D. Sales taxes and excise taxes are progressive taxes.

Connect with the Article

▶ **Write your answer to each question.**

12. Why do states compete to attract businesses that are considering relocating? Relate your answer to what you have learned about government and taxes.

_____

13. Think about the costs of government policies such as entitlements. Revisit the graphs on page 158. What is your opinion on how the government is spending tax revenues?

_____

_____

PUBLIC POLICY

Vocabulary

public policy

employee benefits

preventive care

Medicare

Medicaid

premium

deductible

Do you have a policy on how you handle certain situations? Perhaps if you babysit, you have a policy to only babysit for people you know.

The United States has several policies on how it operates and the way it approaches certain issues. For example, regarding climate change, the United States has enacted some policies to help reduce our carbon footprint. Major goals of the policies include finding ways to be both environmentally friendly and economically wise when conducting business. Public policies like this shape the way other countries see America.

Relate to the Topic

This lesson is about contemporary public policy in the United States. Public policy is ever changing depending on the issues that the country is facing at a given time. What topics in public policy have you heard about recently?

_____

_____

_____

Reading Strategy

SCANNING A GRAPH   Graphs of many types are used to present social studies information. Previewing a graph can give you a good glimpse of what you will read. Scan the graph on page 163. Then answer the questions.

1. What data is shown in the graph?

_____

_____

Hint: Look at the title.

2. How is the data arranged?

_____

_____

Hint: Compare the bars.

Healthcare Public Policy and the United States

Public policy is the system of laws and actions on a particular topic. A major area of public policy for the U.S. government is healthcare. The United States is the wealthiest nation in the world by many measures. You would not, however, know this by looking at healthcare statistics. Even though the United States spends more than any other country on healthcare, it is not seeing great benefits.

In 2011, the United States spent 17.7% of its gross domestic product on healthcare. That works out to $8,508 for every person. While the price of healthcare has gone up, the health of Americans has gone down. In 1960, life expectancy in the United States was one and a half years more than the average of the 34 countries that are part of the Organization for Economic Cooperation and Development (OECD). In 2011, it was one and a half years *below* the average.

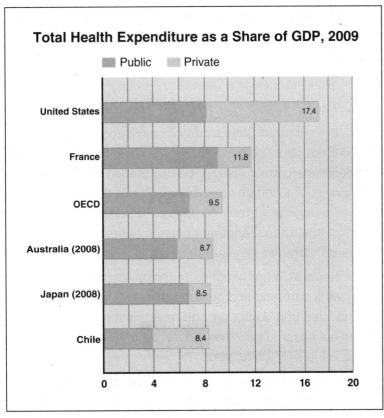

All other countries in the OECD spent considerably less of their GDP than the United States on healthcare in 2009.

▶ **Reading a Bar Graph** A bar graph is most useful for making comparisons. The title gives information about the data that is displayed in the graph. The values on the *x*-axis and the *y*-axis tell the categories of data. Look at the bar graph on this page. Compare the total expenditures as a share of GDP for each country. Which country spent half the amount that the United States spent on healthcare as a share of GDP?

    A. Japan   B. Australia

Check your answers on page 246.

So what's going on? Well, for one, the United States doesn't match up to countries around the world in value for healthcare. We are paying more, but we still have fewer doctors per person than most other countries in the OECD. But, we have more machines! The number of MRIs (magnetic resonance imaging scans) done in the United States is more than two and a half times the OECD average. Although this might seem like a good thing, an MRI is very costly. They cost much more in the United States than in other OECD countries. Sometimes they aren't even necessary. Even though we're doing more MRIs, we aren't catching any more illnesses or injuries than before. Clearly, the delivery of healthcare in the United States is not as effective as it should be.

The population of the United States is also changing. There are half as many smokers as there were 30 years ago, which is better for everyone's health. But obesity rates are higher in the U.S. than most other places. Over one third of Americans (36.5% in 2011) are obese. In other OECD countries, the obesity rate was 22.8% in 2011. Obesity, unfortunately, increases a person's risk for many other illnesses. These illnesses, such as diabetes, often lead to increased healthcare costs in the future.

Health Insurance and the Uninsured

In the United States, traditionally people have gotten health insurance through their employers. Health insurance is most often part of employee benefits. **Employee benefits** are extra employee compensation that comes with a job. For example, an employee of a certain company may have the benefit of free daycare if they use the daycare provider at their company. Retirement benefits include payments after a person has retired. Another common benefit is vacation—a certain number of paid days off. Benefits vary with different jobs and companies.

However, what happens to those Americans who do not have jobs? Or those who only work part-time and do not qualify for benefits? What about those who work for companies that do not provide health insurance? In most cases, before the Affordable Care Act became law, they did not have health insurance. In 2011, 48.6 million Americans were uninsured.

People that are uninsured often postpone visiting the doctor, or skip it all together because they cannot afford it. They are also more likely to skip preventive care.

Preventive care includes regular checkups and childhood immunizations. Preventive care helps to catch medical problems early. Many conditions are treatable when they are caught early. However, when these same conditions are identified later rather than earlier, then they are more difficult to treat. In addition, they are also often more costly to treat. Part of the debate on public policy related to healthcare centers around just this situation. Should the healthcare system focus on preventive care or diagnosing and treating illnesses? Where is money and time best spent?

The Affordable Care Act

Public policy regarding healthcare in the United States is changing dramatically. On March 23, 2010, President Obama signed the Affordable Care Act. The law includes a set of reforms designed to make healthcare more affordable and available.

The graph on page 163 divides the amount spent on healthcare into the categories of private and public funding sources. Public means the government provided this money. In the United States, people that meet the age or income requirements can get health coverage through Medicare or Medicaid. **Medicare** provides insurance for the elderly, and **Medicaid** provides insurance for low-income individuals and families. Still, compared to other countries, much more health insurance is purchased using private funds (through employers) than in any other country.

However, as noted before, this still leaves millions of people uninsured. The Affordable Care Act provides affordable insurance exchanges where people can shop for individual health insurance. If a person qualifies, they can receive assistance in paying their health insurance premiums. A **premium** is the amount a person pays each month for their health insurance coverage.

Additional policies in the Affordable Care Act make it easier for people to get the healthcare they need. Insurers must now provide benefits for preventive care without charging copays or making customers pay a deductible. A **deductible** is a set amount that a person must pay in a year before insurance will cover any costs.

The Affordable Care Act has also helped the millions of Americans who could not get health coverage because of pre-existing conditions. As of 2014, it is illegal for insurance companies to deny someone coverage because of their pre-existing condition. Pre-existing conditions include things like asthma and cancer.

▶ Finding the Implied Main Idea The topic sentence of a paragraph most often tells the main idea. Other times, the main idea is not stated, but implied. The reader must figure out the main idea. Reread the second paragraph under the heading "The Affordable Care Act." Which sentence below describes the main idea of the paragraph?

    A. Healthcare is paid for by either private or public funds.

    B. Americans pay mostly for health insurance through private funds.

The Shaping of Public Policy

The Affordable Care Act became a law because of the work of many groups and individuals over many years. People can shape public policy by advocating in favor of or against certain policies. Many people were in favor of the Affordable Care Act, and many others were against it. In fact, the Affordable Care Act was nearly defeated more than once on its way to becoming law. Public policy is shaped by laws like these. In turn, public policy then reflects the values of a nation.

Thinking About the Article

Practice Vocabulary

▶ **The words below are in the passage in bold type. Study the way each word is used. Then complete each sentence by writing the correct word.**

employee benefit	premium	public policy
preventive care	deductible	Medicare

1. A certain number of sick days off from work in a year is an example of a(n)

_____

2. Most people must pay a _____ first before their insurance company will begin covering their medical expenses.

3. _____ is a program to provide health coverage to the elderly in the United States.

4. People that receive _____ are more likely to stay healthy than those that do not.

5. An insurance _____ is the amount a person pays each month for insurance.

6. _____ is the set of laws and actions a government takes on a specific topic.

Understand the Article

▶ **Write your answer to each question.**

7. What are two reasons why preventive care is important?

_____

_____

8. How does the Affordable Care Act change the lives of people living with long-term illnesses?

_____

_____

9. Name at least two issues specific to healthcare that would likely be included in the United States' public policy on healthcare?

_____

_____

Apply Your Skills

▶ **Circle the letter of the best answer for each question.**

10. Which fact or facts about the Affordable Care Act does the author avoid to make it appear that it does not have any disadvantages?

    A. how often most people visit the doctor

    B. how long the policies will remain in effect

    C. how many people qualify to receive assistance

    D. how much the program costs

11. Look at the graph on page 163. Which of these countries spends about the same share of GDP in public funds on healthcare as the United States?

    A. Mexico

    B. Chile

    C. Canada

    D. Hungary

12. Which claim is supported by the article?

    A. The Affordable Care Act will be costly.

    B. The Affordable Care Act became a law smoothly.

    C. The Affordable Care Act will greatly benefit Americans.

    D. The Affordable Care Act was favored by most Americans.

Connect with the Article

▶ **Write your answer to each question.**

13. Why do you think it took so long for a healthcare bill to be finally passed into law?

14. Some countries provide healthcare to all of their citizens at no additional cost to the citizens. They pay for healthcare through the taxes that the citizens pay. Compare this system to public policy in the United States on healthcare. Which do you prefer? Why?

CIVICS AT WORK

SERVICE: COMMUNITY WORKER

They may work for environmental groups, political organizations, social service agencies, or neighborhood and grassroots organizations. Who are they? They're community workers. Community service work is usually challenging, but it is also rewarding. There is often a lot of work to do, and the hours can be unpredictable. But if you care about the well-being of your community, then this may be the type of job for you.

A broad range of community service work exists. Some workers help clients obtain basic services such as housing assistance, job placement, medical care, and child care. Others may focus their efforts on community safety or environmental protection. Still other community workers may help residents speak up for their personal and political rights.

Community workers must be familiar with the laws and rules affecting the work they perform. They need to be good listeners and speakers, and to be able to put their ideas and the ideas of others into writing.

Look at the Some Careers in Community Service sidebar.

- Do any of the careers interest you? If so, which ones?
- What information would you need to find out more about those careers?

On a separate piece of paper, write some questions that you would like answered. You can find more information about those careers in the *Occupational Outlook Handbook* at your local library or online.

Food Bank Worker collects and distributes food and other products to community residents

Community Outreach Worker helps local residents organize for their rights or against unfair or discriminatory practices

Shelter Coordinator oversees providing shelter, clothing, food, and counseling to the homeless and to victims of domestic violence

MEMO

To: Evan, Project LINK Director

From: Anita, Community Outreach Worker

Re: Election Efforts

Last Thursday evening I was distributing election flyers at Stone Elementary School. I was asked to leave the site by the school's principal and a police officer. When I asked them why, they gave no explanation. They grabbed me by my elbows and escorted me to my car.

I know by now you have heard about this incident. I would like you to know that I followed all the laws that you explained to me. I stood more than 15 feet from the school's entrance. I did not give a flyer to anyone under the age of 18. I did not force anyone to take a flyer.

This troubles me. I know that the First Amendment to the Constitution guarantees me the right to freedom of speech. I think this action violates my rights. Please let me know what I can do about this situation.

1. What was Anita's assignment for Thursday evening?

    A. to guard the entrance of Stone Elementary School

    B. to help the principal at Stone Elementary School

    C. to distribute election flyers at Stone Elementary School

    D. to get arrested by the police at Stone Elementary School

2. Which of the following is a right guaranteed Anita by the First Amendment?

    A. voting, if she is at least 18 years old

    B. giving flyers about the election to interested adults

    C. refusing to let police search her car unless they show a warrant

    D. receiving an explanation of the reason for her arrest

3. Why is it likely that Anita stood more than 15 feet from the entrance of the school?

    A. She was able to talk to more people before they entered the school.

    B. She was nervous that the principal would make her leave.

    C. The local law specified she must be that distance.

    D. The First Amendment requires her to stand that distance.

The Miranda Decision

In March 1963, a man kidnapped and raped a young girl. Ten days later the police arrested Ernesto Miranda. After police questioned Miranda alone for two hours, he confessed to the crime. Prosecutors used Miranda's confession as evidence against him at the trial. The jury found Miranda guilty. In 1966 the Supreme Court overturned, or set aside, Miranda's conviction. The justices believed police had violated Miranda's constitutional rights. Police had not told Miranda that, as a suspect in a crime, he had the right to talk to a lawyer before they questioned him. This Supreme Court ruling is called the Miranda Decision.

As a result of the Court's ruling, police must tell people they arrest about three of their constitutional rights: First, people have the right to remain silent. Second, anything they choose to say can be used against them in court. Third, they have the right to have a lawyer present while police question them. These rights are known as the Miranda rights.

In 1986, another case about suspects' rights reached the Supreme Court. The New York City police chased a man suspected of rape into a store. When the officers checked to see if the man had a weapon, they found an empty holster. When police asked him where his gun was, the suspect told them. After police found the gun, they read the suspect his Miranda rights. The gun and the man's statement were used as evidence against him. The Supreme Court decided that "public safety outweighs the need for the rule protecting the Fifth Amendment's privilege against self-incrimination."

▶ **Write the answers to the question.**

1. What are two ways the two cases described in the article are alike?

▶ **Circle the letter of the best answer for each question.**

2. At which point during an arrest do police need to notify the suspect of their Miranda rights?

    A.   after they question the suspect

    B.   when the suspect is in court

    C.   before they question the suspect

    D.   when they are releasing the suspect

The Rule of Government in Education

In the United States, the role of the federal government in education is complex. The Tenth Amendment to the Constitution gives the power to make education policy to state and local governments. However, about 2% of the federal budget is spent on education each year. The U.S. Department of Education oversees public policy of the federal government regarding education in the United States.

In an effort to improve the quality of education in the United States, the No Child Left Behind Act (NCLB) was passed in 2001. The main goal of the program was to ensure exactly what its title says—that no child would get left behind in the education system.

Many people believe the law is not perfect. President Obama laid out ideas for how to change NCLB including several goals to be included before reauthorization of the law. They include:

- Preparing students for college and careers.
- Striving for strong principals and teachers.
- Giving all students the same opportunities.
- Rewarding excellence.
- Promoting creativity and improvement.

These changes are part of the education public policy discussion. Hopefully, these changes will finally point the public education system in the right direction.

▷ **Circle the letter of the best answer for each question.**

3. Which language in the article shows the author's bias that public education in the United States is heading in the wrong direction?

    A. "spent on education" in the first paragraph

    B. "effort to improve" in the second paragraph

    C. "law is not perfect" in the third paragraph

    D. "hopefully" and "finally" in the last sentence

4. Which is the most likely meaning for the term "reauthorization"?

    A. to write from scratch

    B. to revise again

    C. to approve again

    D. to pay for again

Voting Makes a Difference

Just before elections, the ads appear. "Don't forget to vote!" "Every vote counts." Many registered voters go to the polls on election day. However, many people who are eligible to vote fail to register. Almost every American citizen who is at least 18 years of age is eligible to vote. To **register** means to complete a form that tells the voter's name, address, and place and date of birth. These forms are often available at the public library and the auto registration office.

Each registered voter goes to a polling place close to his or her home on election day. There, election workers check the voter list to make sure the person is registered. This prevents people from voting in the wrong place or more than once. In some polling places, voters step into a booth where they pull levers on a machine. In other places, voters use a punchpin to punch holes in computer cards, use a pencil to mark a paper ballot, or make selections on a computer screen.

Does your vote make a difference? Studies show it does. A handful of votes decides many elections. Even in nationwide presidential elections, a small number of votes have made a big difference.

Experts say that a majority of the voting-age population has never elected a president because not enough people of voting age actually vote. Abraham Lincoln received 55 percent of the vote when he was reelected President in 1864. But Native Americans, African Americans, and women could not vote then. So those votes represented only 13 percent of the voting-age population at the time. In 2000, only 51 percent of voting-age Americans went to the polls. Al Gore won the popular vote by one-half of one percent. Because the states in which George W. Bush won had 271 electoral votes compared with the 266 electoral votes in the states that Gore won, Bush became President. Would the results have been different if all eligible voters had taken time to vote? No one will ever know.

▶ **Write the answer to each question.**

   5. Where can an eligible voter go to register to vote?

----

   6. Why is a person's date of birth important on the voter's registration form?

▶ **Circle the letter of the best answer for the question.**

   7. Which statement does the article support?

     A. If you pay taxes, you must register to vote.

     B. Registering is a way of helping people vote.

     C. Most people register to vote.

     D. Votes can make a difference in all kinds of elections.

The Right to Privacy

▶ **Write the answer to each question.**

8. What does the woman represent?

_____

9. What does the man with the hat represent?

_____

▶ **Circle the letter of the best answer for the question.**

10. What does the cartoon imply about the government's respect for Americans' right to privacy in the world today?

    A.   The government takes the right to privacy very seriously.

    B.   The government protects Americans' right to privacy.

    C.   The right to privacy is threatened because the government can get information.

    D.   The right to privacy is guaranteed because the federal government and the military promise not to abuse this right.

SOCIAL STUDIES EXTENSION

Attend a meeting of your local city council, county commission, or school board. List all the topics the officials discuss and circle those that lead to a decision by the group.

© Houghton Mifflin Harcourt • Image Credits: ©Kirk Anderson/Artizans

Check your answers on page 247.

MINI-TEST

 This is a 15-minute practice test. After 15 minutes, mark the last number you finished. Then complete the test and check your answers. If most of your answers were correct but you did not finish, try to work faster next time.

▶ **Directions: Choose the <u>one best answer</u> to each question.**

Questions 1 and 2 refer to the following information.

During George Washington's first term as President, the government imposed an excise tax on whiskey. Whiskey makers felt that the tax was an attack on their liberty. In 1794, the Whiskey Rebellion began. There were riots, and some federal tax agents were tarred and feathered. The President called out troops to stop the protests. When two rioters were convicted of treason, however, he pardoned them.

1. Which information best supports the conclusion that the Whiskey Rebellion was a violent protest against the U.S. government?

   A. Washington taxed whiskey.

   B. Rebels assaulted federal workers.

   C. The revolt did not last long.

   D. The whiskey tax was removed.

2. The right of the people to protest was protected by

   A. the Emancipation Proclamation.

   B. the Bill of Rights.

   C. the system of checks and balances.

   D. the separation of powers.

Question 3 refers to the following illustration.

3. The people in the illustration are exercising a right that is protected by the Constitution. Which of the following would involve exercising the same right?

   A. members of a jury listening to a case in court

   B. demonstrators protesting U.S. involvement in a war

   C. worshippers attending an interfaith prayer service

   D. a newspaper printing an article about an election

UNIT 3 CIVICS AND GOVERNMENT

Questions 4 and 5 refer to the following quotation from the Declaration of Independence.

"The history of the present King of Great Britain is a history of repeated injuries and usurpations, all having in direct object the establishment of an absolute Tyranny over these States. To prove this, let Facts be submitted to a candid world.

He has refused his Assent to Laws, the most wholesome and necessary. . . .

He has forbidden his Governors to pass laws of immediate and pressing importance, unless suspended in their operation till his Assent should be obtained. . . . "

4. Based on the quotation, which statement is a fact rather than an opinion?

   A. The king is a tyrant.

   B. Representative government is good.

   C. The colonists would make better laws than the British king.

   D. The king has restricted the powers of the colonial governers.

5. For which statement does the quotation provide adequate factual support?

   A. Some colonists were very angry with the King of Great Britain.

   B. The king wanted to give up his American colonies.

   C. The king imposed unfair taxes upon the American colonists.

   D. The king's actions were based on hatred of the American colonists.

Questions 6 and 7 refer to the following information and political cartoon.

Politicians can run positive or negative campaigns. In positive campaigns, politicians focus on their own qualifications and accomplishments. In negative campaigns, they focus on attacking their opponents.

6. Which of the following ideas is implied by this cartoon?

   A. Americans watch too much television.

   B. There should be more political ads on television.

   C. During election season, attack ads insult television viewers.

   D. Many people who run for public office have low moral standards.

7. What is the cartoonist trying to persuade people to do?

   A. stop eating pork and pork products

   B. stop watching campaign ads

   C. urge television networks to have more family-friendly shows

   D. be ashamed of the nastiness of negative political campaigns

Check your answers on page 248.   175

Have you ever bought something that you wanted but didn't really need? Do you make rent or car payments? These are examples of individual choices that involve money. **Economics** is the study of how people satisfy their wants and needs by making choices about how to use limited resources.

Would you describe yourself as a good money manager? A cost-conscious shopper? A saver? Explain.

_____

_____

Thinking About Economics

You may be surprised to see how much you already know about economics. Think of news reports that you have seen on television, for example. How many of those reports involve information about money? In what other ways does television keep you thinking about your economic choices? Think about what you know about economics from daily life.

Check the box for each fact that you already know.

☐ When there is a sudden demand for a product, the price of that product usually rises.

☐ Two of the largest monthly expenses for an average American family are food and housing.

☐ Smart shoppers consider the quality of an item as well as its price.

☐ Today many jobs require the ability to use computers or other technology.

☐ Restaurant workers, sales clerks, and nurses are examples of people who work in service industries.

☐ A country's government wants businesses to export more goods than are imported from other countries.

Write one economic decision that you make at least once each week and one that you make only once or twice each year.

_____

_____

Previewing the Unit

In this unit, you will learn:

- about economic concepts and the differences between microeconomics and macroeconomics

- how a free enterprise system works

- what kinds of decisions help you use your money wisely

- how supply and demand affect prices

Lesson 23	**Fundamental Concepts**
Lesson 24	**Free Enterprise**
Lesson 25	**Money Management**
Lesson 26	**Supply and Demand**

FUNDAMENTAL CONCEPTS

Vocabulary

incentive

positive incentive

negative incentive

entrepreneur

profit

specialization

comparative
    advantage

interdependence

inflation

deflation

unemployment

The modern world revolves around economics and economic systems. Thousands of years ago, people produced what they needed on their farms. Slowly, as communities grew, people began to specialize and then bartered and traded for what they needed. Eventually, currency was used. Livestock and mollusk shells were used as currency in the past. About 1000 B.C., the first metal money and coins came into use.

Today, economics connects the entire world like never before. The food and clothes you buy may come from countries around the world. A particularly cold winter in Florida may mean the price of orange juice skyrockets. We are all connected economically.

Relate to the Topic

Economics is the study of what we produce, what we consume, and how we exchange money to get what we need and want. Have you purchased a good or service in the last week? How did you decide what to purchase, when to purchase it, and how much you were willing to pay for it?

_____

_____

_____

Reading Strategy

USING PRIMARY RESOURCES   Primary sources include sources such as diaries, speeches, letters, interviews, poems, novels, and art. A primary source gives you a direct view of a particular event or opinion. In contrast, a secondary source, such as this book, interprets and analyzes a primary source. Read the two quotations on page 180 and answer the questions.

1. What do the quotations discuss?

_____

Hint: How could you summarize each quotation?

2. What is Senator Elizabeth Warren's opinion on wealth in America?

_____

Hint: Consider her tone.

The Fundamentals of Economics

Economics can be divided into two types—microeconomics and macroeconomics. Microeconomics is the part of economics that deals with single factors and the effects of individual decisions. It explores the interactions between buyers and sellers. Macroeconomics is the part of economics that deals with the big picture. It explores the economy of an entire country, such as the United States. People that study macroeconomics are able to interpret economic indicators to determine how well the economy is doing.

Incentives

People make economic decisions every day. Today alone, you've likely decided what to eat for breakfast, what clothes to wear, and what toothpaste to use. These decisions are all linked to the economy. So, how do people make these decisions? People make decisions based on incentives. An **incentive** is something that influences behavior.

You might work extra hours at your job because you'll get paid overtime at the end of the week. Or you might work extra hours because you're not permitted to leave your job site until certain tasks are completed.

These examples describe the difference between a positive economic incentive and a negative economic incentive. A **positive incentive** rewards a person for making a certain choice. A **negative incentive** punishes a person for making a certain choice. Micoeconomists study how people respond to incentives to learn more about the economic choices people make.

Why do microeconomists care about the decisions people make? Remember, microeconomics is the study how buyers and sellers interact. A big part of these interactions is based on incentives. In addition to microeconomists, entrepreneurs rely on this information to help them make decisions about what to produce and how much of it to produce. An **entrepreneur** is a person who starts and runs a business. Entrepreneurs are important to the economy.

Profits

An entrepreneur often takes on all of the risk involved in running a business. The reward for taking this risk is the profit the entrepreneur may make if the business is successful. **Profit** is the money a business makes after paying all of its expenses. Profit is the result of successful buyer and seller interactions. Profit is also an incentive—an incentive for an entrepreneur to do business. Although many businesses work hard to develop innovative and important products, a main goal is making a profit.

The fact that businesses are mostly free from government regulations to conduct business as they choose means there is no limit to the profits that a business may make. In other types of economies, businesses are under greater government control. There is often debate in the United States over profits and what level of profits is socially acceptable. Some believe that hard work should be rewarded and ultimately benefits all.

"America's abundance was created not by public sacrifices to the common good, but by the productive genius of free men who pursued their own personal interests and the making of their own private fortunes. They did not starve the people to pay for America's industrialization. They gave the people better jobs, higher wages, and cheaper goods with every new machine they invented, with every scientific discovery or technological advance—and thus the whole country was moving forward and profiting, not suffering, every step of the way."

—Philosopher Ayn Rand

Others are furious over the sky-high profits that some companies make, believing they come at the expense of the many.

"There is nobody in this country who got rich on their own. Nobody. You built a factory out there—good for you. But I want to be clear. You moved your goods to market on roads the rest of us paid for. You hired workers the rest of us paid to educate. You were safe in your factory because of police forces and fire forces that the rest of us paid for. You didn't have to worry that marauding bands would come and seize everything at your factory....Now look. You built a factory and it turned into something terrific or a great idea—God bless! Keep a hunk of it. But part of the underlying social contract is you take a hunk of that and pay forward for the next kid who comes along."

—United States Senator Elizabeth Warren

▶ **Using Primary Sources** When you use a primary source, it is important to know and understand the origin of the source. The opinion of the speaker or writer is often clear in a primary source. Pay attention to the tone of the quotations. How would you describe the tone of each quotation?

A. They are both content.

B. They are both irritated.

Senator Warren touches on two important microeconomic concepts—specialization and interdependence, both of which contribute to a business's potential profit. **Specialization** is focusing on what one does best. This is why you don't often see frozen food companies also selling car tires. Together as an economy, specialization improves efficiency. What causes businesses to specialize? **Comparative advantage** leads to specialization. A business has a comparative advantage if it can produce something at a lower cost than anyone else.

Specialization is a cause of interdependence. **Interdependence** refers to the idea that the businesses in an economy are dependent on each other. For example, if you own an ice cream shop where you make your own ice cream, chances are you do not also own a dairy farm to produce the milk to make the ice cream. You need to buy the milk and other ingredients to make your ice cream. You are therefore dependent on dairy farms and other suppliers.

Economic Indicators

Macroeconomists watch economic indicators, which are pieces of economic data, to help them make predictions about the entire economy. You may hear about economic indicators such as unemployment and inflation reported on the news. They give a good indication of how the economy is doing and where it is headed.

One economic indicator is inflation. **Inflation** is a rise in prices relative to money available. If prices rise, but your salary does not, you will get less for your money than you once could. In the United States, the rate of inflation is usually measured using the Consumer Price Index (CPI). The CPI is a representative "basket of goods." The Bureau of Labor Statistics keeps track of the cost of the goods in the basket. The inflation rate is reported as a percentage. If the inflation rate from 2013 to 2014 is 2.5%, it means that the items in the CPI cost 2.5% more in 2014 than in 2013. If the inflation rate is negative, it shows **deflation**, which is a decrease in prices relative to money available. Deflation happens rarely compared to inflation.

Another economic indicator is unemployment. **Unemployment** is a measure of the number of unemployed persons in the United States. It is given as a percentage. If the unemployment rate is 8.2%, it means that 8.2% of the people in the United States who are available to work do not have jobs. It does not include people who choose not to be in the workforce, like stay-at-home parents or the disabled who are unable to work. If the unemployment rate is high, the economy is not growing, because jobs are being lost instead of gained. This means businesses are cutting back. If the unemployment rate is low, the economy is growing.

▶ Comparing and Contrasting Comparing and contrasting two or more people, events, or things helps you to understand how things are alike and different. Which is true of the article?

  A. It compares inflation and deflation.

  B. It contrasts inflation and deflation.

Thinking About the Article

Practice Vocabulary

▶ **The words below are in the passage in bold type. Study the way each word is used. Then complete each sentence by writing the correct word.**

incentives	profit	entrepreneur
specialization	comparative advantage	interdependence

1. A company has a(n) _____ if they are able to produce a product at a lower cost than other companies.

2. A(n) _____ is a person who starts and runs a business.

3. Businesses and companies around the world are connected due to their

_____ .

4. People make decisions based on _____ .

5. _____ is the amount of money a business has left after paying its expenses.

6. Businesses focusing on what they do best is called _____ .

Understand the Article

▶ **Write your answer to each question.**

7. How do the views expressed by Ayn Rand and Elizabeth Warren in the quotations differ?

_____

_____

8. How is a positive incentive different from a negative incentive?

_____

_____

9. Is a person who is not looking for a job part of the unemployed persons counted to determine the unemployment rate? Explain.

_____

_____

Apply Your Skills

▶ **Circle the letter of the best answer for each question.**

10. Suppose you create a line graph by plotting the unemployment rate on the x-axis and the number of people who are unemployed on the y-axis. Which best describes how the two are related?

   A. As the number of people who are unemployed increases, the unemployment rate increases.

   B. As the number of people who are unemployed decreases, the unemployment rate increases.

   C. As the number of people who are unemployed increases, the unemployment rate decreases.

   D. As the number of people who are unemployed increases, the unemployment rate stays the same.

11. Which cause and effect relationship is true in economics?

   A. Incentives lead to profits.

   B. Interdependence leads to comparative advantage.

   C. Specialization leads to interdependence.

   D. Profits lead to entrepreneurship.

12. In country X, it takes 10 hours of labor to produce wheat and 20 hours of labor to produce corn. In country Y, it takes 20 hours of labor to produce wheat and 10 hours of labor to produce corn. According to the idea of comparative advantage, which country should produce wheat?

   A. Neither country X or Y should produce wheat.

   B. Both country X and country Y should produce wheat.

   C. Country X should produce wheat.

   D. Country Y should produce wheat.

Connect with the Article

▶ **Write your answer to each question.**

13. Think about starting your own business. What aspects of entrepreneurship appeal to you?

_____

14. What effect would a high rate of inflation likely have on a small business?

_____

FREE ENTERPRISE

Vocabulary

free enterprise
    system

consumer

market

incentive

demand

subsidy

efficiency

cooperative

Each day in the United States, people choose how they will spend the money they have earned. For example, some people travel several miles to buy groceries from a supersized grocery-hardware-clothing store. Others decide to shop at a supermarket in their neighborhood. Factors such as price, convenience, and good service influence their decisions.

Businesses make economic decisions, too. They note which products are selling well and which are not. They study which supplier offers the lowest prices, the best quality, and the fastest delivery. Americans are free to buy, and American businesses are free to sell, what they want. All of this buying and selling impacts the U.S. gross domestic product, which is the total market value of all the finished goods and services produced within a country's borders in a year.

Relate to the Topic

This lesson uses farming to explain how the economy in the United States works. Think back to your childhood. Recall two specific food products or toys that your parents bought for you. Are those items still available? Why do you think that they are—or are not—for sale today?

_____

_____

_____

Reading Strategy

PREVIEWING LINE GRAPHS   A line graph can show changes in a situation. Previewing line graphs can help you understand important information in a passage. Look at the line graphs on pages 186 and 187. Then answer the questions.

1. What general topic are both line graphs about?

_____

Hint: Look for words that appear in both graph titles.

2. What specific types of changes do you expect to see on each graph?

_____

_____

Hint: Look at the titles and at vertical scales.

How Free Enterprise Works

The United States has an economic system called the **free enterprise system.** In this type of economy, **consumers,** or buyers, buy products and services from privately owned businesses. Producers determine the kinds, the amounts, and the prices of goods based on what consumers want to buy. In other words, Americans make economic choices based on opportunities in the market. A **market** is all the potential customers for a particular product or service. In the free enterprise system, the U.S. government does not make a plan for the nation's economy. However, it does make laws and regulations that limit freedoms, but for the purpose of keeping the economy running smoothly. Farming is a good example of how free enterprise works in the United States.

Farming as a Market

How do farmers decide what crops to grow and animals to raise? Farmers try to find answers to these questions by watching consumers. For example, American consumers today are buying more cheese than they did in the past. In 2008 the average American consumed 33.5 pounds of cheese. That figure is up from 30.5 pounds per person in 2002 and 27.5 pounds per person in 1997. It is about three times as much cheese as Americans consumed in 1975. As a result, dairy farmers raised more cows, whose milk was used to make more cheese.

Farmers have an **incentive**, or good reason, to produce the kinds of goods people want. Farmers want to make as much money as possible. By looking at what consumers buy, farmers learn what to produce and how much. The amount of goods or services consumers are willing to buy at a certain price at a given time is called **demand**. If people prefer potatoes over beets, then demand is higher for potatoes. This gives farmers an incentive to grow potatoes. As a result, more farmers grow potatoes than beets.

The government also sometimes steps in to control price and production in the form of subsidies. A **subsidy** is assistance in the form of money. Government subsidies provide farmers security in case of market failures. An example of market failure would be a case where the market prices would not allow the farmer to make even a small profit and might actually result in a loss for farmers. But we need farmers, so the government steps in and subsidizes the market price in order to support farmers. Subsidies cost the government billions of dollars each year, however. Whether they are effective should be carefully studied.

▶ Making Inferences It is important to look for main ideas and details as you read. Sometimes you can use that information to figure out things that are not actually stated. This is called making an inference. Reread the first paragraph under the heading "Farming as a Market." Which inference can you make from details in the paragraph?

    A. The market determines what products are produced.

    B. Consumers will pay any price for cheese.

How Competition Leads to Efficiency

Farmers sell their goods in a market where there is competition from other farmers. Because many buyers and sellers are in the market, no one buyer or seller sets the price. In a competitive market, sellers have an incentive to keep prices low. Suppose one farmer's price for corn is higher than another farmer's price. The consumer will buy the corn at the lower price. So a farmer has to sell at the lowest possible price. But the price must not be so low that the farmer cannot recover the costs of growing the corn, such as supplies, equipment, and labor. Each farmer wants a price that allows him or her to make some money after paying expenses.

A competitive market requires efficiency. **Efficiency** means that the time, energy, and money put into a job results in a great deal of production without much waste. Over the years American farmers have become more efficient. In the 1850s, one farmer produced enough food to feed five people. About 50 percent of Americans were farmers. Today however, the average farmer feeds about 139 people. Only 0.8 percent of Americans today make their living as farmers.

So few farmers can produce so much food because of technology, which includes the tools and methods used to increase production. Today, farmers use more machines. They also have special seeds, fertilizers, and weed killers. As a result, it takes fewer farmers to produce a larger food supply. The graph on page 187 shows that farms today are larger than they were in the past. But as the graph below shows, there are fewer farms. Many farms are now owned by corporations rather than by individuals.

Number of Farms in the United States, 1900–2010

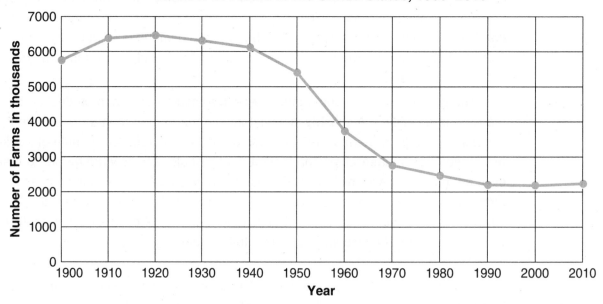

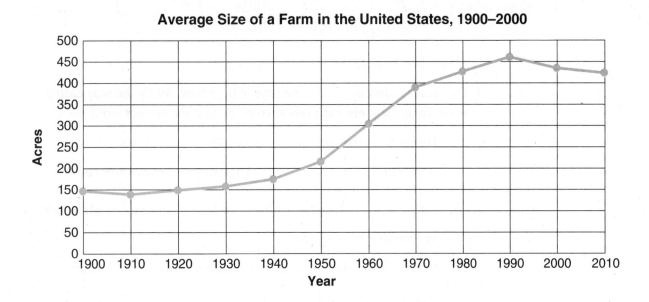

Average Size of a Farm in the United States, 1900–2000

▶ Comparing Line Graphs A line graph usually shows changes over time. A change may be an increase or a decrease. Look at the line graphs on page 186 and above. They show changes in the number and average size of U.S. farms over 110 years. During different periods farms changed in different ways. How did farms change overall between 1900 and 2010?

A. The number of farms stayed the same while the size of farms decreased.

B. The number of farms decreased while the size of farms increased.

How Competition Affects Farmers and Consumers

Competition among farmers benefits consumers in many ways. In 1900, the average American family spent more than 45 percent of its income on food. They ate nearly every meal at home. Today, the average family spends only about 16 percent of its income on food. More than 45 percent of the money in the food budget is spent on meals away from home. Competition has kept food prices down and given consumers more choices in how to spend their food money.

However, individual farmers have a hard time competing with large, corporate farms. As a result, some individual farmers have left the market. Others sign contracts with canneries, frozen-food companies, schools, colleges, hospitals, and government agencies. These contracts provide farmers with secure markets for their products. Still other individual farmers join cooperatives. A **cooperative** is an institution formed by people who join together to ensure the best price for their products. Many orange and grapefruit growers in California and Florida belong to cooperatives. Some cooperatives advertise to encourage consumers to buy their products. Cooperative financial institutions help farmers finance their businesses by offering loans.

Check your answers on page 249.

Thinking About the Article

Practice Vocabulary

▶ The words below are in the passage in bold type. Study the way each word is used. Then complete each sentence by writing the correct word.

free enterprise system	market	subsidies
demand	efficiency	cooperative

1. An economy in which the buyers and sellers determine what goods are produced is called a(n) _____.

2. One indicator that farming in the United States is not a completely free enterprise is the use of government _____.

3. A(n) _____ represents all the potential customers for a particular product or service.

4. If few people are buying a product, it has a low _____.

5. Farmers may take out loans from a financial _____, an institution that can help farmers run their businesses.

6. Farms in the United States are known for their _____, because they produce more farm products with fewer farmers than in the past.

Understand the Article

▶ Write the answer to each question.

7. How does new technology affect farmers?

_____

_____

8. Think about the definition of gross domestic product. Do agricultural products that are imported from Canada count toward the U.S. gross domestic product? Why or why not?

_____

_____

9. How does the relationship between farmers and institutions benefit farmers?

_____

_____

Apply Your Skills

▶ **Circle the letter of the best answer for each question.**

10. Look at the graph on page 186. Which is closest to the average number of farms in the United States between 1960 and 2010?

    A. 1,500,000

    B. 2,000,000

    C. 2,500,000

    D. 3,000,000

11. Look at the graphs on pages 186 and 187. What do the graphs suggest might be true by 2020?

    A. Farms will be about the same size as in 2010, and there will be about the same number of them.

    B. There will be more family-owned farms than in 2010.

    C. Farms will be much larger than in 2010, and there will be fewer of them.

    D. There will be fewer farms than in 2010, and individual families will own most of them.

12. How does the federal government help prevent the effects of market failures in agriculture?

    A. It decreases competition among farmers.

    B. It buys farms that go out of business.

    C. It controls the prices of agricultural goods.

    D. It provides subsidies to farmers.

Connect with the Article

▶ **Write your answer to each question.**

13. How would you describe the author's point of view on agricultural subsidies?

_____

14. Apply what you have learned to other products. How does competition among cellular phone companies help you choose which one to use?

_____

MONEY MANAGEMENT

Some families have to guard every penny. They carefully keep track of expenses. They save money to reach their financial goals. Other families enjoy spending. They often give gifts. They may buy a bigger house when a new baby arrives. Some families are willing to take additional risks with their money. They like to invest if there seems to be a chance to make even more money.

What young people learn about money influences the role that money plays later in their lives. It helps determine how they spend money and what financial risks—if any—they take.

Relate to the Topic

This lesson is about wise money management. Think about what you've just read about ways different families manage money. Name something you learned from your family about money management.

_____

_____

Reading Strategy

RELATING TO WHAT YOU KNOW   As you read informational material, compare the facts with what you already may have learned—from a book, for example, or from personal experience. Read the paragraph on page 191 that begins the article. Then answer the questions.

1. Of the people you know, whom would you call a money manager?

_____

_____

Hint: According to the paragraph, what does a money manager do?

2. What do you already know about borrowing money wisely?

_____

_____

Hint: Think about interest rates and monthly payments.

Getting the Most for the Money

Few people have as much money as they would like. To get the most out of what they earn, people must become money managers. This requires that they use their money wisely. People who manage their money well follow similar rules. First, they create and follow a spending plan. Second, they consider all the costs involved in a purchase before deciding to buy something. Third, they do not borrow money often. And last, if they <u>must</u> get a loan, they borrow carefully.

Follow a Plan

People who manage their money make a budget. A **budget** is a detailed spending plan. It shows how much money comes in and goes out each month. To prepare a budget, first list your net income. **Net income** is money left after taxes are paid. It is also called take-home pay. Then list all expenses, or money that is owed. Start with **fixed expenses,** which are payments that stay the same each month. Rent and car payments are fixed expenses. Next list expenses that vary from month to month. This kind of expense is called a **flexible expense.** Clothing is a flexible expense.

The chart below is an example of a budget. The amounts the family planned to spend in a month are in the left-hand column. The amounts actually spent are in the right-hand column. A budget contains categories of expenses. Utilities generally include electricity, natural gas, water, sewer, and trash removal. Transportation may include gasoline, bus fare, and an emergency auto repair fund.

Fixed expenses are usually easy to budget. However, sometimes fixed expenses are due only a few times a year and are forgotten until the bill comes in the mail. Property taxes are an example of this type of periodic expense. It is important to set aside money each month for periodic expenses. Then these bills can be paid when they are due.

Savings is an important category. Savings can be used for unexpected expenses, such as major car repairs. You may also be saving for a major purchase such as a house, or for retirement.

A budget helps people decide what they can and cannot afford. They see how each purchase could affect other things they want or need. They may find places where they can cut costs.

Many people are surprised when they prepare a budget. They see how much money they spend on things they do not really need. Some people give up smoking, drinking alcohol, or expensive entertainment after they realize how much income these activities use up.

Budget for the Rivera Family
Net Monthly Income $3,200

Fixed Expenses	Planned	Actual
Home mortgage	$760	$760
Car payment	$280	$280
Insurance	$110	$110
Flexible Expenses		
Utilities	$205	$205
Transportation	$320	$320
Food	$440	$475
Credit card payments	$250	$250
Health Care	$180	$200
Clothing	$170	$170
Entertainment	$180	$140
Savings	$150	$125
Other	$155	$165
Total	$3,200	$3,200

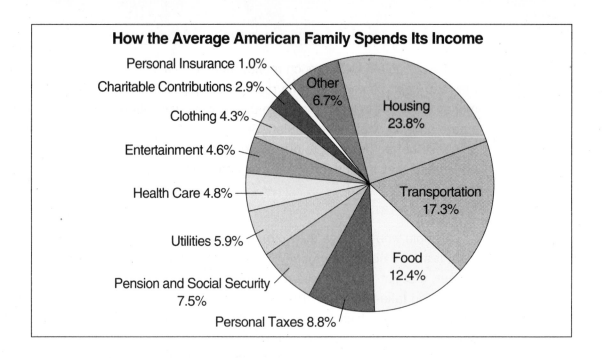

How the Average American Family Spends Its Income

Personal Insurance 1.0%
Charitable Contributions 2.9%
Clothing 4.3%
Entertainment 4.6%
Health Care 4.8%
Utilities 5.9%
Pension and Social Security 7.5%
Personal Taxes 8.8%
Other 6.7%
Housing 23.8%
Transportation 17.3%
Food 12.4%

▶ Reading a Circle Graph A circle graph is used to compare parts to a whole and to each other. Circle graphs are sometimes called pie charts. Each section of the graph looks like a slice of a pie. The sections can be compared to one another or to the whole amount. The larger the section, the greater the amount. Often a circle graph is presented using percents. The whole circle is always 100 percent. Look at the circle graph above. It shows the percent of income the average family spends on various goods and services. What expense takes up the largest percentage of the average family's income?

    A. transportation   B. housing

Consider the Costs

It is important to look at all the costs involved before deciding on a purchase. The cost of a new pair of shoes is not just the price of the shoes. There is also an opportunity cost. **Opportunity cost** is the cost of choosing one thing over another. For example, as a result of buying shoes, the shopper may have less money for a new winter coat. Sometimes opportunity cost is called a trade-off. In making choices, a person knows that he or she gives up one thing in order to get something of greater value. Good money managers know what the results of most of their buying decisions will be.

Let's look at an example. There is also an opportunity cost in spending money instead of saving money. When people place money in savings accounts, the bank borrows the money to loan to other people. Banks pay **interest**, which is a fee for borrowing money, on money in savings accounts. If Mrs. Rivera chooses to spend $75 on shoes and takes the additional $30 from her savings account, the opportunity cost is more than $30. It is also her lost interest. Banks offer many options that earn interest. A money market fund will pay higher interest, but sometimes you must maintain a higher balance. A certificate of deposit will earn the highest interest, but you must leave your money in the bank for a certain amount of time.

▶ **Identifying Cause and Effect** Every event has at least one cause and one effect. The cause is <u>why</u> something happened. The effect is <u>what happened</u> as a result of the cause. Words such as *because, reason,* and *since* suggest a cause. Such words or phrases as *as a result, cost,* and *for this reason* signal effects. Reread the first paragraph under the heading "Consider the Costs." What would be an effect of ignoring opportunity cost when deciding to buy something?

    A. The purchase would cost more than the budget allows.

    B. The family might have no money for something else it wants or needs.

Careful Borrowing

People do not always have enough cash on hand to pay for the things they want or need. They may decide to borrow the money now and pay it back later. Borrowing money can be more expensive than combining the price of the item and the opportunity cost. The loan's interest, or the fee for borrowing the money, must be considered, too.

Some experts suggest that a person should borrow no more than one-fifth of his or her net income. In other words, a person who takes home $20,000 a year should limit debts to $4,000. Borrowing includes anything bought on a payment plan, paid for with a credit card, charged at local stores, or borrowed from a bank.

Knowing the cost of borrowing helps people get the most for their money. Interest rates can vary greatly. One study of new-car loans showed that some lenders charged ten percent more interest than others. Many loans had hidden costs. In some cases, borrowers had to pay a fee just to apply for the loan. In other cases, they had to pay extra money if payments were late. Some lenders charged a penalty if borrowers paid off their loans early.

A smart borrower never signs a loan agreement without reading and understanding the contract. Consumer credit laws protect borrowers. By law, lenders have to tell people what a loan will cost. Borrowers have a right to know the interest rate on the loan. A borrower also needs to know the annual percentage rate. The **annual percentage rate,** or APR, is the percent of interest a lender charges per year for the money that is borrowed. By knowing the APR, borrowers can compare loans.

People who are good money managers take charge of their finances. They know what they spend their money on and how much they spend. They not only take advantage of opportunities but also make the most of those opportunities.

Thinking About the Article

Practice Vocabulary

▶ **The words below are in the passage in bold type. Study the way each word is used. Then complete each sentence by writing the correct word.**

budget	fixed expense	net income	flexible expense

interest   opportunity cost   annual percentage rate

1. The _____ of buying a new car is that a family may have to wait another year to go on vacation to Disney World.

2. Take-home pay is often called _____.

3. Unfortunately the rate of _____ that banks give for saving money is not as high as the rate they charge for lending money.

4. Before making a loan, a lender must tell the borrower the loan's _____, or the amount of interest a lender charges each year.

5. An example of a(n) _____ is a mortgage payment.

6. The first step in managing money is setting up a(n) _____.

7. A grocery bill is an example of a(n) _____.

Understand the Article

▶ **Write the answer to each question.**

8. Against which items in a budget is the author biased? What do you think the author would recommend doing with this money instead?

9. What is the advantage and disadvantage of placing money in a certificate of deposit compared to placing money in a savings account?

10. What are four rules that help people become better money managers?

Apply Your Skills

▶ **Circle the letter of the best answer for each question.**

11. Which of the following is the author's opinion and not a fact?

    A.   A budget shows how much money comes in and goes out each month.

    B.   Borrowers have a right to know the interest rate on a loan.

    C.   People should not spend money on smoking or alcohol.

    D.   Lenders have to tell people what a loan will cost.

12. The author of the article would have the most credibility if he or she was

    A.   a financial advisor.

    B.   a loan officer.

    C.   a bank manager.

    D.   a tax collector.

13. What does the circle graph on page 192 show about the average American family's spending habits?

    A.   It spends more on taxes than anything else.

    B.   It spends one-half its income on housing and food.

    C.   It spends about the same on transportation as it does on clothing.

    D.   It spends less on health care than it does on electricity, gas, telephone, and other utilities.

Connect with the Article

▶ **Write your answer to each question.**

14. Why do you think some lenders charge a fee if a loan is paid off early?

_____

_____

15. Some lenders argue that consumer credit laws are unfair to the lender. Choose the side of the lender or the consumer and argue against or in favor of consumer credit laws. Cite information from the article to support your argument.

_____

_____

_____

SUPPLY AND DEMAND

Vocabulary

supply

estimate

profit

elastic demand

inelastic demand

elastic supply

inelastic supply

scarce

A weekend trip to the video store can be frustrating. Family members plan to watch a movie they missed in the theater. They scan the shelves and see the title, but they find the case empty. "Why didn't the store order enough of these?" they wonder.

Stocking the right number of movies is not easy. A store owner may expect demand for a new video or DVD to be high—but how high? The owner wants to order enough copies to satisfy customers, but not so many that unrented copies sit on the shelves. When copies are not rented, the store loses money. This is an example of an economic choice that results in making money or losing it.

Relate to the Topic

This lesson discusses the economic laws of supply and demand. List the last item that was marked so low you bought an extra one. Was that item a want or a need? Then list an item that you refused to buy because the price was too high. Was that item a want or a need?

Did buy _____   Did not buy _____

Want or need _____   Want or need _____

Reading Strategy

PREVIEWING A TABLE   Tables present information. They can also help you prepare to read an accompanying article. Look at the table on page 198. Consider why that information might be given. Then answer the questions.

1.   What information in this table is related to economics?

_____

Hint: Look at the first and fifth columns.

2.   How might this table relate to the article title, "Supply and Demand"?

_____

Hint: Look at the subheadings and skim the article.

It's All in the Cards

Two things determine the price of goods. One is the consumers' demand for the goods. The other is the **supply,** or the amount of goods and services sellers offer at certain prices at a given time. People who study the market economy look closely at how supply and demand affect each other.

A Changing Market

Ideally, sellers would supply the same amount of goods and services that the consumers will buy. But, just like the owner of the video store, business owners can only **estimate** how much to order or produce. Sometimes they are right, and sometimes they are wrong. Considering the past and their business knowledge, sellers learn to predict what and how much to sell. Stadium vendors predict how many fans a team will draw so they can order enough hot dogs.

More sellers enter a market when prices are high. They have seen the success of others and want to make money selling the goods, too. Sellers usually increase production when prices are high. That is what generally happens with baseball cards.

Young people have been collecting baseball cards for decades. A photo of a baseball player appears on the front of each card. On the back are facts about the player. In the past, young people traded cards with friends to get a favorite player or a set of their favorite team. Some young card traders kept collecting cards even after they had grown up. Today, in fact, more than half of all card collectors are adults.

Card collectors sometimes **profit,** or make money, by selling cards at prices higher than what they paid for them. Old baseball cards, especially, can earn an amazing profit. For example, a person who paid one cent for a Yogi Berra card many years later sold that card for $6,000! The value of some old baseball cards shows how supply and demand affect each other.

A Matter of Supply and Demand

How a price change affects supply or demand is called elasticity. The supply and demand of certain products are either elastic or inelastic. An **elastic demand** means that a change in price affects the number of people who will buy the product. When steak goes up in price, for example, fewer people buy it. When the price drops, people buy more. A product has an **inelastic demand** if a price change does not affect the number of people who buy it. Products with an inelastic demand are generally things that are always needed. When the price changes for bread and milk, for example, shoppers still buy about the same amount. Because they need the product, its demand stays about the same despite a price change.

An **elastic supply** means that sellers can increase the supply of a product that has increased in price. Sports-card producers tend to increase supplies when cards are selling at high prices. This means the supply of new baseball cards is elastic.

On the other hand, an **inelastic supply** is limited. The supply of older baseball cards is inelastic. The supply cannot increase regardless of what happens to the price. For example, Topps, a sports-card producer, made a certain number of rookie baseball cards for Mark McGwire in 1985. At the beginning of the 1998 baseball season, that card was worth $30. Later that year, after McGwire broke Roger Maris's home-run record, the card's value rose to $200. However, when Barry Bonds broke McGwire's record three years later, the value of McGwire's rookie card dropped to $80—the demand for McGwire's card had declined.

The law of supply says that if prices are high, suppliers will make more products for the market. If prices are low, they will cut back production. Prices go up if the demand is greater than the supply. So prices for old baseball cards are generally high. Below are recent values for some baseball cards in near-perfect condition.

▶ Reading a Table A table organizes information in columns and rows. The title tells what kind of information is in the table. Look at the table below. For example, to find the mid-2002 value of a 1951 Willie Mays rookie card, read down the column under the heading "Player." When you come to *Mays, Willie,* read across the row to the column labeled *Mid-2002* Value. The Willie Mays card is valued at $3,000. Which of the two Mickey Mantle baseball cards has a higher value?

A. the Topps edition   B. the Bowman edition

| Baseball Cards for Investment | | | | RC = Rookie Card |
Player	Card Year	Card Producer	Card No.	Mid-2002 Value
Mantle, Mickey	1951 RC	Bowman	253	$8,500.00
Mays, Willie	1951 RC	Bowman	305	$3,000.00
Mantle, Mickey	1952	Topps	311	$18,000.00
Aaron, Hank	1954 RC	Topps	128	$1,500.00
Ryan, Nolan	1968 RC	Topps	177	$700.00
Clemente, Roberto	1973	Topps	50	$50.00
Clemens, Roger	1984 RC	Fleer Update	U27	$200.00
Clemens, Roger	1985	Donruss	273	$30.00
McGwire, Mark	1985 RC	Topps	401	$80.00
Bonds, Barry	1987 RC	Topps	320	$10.00
Sosa, Sammy	1990 RC	Upper Deck	17	$8.00
Jeter, Derek	1993 RC	SP	279	$120.00
Rodriguez, Alex	1994 RC	Fleer Update	86	$40.00
Wood, Kerry	1997 RC	Bowman	196	$5.00
McGwire, Mark	1998	Fleer	25	$2.50
McGwire, Mark	1998	Leaf	171	$12.00
Suzuki, Ichiro	2001 RC	Upper Deck	271	$20.00
Bonds, Barry	2001	Donruss Classics	2	$5.00
Jeter, Derek	2002	Topps	75	$1.50
Sosa, Sammy	2002	Upper Deck	301	$1.25

A Honus Wagner baseball card in near perfect condition sold for $1.265 million in 2000.

The Mickey Mantle 1952 baseball card is scarce, and people are willing to pay a lot of money to get it. **Scarce** means that the demand for the item is much greater than the supply. People will pay even more money for cards that are extremely rare.

Scarcity and Price

In 2000, a baseball card of Honus Wagner sold at auction for $1.265 million. Wagner was a popular shortstop for the Pittsburgh Pirates in the early 1900s. Why is his card so valuable? In the early 1900s, tobacco companies distributed baseball cards. They printed cards of Honus Wagner. Wagner did not want to encourage tobacco use, so he refused to let the company distribute his card. Today less than 75 Wagner cards are known to exist. Their scarcity makes them rare. The few that are in excellent condition are rarer still. It was one of these cards that sold for $1.265 million.

A controversial purchase shows what can happen when a rare card becomes one of a kind. A 13-year-old boy bought a 1968 Nolan Ryan rookie baseball card for $12 at a store. The card was worth $1,200, but the store clerk did not read the price correctly. The store had a big sign that read "All sales final," but the store owner took the boy to court anyway. He wanted the other $1,188 from the boy.

During the trial, the boy told the judge that he had already traded the Ryan card. He had traded it for two cards that were worth about $2,200. The judge ordered that the Nolan Ryan card be brought to court as evidence.

▶ Predicting Outcomes Trying to figure out what will happen next is called **predicting outcomes.** As you read, try to guess something based on what you have read so far. Use what you already know from past experiences to help make predictions. Reread the paragraphs above. How do you think the court case affected the value of the Nolan Ryan card?

    A. The value of the card increased.

    B. The value of the card went down.

The new owner agreed to bring the card to court. But he asked that the court's "Exhibit 1" sticker remain on the card after the case was settled. The card, with the sticker, could be worth as much as $3,000. The trial and the sticker made the card one-of-a-kind, so it has increased in value.

Today many collectors continue to buy cards, hoping to find a rare one and strike it rich. Critics doubt that anyone will get rich from cards produced in the last few years. They say the supply of new cards is far too great. They point out that in 1951, only two major companies, Topps and Bowman, made baseball cards. Today there are several companies. Many of them produce more than one series of baseball cards.

Other baseball-card experts disagree with this idea. They believe that baseball cards will never lose value. One trader said, "As long as there are baseball fans, there will be baseball cards, and those cards will be worth something."

Thinking About the Article

Practice Vocabulary

▶ The words below are in the passage in bold type. Study the way each word is used. Then complete each sentence by writing the correct word.

inelastic demand	elastic demand	supply	profit
elastic supply	inelastic supply	scarce	

1. Mickey Mantle's baseball cards are an example of a(n)

   _____.

2. A collector who sells a rare baseball card is likely to

   _____.

3. If the amount of a product increases when its price goes up, the

   product has a(n) _____.

4. When the supply of a product is very low, the product is considered

   _____.

5. Products and services with a(n) _____ are generally
   necessities.

6. Fewer people buy a product with a(n) _____ when its
   price goes up.

7. A seller increases the _____ of a product when its price
   goes up.

Understand the Article

▶ Write the answer to each question.

8. The author believes the boy that bought the 1968 Nolan Ryan card should
   not have been taken to court. How might the author's viewpoint change if
   10 or 20 years from now, the card is worth $5,000 or $10,000?

   _____

9. Why is the word *elastic* used to describe products with a changing supply
   or demand?

   _____

10. What happened after the store owner realized one of his baseball cards
    had been sold for much less than its actual price?

    _____

Apply Your Skills

▶ **Circle the letter of the best answer for each question.**

11. Reread page 199. Which prediction would the information in the paragraphs support?

A. There is only one 1968 Nolan Ryan rookie card marked "Exhibit 1."

B. The "Exhibit 1" sticker on the card will lower the card's value.

C. The store owner received his $1,188 from the boy.

D. The new owner of the Ryan card will make a profit.

12. Look at the table on page 198. Which best explains why the two Roger Clemens cards have different values?

A. Clemens' trade to another team after the 1984 season caused the value of the 1985 card to decline.

B. The demand for the 1985 Clemens card correlates to an increase in price over time.

C. The value of the Donruss card correlates to a worse baseball season.

D. The shorter supply of Clemens' Fleer Update card caused the higher price.

13. Look at the mid-2002 values of the cards in the table on page 198. If the values make up a data set, what is the mode of the data?

A. $1.50   C. $50.00

B. $5.00   D. $120.00

Connect with the Article

▶ **Write your answer to each question.**

14. How do supply and demand cause companies that make a product to enter or leave a market?

_____

_____

_____

15. Would you advise someone to invest his or her money in baseball cards? Explain your answer clearly.

_____

_____

_____

ECONOMICS AT WORK

HORTICULTURE:
FLOWER SHOP MANAGER

Do you like working with plants and flowers? You may enjoy managing a flower shop. However, being a florist involves more than customer service and arranging flowers. It also requires a good understanding of the economics of running a store.

Flower shop managers are responsible for ordering and maintaining cut flowers and green plants. They must be aware of the best sources for economically priced flowers. They must also know what prices to charge for the flowers so that they can make money while competing with other stores.

A major part of each day is spent ordering, caring for, and arranging cut flowers. Managers must be familiar with each type of plant and be able to recommend plant and bouquet selections to their customers.

Look at the Some Careers in Horticulture sidebar.

- Do any of the careers interest you? If so, which ones?

- What information would you need to know more about those careers?

On a separate piece of paper, write some questions that you would like answered. You can find more information about those careers in the *Occupational Outlook Handbook* at your local library or online.

SOME CAREERS IN HORTICULTURE

Garden Planner
uses knowledge of green plants and flowers to plan gardens for individuals and companies

Garden Center Worker
takes care of plants, assists customers, stocks supplies

Groundskeeper
cares for flowers, grass, trees, and shrubs in public and private settings

Landscape Worker
plants flowers, shrubs, and trees according to design plans

Lawn Service Worker
tends lawns flower beds, and shrubs

▶ **Use the material below to answer the questions that follow.**

     Maria is a floral shop manager. She reviewed all the invoices from the past year and recorded the highest and lowest prices she paid for the best-selling flowers. In general, the law of supply and demand dictates that flowers cost more when they are out of season and in scarce supply. Maria made a table of information from the invoices.

Flower	Highest Price Paid	Lowest Price Paid
Calla lily	$2.50 per stem	$1.20 per stem
Carnation	$5.35 per bunch	$1.25 per bunch
Delphinium	$7.95 per bunch	$4.95 per bunch
Hyacinth	$3.95 per bulb	$1.25 per bulb
Poppy	$6.25 per bunch	$2.25 per bunch
Tulip	$2.25 per stem	$0.65 per stem

1. Below is a list of prices Maria paid for each flower. Determine if each flower was purchased in season or out of season. Circle the correct answer.

Calla lily—$1.25 per stem	in season	out of season
Carnation—$5.19 per bunch	in season	out of season
Delphinium—$6.95 per bunch	in season	out of season
Hyacinth—$3.45 per bulb	in season	out of season
Poppy—$2.55 per bunch	in season	out of season
Tulip—$0.72 per stem	in season	out of season

2. Which of the following prices indicates that the plant is out of season?

    A. Tulip—$0.70 per stem

    B. Calla lily—$2.25 per stem

    C. Delphinium—$5.25 per bunch

    D. Carnation—$1.75 per bunch

3. Have you ever noticed how certain items are more expensive during certain times of the year? You may be aware of this when you go grocery shopping or when you buy certain types of clothing. Use a separate piece of paper to describe at least one seasonal pricing difference that you've encountered.

ECONOMICS AT WORK   *Check your answers on page 252.*   203

Increasing Demand

Producers of goods and services are always looking for ways to increase demand. When consumers want to buy more products and services, producers and sellers are able to make higher profits. One way to increase demand is to find new uses for products. New uses for a product attract new customers. Farm products are a good example. In recent years scientists have found ways to increase the demand for many crops. Take corn, for example.

For years, people bought corn as a food product. Today, however, corn is used to make everything from paint to diapers. In some cases, corn is a good substitute for oil in making paint. It is an ingredient in coatings for wood and metal. Adding a small amount of cornstarch to plastic can help protect the environment. Ordinarily plastic does not decompose or break down. It lasts forever—unless a small amount of cornstarch is added during the plastic-making process. Then the plastic will decompose. As a result, cornstarch is an additive to such products as disposable diapers and plastic bags.

No one is sure how many other products could be improved with a little corn. But scientists continually research the possibilities. As the demand grows, farmers have more reasons to grow corn.

▶ **Circle the letter of the best answer for each question.**

1. According to the article, which of the following would be most likely to encourage the new uses of corn?

    A. people who like to eat corn

    B. people who use corn as animal feed

    C. gasoline producers

    D. people concerned about the environment

2. Which of the following is the best conclusion that can be drawn from the passage?

    A. Demand for corn is likely to increase.

    B. Demand for corn is likely to decrease.

    C. The supply of corn is likely to stay the same.

    D. The supply of corn is likely to decrease.

A Wedding Budget

Josh and Jennifer Lee's Wedding Expenses			
Expense	Planned	Actual	Percentage of Actual Amount Spent
Clothing	$1,600	$1,670	12%
Wedding rings	450	650	5%
Wedding stationary	350	335	2%
Limousine rental	500	560	4%
Chapel Fee	200	200	1%
Flowers	1,250	1,225	9%
Reception	7,050	6,975	50%
Wedding photographs	1,500	1,140	10%
Wedding video	250	250	2%
Music	250	450	3%
Other	350	275	2%
Total	13,750	13,730	100%

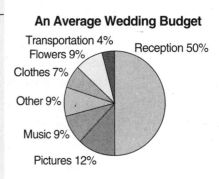

An Average Wedding Budget

Transportation 4%
Flowers 9%
Clothes 7%
Other 9%
Music 9%
Pictures 12%
Reception 50%

▶ **Write the answer to each question.**

3. The Lees opted for wedding rings that cost more than they had planned. According to their budget, what could be the opportunity cost of more expensive rings?

_____

4. According to their budget, what can you conclude about the incentive the Lees had to book the wedding photographer they did?

_____

_____

▶ **Circle the letter of the best answer for the question.**

5. Which of the following is best supported by the graph and the table?

A. The Lees spent less on music than they had planned.

B. The Lees spent about an average amount on flowers but less than average on music.

C. For both the average wedding budget and for the Lee's wedding budget, flowers and pictures account for 15 percent of the total expense.

D. Wedding flowers cost too much money.

Deceptive Selling

Almost everyone has been the victim of deceptive selling methods. Perhaps you paid too much for an item. Maybe the product you bought was not worth as much as you thought it was. Smart shoppers learn to be cautious. They watch for one or more of the following selling practices. In many places, consumer credit laws exist to make these practices illegal.

Special Pricing.   A seller offers a product at a "special low price." The seller tells the customer to buy now because the price will go up soon. However in many cases, the "special" price is actually higher than the price of the same item at other stores.

Bait and Switch.   An ad offers an item at a very low price. When customers go to buy that item, they are told that the item is an inferior product. The seller then suggests switching to a more expensive model of the same item. The seller may also tell buyers that the advertised item is "out of stock." The seller then urges the customer to buy the more expensive model that just happens to be "in stock."

Chain Referrals.   Customers are told that if they buy a product and then refer other customers, they will receive a gift or a reduced price. Often the price of the product, even with the gift or discount, is higher than the price of the same item at other stores.

▶ **Write the answer to each question.**

6. An ad offers a deal on a TV. When the customer goes to buy the item, the seller says it is out of stock. The seller notes that a more expensive model is in stock. Which sales method is the seller using?

_____

7. A seller tells a buyer that they should make a car purchase now because the interest rate on the loan will be going up next month. There will never be a better time to buy than now. Which sales method is the seller using?

_____

▶ **Circle the letter of the best answer for the question.**

8. Which of the following statements is supported by the article?

   A.   All sellers are dishonest.

   B.   Be alert to unlawful practices.

   C.   If a deal sounds good, buy the item.

   D.   Never check prices in other stores.

Microfinance

Microfinance is making loans, savings, and other basic financial services available to the poor. "Micro" means small and microfinance involves small amounts of money. Typical financial institutions were designed to help those who already have money, not those that have very little. Some people find it impossible to imagine that a poor person could use a $20,000 loan to start a small business or use $1,000 to start a savings account. Microfinance institutions provide microfinance services to poor people on a scale they can use.

Microfinance institutions may be small non-profit organizations or large banks. Microfinance took off in the 1980s when people began experimenting with providing poor women, usually in developing countries, with loans to invest in small businesses. By running their own businesses, these women could make a living.

To determine the interest rates on microloans a microfinance institution calculates the cost of the money it lends and the cost of loan defaults. For example, if it costs 8% to loan the money and the institution experiences defaults of 1% of the amount lent, the interest rate on the loan would be 9%, which is reasonable. However, transaction costs are the same for any loan, big or small. With the high number of small loans these institutions make, the transaction costs add up, and these costs are reflected in the interest rate. As a result, interest rates for microloans are typically higher than for conventional loans. Around the world, they average about 35%. However, this is still usually lower than rates charged by informal moneylenders.

▶ **Write the answer to each question.**

9. How are microfinance institutions different from typical financial institutions?

_____

10. Which language from the article shows the author is in favor of microloans despite their high interest rates?

_____

▶ **Circle the letter of the best answer.**

11. Why do microloans usually cost more than typical loans?

    A.   Institutions do not make any money on microloans.

    B.   Most microloans are not repaid.

    C.   Financial institutions are nervous about lending money to the poor.

    D.   The transaction costs are higher because there are many loans.

SOCIAL STUDIES EXTENSION

Some microfinance institutions enable anyone to loan money through a microloan. Explore online to find a website that makes this possible. Look through the options for loans. Which loan would you choose to fund? Why?

MINI-TEST

This is a 15-minute practice test. After 15 minutes, mark the last number you finished. Then complete the test and check your answers. If most of your answers were correct but you did not finish, try to work faster next time.

▶ **Directions: Choose the <u>one best answer</u> to each question.**

Questions 1 and 2 refer to the following information.

A wise shopper often thinks about unit price—the cost of an item in terms of its unit of measurement. For example, a unit price for a bag of apples might be the price per pound.

In the past, consumers had to figure out unit prices themselves. Today, most supermarkets post the unit price along with the item's price on the item's shelf display.

1. What do you infer is the reason supermarket owners post unit prices?

    A. to help shoppers compare the value of similar items in order to decide which to purchase

    B. to advertise the highest quality items

    C. to announce price changes

    D. to keep shoppers from buying items they cannot afford

2. What are consumers likely to notice in unit prices if the economy is in a period of steep inflation?

    A. The unit prices would decrease.

    B. The unit prices would increase.

    C. The unit prices would stay the same.

    D. The unit prices would no longer be available.

Question 3 refers to the following line graph.

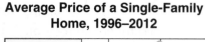

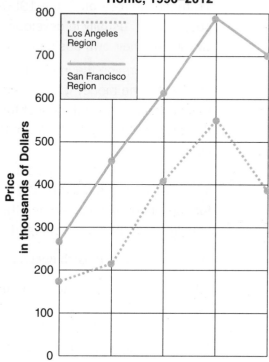

3. Which of the following is a valid conclusion based on the graph?

    A. Prices of homes rose steadily in both San Francisco and Los Angeles between 1996 and 2012.

    B. Prices of homes declined steadily in both San Francisco and Los Angeles between 1996 and 2012.

    C. Between 2000 and 2012, home prices in both San Francisco and Los Angeles rose and then fell.

    D. Between 2004 and 2008, homes in San Francisco and in Los Angeles gained little or no value.

UNIT 4 ECONOMICS

Questions 4 and 5 refer to the following table.

How We Pay—and May Pay Tomorrow

Method of Payment (Partial Listing)	Billions of Transactions		Percent of Transactions	
	1999	2005	1999	2005
Personal Checks	29.4	23.8	27.9	17.6
Money Orders	1.2	1.4	1.1	1.1
Credit Cards	18.4	23.2	17.4	17.2
Debit Cards	6.4	18.4	6.1	13.6
Cash	46.6	58.6	44.2	43.4

4. Which information best supports the conclusion that cash and personal checks continued to be very popular ways to pay for purchases?

   A. The use of debit cards declined between 1999 and 2005.

   B. There were more transactions of all kinds in 2005 than in 1999.

   C. Credit cards and checks were used almost equally in 2005.

   D. As in 1999, cash and checks were used for most purchases in 2005.

5. Based on the table, which of the following is a reasonable prediction for the year 2015?

   A. Cash transactions will increase while money order transactions decrease.

   B. Money order transactions will increase while cash transactions decrease.

   C. Personal check transactions will decrease while debit card transactions increase.

   D. Cash transactions will increase while credit card transactions decrease.

Questions 6 and 7 refer to the following information.

When stock analysts talk about a bear market, are they giving you good news? What about a bull market? These "animal" terms have important meanings.

In a bear market, stock prices go down. The drop isn't sudden, as in a crash; rather, investors expect stock prices to decline and to stay low. A bear market, which may last for many months, reflects a generally slow economy.

A bull market is just the opposite—stock prices are going up, and experts predict that the trend will last for a while. A bull market indicates a growing economy and a good chance for investors to profit.

6. Why are these animal names appropriate for the stock market conditions they refer to?

   A. Bears are furry and bulls are not.

   B. Bears are wild animals and bulls are domesticated animals.

   C. Bears have sluggish periods and bulls sometimes charge or stampede.

   D. Bears hunt and bulls graze.

7. Which of the following is most likely to lead to a bear market?

   A. growth in the amount of exports

   B. poor earnings predictions from major companies

   C. a high demand for a new product

   D. stockholders buying more stock instead of selling the stock they have

ANSWER SHEET

Posttest
Social Studies

Name: _____ **Class:** _____ **Date:** _____

1 Ⓐ Ⓑ Ⓒ Ⓓ

2 Ⓐ Ⓑ Ⓒ Ⓓ

3 Ⓐ Ⓑ Ⓒ Ⓓ

4 Ⓐ Ⓑ Ⓒ Ⓓ

5 Ⓐ Ⓑ Ⓒ Ⓓ

6 Ⓐ Ⓑ Ⓒ Ⓓ

7 Ⓐ Ⓑ Ⓒ Ⓓ

8 Ⓐ Ⓑ Ⓒ Ⓓ

9 Ⓐ Ⓑ Ⓒ Ⓓ

10 Ⓐ Ⓑ Ⓒ Ⓓ

11 Ⓐ Ⓑ Ⓒ Ⓓ

12 Ⓐ Ⓑ Ⓒ Ⓓ

13 Ⓐ Ⓑ Ⓒ Ⓓ

14 Ⓐ Ⓑ Ⓒ Ⓓ

15 Ⓐ Ⓑ Ⓒ Ⓓ

16 _____

17 _____

18 _____

19 _____

20 Ⓐ Ⓑ Ⓒ Ⓓ

21 Ⓐ Ⓑ Ⓒ Ⓓ

22 Ⓐ Ⓑ Ⓒ Ⓓ

23 _____

_____

_____

_____

_____

_____

_____

_____

_____

_____

Directions

This is a 40-minute practice test. After 40 minutes, mark the last number you finished. Then complete the test and check your answers. If most of your answers were correct but you did not finish, try to work faster next time.

The Pre GED® Social Studies Posttest consists of multiple-choice and short answer questions that measure general social studies concepts. The questions are based on short readings and/or illustrations, including maps, graphs, charts, cartoons, or other figures. Study the information given and then answer the question(s) following it. Refer to the information as often as necessary in answering the questions.

Record your answers on the answer sheet on page 210, which you may photocopy. For multiple-choice items, fill in the lettered circle on the answer sheet that corresponds to the answer you select for each question in the Posttest. For fill-in-the-blank and extended-response items, write your answers on the lines provided.

After you complete the Posttest, check your answers on pages 254–256. Then use the Posttest Evaluation Chart on page 223 to identify the social studies skills and content areas that you need to practice more.

EXAMPLE

The Declaration of Independence was drafted by Thomas Jefferson in which year?

A. 1620
B. 1700
C. 1776
D. 1789

(On Answer Sheet)

Ⓐ Ⓑ ● Ⓓ

The correct answer is "1776"; therefore, answer space C would be marked on the answer sheet.

If you do not use the answer sheet provided, mark your answers on each test page by circling the correct answer for each question.

▶ **Directions: Choose the <u>one best answer</u> to each question.**

Questions 1 and 2 are based on the information and the photograph below.

　　The first televised presidential debates were between Senator John F. Kennedy and Vice-President Richard M. Nixon. Nixon was recovering from a knee injury and came to the first debate looking pale and underweight. Kennedy, on the other hand, had taken time off the day before the debate. He had been campaigning out-of-doors in California and looked tanned and relaxed. People who listened to the first debate on the radio heard two politicians who were quite close in their views. People who watched the debate on television saw great contrasts in the way the two candidates presented themselves on camera.

1. Based on the information and the photograph, what difference between the two candidates did televising the debates highlight?

   A. their debate experience

   B. their political views

   C. their understanding of key issues

   D. their physical appearance and poise

2. In an extremely close race, John F. Kennedy won the 1960 presidential election. What can you infer about the impact of the debates on the outcome of the election?

   A. The debates had no effect on the outcome.

   B. Richard Nixon's greater experience impressed voters.

   C. Televising the debates prompted voters to be influenced by the candidates' appearance.

   D. Voters felt that they could support a senator over the vice-president.

Question 3 is based on the following paragraph from the U.S. government's *Occupational Outlook Handbook.*

"Applicants for reservation and transportation ticket agent jobs are likely to encounter considerable competition because the supply of qualified applicants exceeds the expected number of job openings. Entry requirements for these jobs are minimal, and many people seeking to get into the airline industry or travel business often start out in these types of positions. These jobs provide excellent travel benefits, and many people view airline and other travel-related jobs as glamorous."

3. Which statement best illustrates the type of information missing from this paragraph?

    A. Ticket agents work varied hours and have flexible schedules.

    B. People who like to travel are likely to be good ticket agents.

    C. Agents must be prepared for unhappy travelers.

    D. Jobs in the travel industry are interesting and exciting.

Question 4 refers to the following information.

The Tenth Amendment to the United States was ratified by three-fourths of the states on December 15, 1791, as part of the Bill of Rights. The Tenth Amendment to the U.S. Constitution reads: "The powers not delegated to the United States by the Constitution, nor prohibited by it to the States, are reserved to the States respectively, or to the people."

4. How does a proposed amendment become part of the Constitution?

    A. It must be proposed by two-thirds of the states.

    B. It must be ratified by three-fourths of the states.

    C. It must be voted on by all of the states.

    D. It must be approved by all of the states.

Questions 5 and 6 refer to the following map of the world.

Oceans and Continents of the World

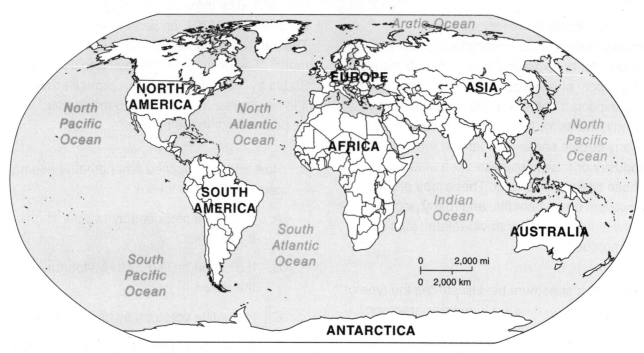

5. Which of the following statements is supported by information on the map?

   A. Every continent is more than 4,000 miles wide.

   B. The continents closest to the equator are the warmest.

   C. Each of the world's oceans is divided into northern and southern regions.

   D. Three of the world's oceans border the continent of Antarctica.

6. Which source for this map is most credible and reliable?

   A. a history teacher's blog

   B. a .com website

   C. nationalatlas.gov

   D. an elementary textbook

Questions 7 through 9 are based on the following passage.

In 1830, Congress passed the Indian Removal Act, authorizing the federal government to take Native American lands in the East; in exchange tribes would receive land in Indian Territory (Oklahoma). By 1833, all of the southeastern tribes except the Cherokee had agreed to move.

In a letter to a principal Cherokee chief, members of the tribe wrote, "We the great mass of the people think only of the love we have to our land . . . . to let [the land] go will be like throwing away . . . [our] mother that gave . . . [us] birth." But, in 1835, federal agents persuaded some chiefs to give up all Cherokee lands for $5.6 million and free passage west.

In 1838, the federal government forcibly removed the Cherokees from their lands. Many had no time to collect their possessions. The trip was harsh; about one-quarter of the people died. The Cherokee called this journey the "Trail of Tears."

7. What was a main reason the Cherokee did not want to move to Indian Territory?

   A. They had deep ties to their land.

   B. They did not like the land in Oklahoma.

   C. They did not have enough time to pack.

   D. There were not enough wagons for them.

8. What information supports the conclusion that Native Americans did not have the same rights as other Americans?

   A. Some tribes agreed to the removal.

   B. Congress authorized the government to take Native American lands.

   C. The Cherokee received only $5.6 million.

   D. The Cherokee had split leadership.

9. Which statement from the article shows the author's bias in favor of the Cherokee and their plight?

   A. In 1830, Congress passed the Indian Removal Act authorizing the federal government to take Native American lands in the East.

   B. In 1838, the federal government forcibly removed the Cherokees from their lands.

   C. Federal agents persuaded some chiefs to give up all Cherokee lands for $5.6 million and free passage west.

   D. Tribes would receive land in Indian Territory (Oklahoma).

Go on to the next page.

Question 10 is based on the following passage.

In 1929, the stock market crashed, and the Great Depression began. In 1930, unemployment grew from 4 million to 7 million people. By 1933, it reached 14 million, about 25% of the population. In the first two months of 1933, over 4,000 banks failed. The day after President Franklin Delano Roosevelt was inaugurated on March 4, 1933, he called a special session of Congress. In 1933, Congress began passing several acts that came to be part of "The New Deal." These acts included the Reforestation Relief Act, which provided jobs for 250,000 in the Civilian Conservation Corps; the Agricultural Adjustment Act, which provided subsidies to farmers; and the Homeowners Refinancing Act, which helped homeowners in danger of losing their homes. The Banking Act of 1933 created the Federal Deposit Insurance Corporation to protect depositors' funds in banks. The last significant New Deal legislation was the Fair Labor Standards Act in 1937 which set a minimum wage for workers and a maximum number of work hours in a week. Some people believe that economic indicators show the New Deal was successful. Others believe that World War II ended the Great Depression.

10. Which evidence would support the opinion that the New Deal was effective?

A. a decrease in bank deposits in the 1930s

B. a decrease in the unemployment rate in the 1930s

C. a decrease in the unemployment rate in the 1940s

D. a decrease in bank deposits in the 1940s

Question 11 is based on this political cartoon about the scandal surrounding the collapse of the Enron corporation in 2001.

11. Which of the following statements is an opinion expressed through this cartoon?

A. A janitor should be Speaker of the House of Representatives.

B. It is not important to investigate corporate scandals.

C. Everyone knows that all politicians are crooks.

D. Washington politicians are too involved with big corporations.

Questions 12 and 13 are based on the following information.

Voter Education Project

Working to Protect the Integrity of the Initiative Process

Think Before You Ink

The Voter Education Project has filed complaints against 10 ballot initiative petitioners so far this election season. As a result, two petitioners have been convicted of forgery. They admitted to state investigators that 70% of the signatures they turned over were invalid. Other investigations are pending.

Protect yourself from signature theft. Take a few simple steps before you sign:

Read the front and back of every petition.

Don't let a petitioner rush you into signing something you don't support.

Be wary when petitioners carry more than two or three initiatives. That means they are paid per signature and that's a high incentive for fraud.

Don't sign an initiative more than once.

Don't sign an initiative unless you are registered to vote at the moment you sign.

If you sign, make sure and fill out your **entire name and address** on every initiative. That makes your signature more difficult to forge.

If a petitioner tries to con you, report it immediately to the Oregon Secretary of State or the Voter Education Project.

12. Which piece of information from the flyer supports the idea that people may behave aggressively in trying to get you to sign a petition?

    A. Don't sign an initiative more than once.

    B. Don't let a petitioner rush you into signing something you don't support.

    C. Fill out your entire name and address if you sign.

    D. Don't sign an initiative unless you are registered to vote.

13. Which of the following statements is an example of faulty logic?

    A. If you are a registered voter, you can sign as many petitions as you like.

    B. Don't sign any petitions because your signature might be stolen.

    C. If you sign a petition, you should include your entire name and address.

    D. Oregon should investigate petitioners who forge signatures.

Go on to the next page.   217

Question 14 is based on the following passage.

In 1985, a photograph of a beautiful Afghan refugee appeared on the cover of *National Geographic* magazine. This became one of the magazine's most famous covers. However, the girl never revealed her name to the photographer, Steve McCurry. Therefore, McCurry was unable to contact the girl to let her know how famous she had become.

Seventeen years later, a team from *National Geographic* traveled to Afghanistan to try to find the now-grown-up woman. Through a list of contacts that finally led to her brother and husband, the woman was identified as Sharbat Gula. Sharbat's husband and brother agreed to let Sharbat be interviewed. To make sure that this was the right person, the magazine staff obtained proof through iris scanning and face recognition technology.

When they met again, McCurry told Sharbat that her image had become a symbol of the people of Afghanistan. "I don't think she was particularly interested in her personal fame," McCurry said. "But she was pleased when we said she had come to be a symbol of the dignity and resilience of her people."

14. When did *National Geographic* identify the girl on its cover?

    A. when her photo was first used in the magazine

    B. seventeen years after the magazine cover was published

    C. following McCurry taking the photograph

    D. before McCurry returned to Afghanistan to find her

Question 15 is based on the timeline.

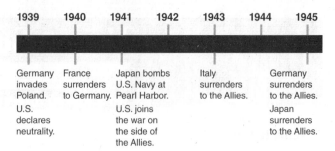

15. The Axis powers—Germany, Japan, and Italy—were finally defeated by the Allies. Which year would you conclude was the turning point in World War II?

    A. 1939

    B. 1940

    C. 1941

    D. 1943

Question 16 is based on the following information.

The United States did not enter World War II until 1941 when the President asked Congress to declare war on Germany.

Write the answer in the blank.

16. The fact that the President cannot declare war himself or herself is an example of separation of _____.

Questions 17 through 19 are based on the following information.

ANARCHISM A philosophy that advocates the abolition of organized authority, and common ownership of land and the means of production

AUTOCRACY/DESPOTISM A supreme, uncontrolled, unlimited authority, where the right of governing is possessed by a single person

DEMOCRACY A form of government in which the supreme power is retained and exercised directly by the people or indirectly by popular representation

LIBERTARIANISM A philosophy of individual freedom, particularly from any unnecessary restraints imposed by governmental authority

SOCIALISM A system in which the means of production, distribution, and exchange are generally owned by the state and used on behalf of the people

17. If the government owns everything, and there is little or no private property, the political philosophy or system that is in effect in the country is _____.

18. A country that has one ruler or a single ruling party bases its government on

_____.

19. "We stress that this opposition to hierarchy is not limited to just the state or government. It includes all authoritarian economic and social relationships as well as political ones, particularly those associated with property and wage labor."

This quote best represents the political philosophy or system of _____.

Question 20 is based on the following line graph.

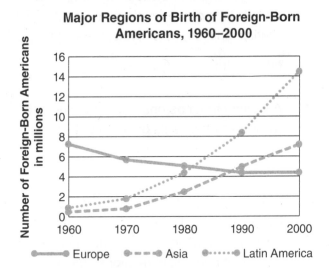

Major Regions of Birth of Foreign-Born Americans, 1960–2000

Legend: Europe ● Asia ● Latin America

20. Based on the graph, which conclusion can you draw?

   A. Political instability in Asia caused more citizens of Asian nations to immigrate to the United States between 1960 and 2000.

   B. Political and economic conditions were better in Latin America and Asia than in Europe during the 1960s, so there were fewer Latin American and Asian immigrants than European immigrants.

   C. More immigrants were from Europe in the 1960s and 1970s, but by 1990 more Latin American and Asian immigrants lived in the United States.

   D. Today, more Asians than Latin Americans want to live in the United States.

Question 21 is based on the following circle graphs.

Annual Budget for St. Petersburg, Florida

Income: Property Tax, Utility & Franchise Tax, Sales Tax, Other

Expenditures: Public Safety, Leisure Services, Non-Departmental, Other

21. Which information from the graphs supports the conclusion that St. Petersburg plans to spend about half of its revenue on police, firefighting, and paramedic operations?

   A. Sales tax and property tax account for about half of the city's income.

   B. Expenditures for public safety account for about half of the city's budget.

   C. The city collects about the same amount for utility and franchise taxes as it spends on parks and other recreational services.

   D. The city has other sources of income in addition to the property tax, utility and franchise taxes, and sales tax it levies.

Question 22 is based on the following transcription.

The executive branch includes many different departments and agencies as well as the President's cabinet. The cabinet is described in Article II, Section 2 of the United States Constitution. The cabinet members are the President's closest advisors.

Section. 2.

The President shall be Commander in Chief of the Army and Navy of the United States, and of the Militia of the several States, when called into the actual Service of the United States; he may require the Opinion, in writing, of the principal Officer in each of the executive Departments, upon any Subject relating to the Duties of their respective Offices, and he shall have Power to grant Reprieves and Pardons for Offences against the United States, except in Cases of Impeachment.

He shall have Power, by and with the Advice and Consent of the Senate, to make Treaties, provided two thirds of the Senators present concur; and he shall nominate, and by and with the Advice and Consent of the Senate, shall appoint Ambassadors, other public Ministers and Consuls, Judges of the Supreme Court, and all other Officers of the United States, whose Appointments are not herein otherwise provided for, and which shall be established by Law: but the Congress may by Law vest the Appointment of such inferior Officers, as they think proper, in the President alone, in the Courts of Law, or in the Heads of Departments.

The President shall have Power to

fill up all Vacancies that may happen during the Recess of the Senate, by granting Commissions which shall expire at the End of their next Session.

22. Which part of Section 2 refers to the President's cabinet?

A. he may require the Opinion, in writing, of the principal Officer in each of the executive Departments, upon any Subject relating to the Duties of their respective Offices

B. He shall have Power, by and with the Advice and Consent of the Senate, to make Treaties, provided two thirds of the Senators present concur

C. and he shall have Power to grant Reprieves and Pardons for Offences against the United States, except in Cases of Impeachment

D. and he shall nominate, and by and with the Advice and Consent of the Senate, shall appoint Ambassadors, other public Ministers and Consuls, Judges of the Supreme Court, and all other Officers of the United States

Go on to the next page.

Question 23 is based on the following transcription.

The Emancipation Proclamation

January 1, 1863
A Transcription

By the President of the United States of America:

A Proclamation.

Whereas, on the twenty-second day of September, in the year of our Lord one thousand eight hundred and sixty-two, a proclamation was issued by the President of the United States, containing, among other things, the following, to wit:

"That on the first day of January, in the year of our Lord one thousand eight hundred and sixty-three, all persons held as slaves within any State or designated part of a State, the people whereof shall then be in rebellion against the United States, shall be then, thenceforward, and forever free; and the Executive Government of the United States, including the military and naval authority thereof, will recognize and maintain the freedom of such persons, and will do no act or acts to repress such persons, or any of them, in any efforts they may make for their actual freedom.

"That the Executive will, on the first day of January aforesaid, by proclamation, designate the States and parts of States, if any, in which the people thereof, respectively, shall then be in rebellion against the United States; and the fact that any State, or the people thereof, shall on that day be, in good faith, represented in the Congress of the United States by members chosen thereto at elections wherein a majority of the qualified voters of such State shall have participated, shall, in the absence of strong countervailing testimony, be deemed conclusive evidence that such State, and the people

thereof, are not then in rebellion against the United States."

23. Describe the political philosophy or philosophies that President Lincoln drew on in issuing the Emancipation Proclamation. Do you feel he was following rule of law (the influence of law on his behavior)? Explain. Support your opinion with evidence.

Posttest Evaluation Chart

The following chart will help you determine your strengths and weaknesses in social studies content areas and thinking skills.

Directions

Check your answers on page 254–256. Circle the number of each item that you answered correctly on the Posttest. Count the number of items you answered correctly in each row. (For example, in the *U.S. History* row, write the number correct in the blank before */5,* which means *out of 5.*)

Complete this process for the remaining rows. Then add the 4 totals to get your *Total Correct* for the whole Posttest.

If you answered fewer than 18 items correctly, determine the areas in which you need further practice. Go back and review the content in those areas. Page numbers for specific instruction appear in the left-hand column.

If you answered 18 or more items correctly, your teacher may decide that you are ready to go on to Steck-Vaughn's Complete Test Preparation for the 2014 GED® Test.

Thinking Skill/ Content Area	Comprehension	Application	Analysis	Evaluation	Total Correct
U.S. History (Pages 14–77)	2		1, 7, **15, 20**		____/5
Geography and the World (Pages 78–129)		5	6, 14		____/3
Civics and Government (Pages 130–175)	4, 16	**17, 18, 19**	8, 9, 11, 13, 23	12, 22	____/12
Economics (Pages 176–209)			**10**	3, **21**	____/3

Total Correct for Posttest _____ **out of 23**

Boldfaced numbers indicate questions based on charts, diagrams, graphs, and maps.

PRETEST

PAGES 1–12

1. **A. Below 1,000 feet** *(DOK Level: 2; Content Topic: G.c.3; Practice: SSP.6.b)* The Coastal Plains are shaded gray on the map. The key shows that the elevation in the gray area is below 1,000 feet.

2. **A. It is nearly impossible to farm in the desert.** *(DOK Level: 2; Content Topic: G.b.2; Practice: SSP.7.a)* Options B, C, and D are all facts from the article. The words "nearly impossible" signal that Option A is an opinion.

3. **D. They move frequently which allows the land to recover.** *(DOK Level: 2; Content Topic: G.b.2; Practice: SSP.2.b)*

4. **B. solar panels** *(DOK Level: 2; Content Topic: G.b.3; Practice: SSP.3.c)* The modern conveniences that nomadic people enjoy are lightbulbs and televisions. They are able to enjoy these modern conveniences because of the electricity produced by solar panels. Their gers, or tents, are not modern, but traditional.

5. **1875** *(DOK Level: 2; Content Topic: GG.f; Practice: SSP.3.a)*

6. **550,000** *(DOK Level: 2; Content Topic: CG.f; Practice: SSP.6.c)*

7. **D. They likely tried to become more "American."** *(DOK Level: 3; Content Topic: CG.f; Practice: SSP.1.a)* If Chinese laborers were not allowed into the United States, one can infer that Chinese already in the United States were discriminated against at that time. So, it is likely that they tried to become more American to fit in.

8. **B. before immigrants lost benefits** *(DOK Level: 2; Content Topic: GG.f; Practice: SSP.3.a)* According to the timeline, exclusions based on beliefs were removed in 1990, which was after the Office of Immigration was established in 1891, Ellis Island opened in 1892, and race was removed in 1952. However, it was before immigrants lost benefits in 1996.

9. **B. Patriot leaders said African American soldiers could no longer serve in the army.** *(DOK Level: 3; Content Topic: USH.b.3; Practice: SSP.1.b)*

10. **C. the loss of so many soldiers at Valley Forge** *(DOK Level: 2; Content Topic: USH.b.1; Practice: SSP.1.a)* Options A and D had no bearing on the policies of Patriot leaders toward African Americans. Option B resulted in Patriot leaders allowing free African Americans, but not slaves, to join.

11. **more** *(DOK Level: 2; Content Topic: CG.b.8; Practice: SSP.6.b)*

12. **C. separate for whites and African Americans** *(DOK Level: 3; Content Topic: USH.d.1; Practice: SSP.4.a)* Segregated means separate. Segregated schools were separate schools for whites and African Americans.

13. **A. state primaries** *(DOK Level: 2; Content Topic: GG.e.3; Practice: SSP.10.a)* According to the diagram, delegates are chosen at state primaries and state caucuses or conventions.

14. **C. electors of the Electoral College** *(DOK Level: 2; Content Topic: GG.e.3; Practice: SSP.10.a)* Voters elect the electors. The electors, in turn, choose the president and vice president from the national candidates.

15. **Students should fully form an opinion either in favor of or against the flat tax. They should support their opinion with data and evidence from the article.** *(DOK Level: 3; Content Topic: E.d.11; Practice: SSP.9.a)*

16. **B. fragile** *(DOK Level: 2; Content Topic: E.c.11; Practice: SSP.5.a)*

17. **A. Hamilton uses Locke's ideas to propose how government should work.** *(DOK Level: 3; Content Topic: CG.b.1; Practice: SSP.8.a)* Locke discusses natural law as giving people freedom and Hamilton discusses how the law protects those rights. So Hamilton's point builds on Locke's point.

18. **D. It shows neither causation nor correlation.** *(DOK Level: 2; Content Topic: E.c.7; Practice: SSP.10.c)* To have correlation or causation, one variable must be independent and the other dependent. In the graph, the year is not dependent on the number of establishments nor is the number of establishments dependent on the year, so there is neither causation nor correlation.

UNIT 1: U.S. HISTORY

LESSON 1

PAGE 16

Relate to the Topic
Answers should indicate your ethnic background and your feelings about how it has affected you.
Reading Strategy
1. Native Americans and new Americans
2. Native Americans arrived in North America before the "new" Americans.

PAGE 18

A

PAGE 19

4, 2, 1, 3

PAGES 20–21

1. **conquistadors** *(DOK level: 1; Content Topic, USH.e; Practice, SSP.4.a)*
2. **indentured servants** *(DOK level: 1; Content Topic, USH.e; Practice, SSP.4.a)*
3. **migrated** *(DOK level: 1; Content Topic, G.d.1; Practice, SSP.4.a)*
4. **missions** *(DOK level: 1; Content Topic, USH.e; Practice, SSP.4.a)*
5. **pueblos** *(DOK level: 1; Content Topic, USH.e; Practice, SSP.4.a)*
6. **Immigrants** *(DOK level: 1; Content Topic, G.d.1; Practice, SSP.4.a)*
7. **The writer is biased toward Native Americans. He or she refers to them as the original Americans and does not seem to like how missionaries thought Native Americans were savages.** *(DOK level: 2–3; Content Topic, G.d.1; Practice, SSP.5.b)*

8. **The Spanish sought wealth. The French sought profit in the fur trade. The British settlers wanted land, a better life, and freedom of religion.** *(DOK level: 2; Content Topic, G.d.1; Practice, SSP.2.a)*
9. **disease, starvation, lack of supplies, and attacks by Native Americans** *(DOK level: 2; Content Topic, USH.e; Practice, SSP.2.b)*
10. **Population statistics that show the numbers of Native Americans declining at the time would support this claim.** *(DOK level: 3; Content Topic, USH.e; Practice, SSP.7.b)*
11. **B. Early English settlements lay north of Spanish settlements.** Option A cannot be determined from the map. Options C and D are false. *(DOK level: 2–3; Content Topic, USH.e; Practice, SSP.6.b)*
12. **D. The English settled at Jamestown, Virginia. In chronological order, the other options are C, A, and B).** *(DOK level: 1–2; Content Topic, USH.e; Practice, SSP.3.a)*
13. **B. 123** *(DOK level: 1–2; Content Topic, USH.e; Practice, SSP.11.a)* To find the average, add the total of each voyage and divide the sum by 2.
14. **Answers should indicate that later settlers were eager to profit from the land and stole the Native Americans' land instead of seeking their help.** *(DOK level: 2–3; Content Topic, USH.e; Practice, SSP.1.a)*
15. **Answers should indicate that most came to make a better living or to escape persecution.** *(DOK level: 1–2; Content Topic, G.d.1; Practice, SSP.9.c)*

LESSON 2

PAGE 22

Relate to the Topic
American colonists might have resisted Great Britain because they wanted to make their own decisions, much like teens resisting their parents' authority.

Reading Strategy

1. Boston, Lexington, and Concord
2. The article will explain why and how two groups of people clashed.

PAGE 23

A

PAGE 25

1. 1765
2. 1770
3. after

PAGES 26–27

1. exports *(DOK level: 1; Content Topic, USH.b.1; Practice, SSP.4.a)*
2. repealed *(DOK level: 1; Content Topic, USH.b.1; Practice, SSP.4.a)*
3. legislature *(DOK level: 1; Content Topic, USH.b.1; Practice, SSP.4.a)*
4. Minutemen *(DOK level: 1; Content Topic, USH.b.1; Practice, SSP.4.a)*
5. appeasement *(DOK level: 1; Content Topic, USH.b.7; Practice, SSP.2.a)*
6. boycotted *(DOK level: 1; Content Topic, USH.b.1; Practice, SSP.4.a)*
7. Angry colonists forced tax collectors out of town, protested the tax, and refused to buy British goods. *(DOK level: 2–3; Content Topic, USH.b.1; Practice, SSP.3.b)*
8. He drafted the Declaration of Independence. *(DOK level: 2–3; Content Topic, USH.b.4; Practice, SSP.2,b)*
9. The author describes Washington's strategy as well-calculated, meaning he was wise, and states that he only engaged when necessary, meaning he was patient. *(DOK level: 2–3; Content Topic, USH.b.3; Practice, SSP.5.a)*
10. Sample answer: If each colony was allowed to create its own laws, then it would be difficult to govern as one nation; a strong central government would allow the colonies to be unified. *(DOK level: 2–3; Content Topic, USH.b.5; Practice, SSP.5.b)*
11. D. the Boston Tea Party *(DOK level: 2–3; Content Topic, USH.b.1; Practice, SSP.3.c)* The British decided to punish the colonists for the Boston Tea Party by passing harsh laws, which the colonists referred to as the Intolerable Acts.
12. C. supposedly *(DOK level: 2–3; Content Topic, USH.b.7; Practice, SSP.5.b)* The word "supposedly" implies that the Native Americans were supposed to have their rights restored, but they didn't.
13. C. The Native Americans *(DOK level: 2–3; Content Topic, USH.b.2; Practice, SSP.2.b)* The Native Americans were the real losers because, after the war, they lost their land and were sent to reservations.
14. Sample answer: I believe that Manifest Destiny was simply an excuse to acquire new land with a clear conscience. At the time, all countries were trying to acquire more land. I think we do still see traces of it today, in America's military actions in other countries. *(DOK level: 2–3; Content Topic, USH.b.6; Practice, SSP.9.a)*
15. Sample answer: People might protest or rebel when laws are unfairly enforced. *(DOK level: 1–2; Content Topic, USH.b.1; Practice, SSP.9.c)*

LESSON 3

PAGE 28

Relate to the Topic

You should briefly describe the situation and how it was resolved.

Reading Strategy

1. It is about war.
2. Sample answer: Slavery and how people's opinions about it differ.

PAGE 29

Underline: My paramount object in this struggle is to save the Union, and is not either to save or destroy slavery.

A

PAGE 31

A

PAGES 32–33

1. Union, Confederacy *(DOK level: 1; Content Topic, USH.c.2; Practice, SSP.4.a)*

2. **Emancipation Proclamation** *(DOK level: 1 Content Topic, USH.c.1; Practice, SSP.4.a);*

3. **Abolitionists** *(DOK level: 1; Content Topic, USH.c.1; Practice, SSP.4.a);*

4. **discrimination** *(DOK level: 1; Content Topic, USH.c.1; Practice, SSP.4.a)*

5. **ratify** *(DOK level: 1; Content Topic, USH.c.3; Practice, SSP.4.a)*

6. **Union** *(DOK level: 1; Content Topic, USH.c.2; Practice, SSP.4.a)*

7. **cash crop** *(DOK level: 1; Content Topic, USH.c.1; Practice, SSP.4.a)*

8. **Plantation owners feared financial ruin if slavery was abolished.** *(DOK level: 1–2; Content Topic, USH.c.1; Practice, SSP.1.a)*

9. **Sample answer: President Lincoln is very clear in his opinion that he is more concerned with saving the Union than he is with ending slavery. However, the article focuses more on slavery, the discrimination against African Americans, and on amendments to help fight discrimination.** *(DOK level: 1–2; Content Topic, USH.c.1; Practice, SSP.8.a)*

10. **The Fourteenth Amendment gave freed slaves the right to vote because it made them citizens. Then, the Fifteenth Amendment was added to protect the rights African Americans had gained in the Fourteenth Amendment.** *(DOK level: 1–2; Content Topic, USH.c.3; Practice, SSP.2.b)*

11. **African Americans were allowed to join the Union military.** *(DOK level: 2–3; Content Topic, USH.c; Practice, SSP.3.b).*

12. **B. The author would likely have been very angry about Reconstruction.** *(DOK level: 2–3; Content Topic, USH.c.4; Practice, SSP.5.c)* Most Southerners were frustrated and felt humiliated by Reconstruction.

13. **C. the Fifteenth Amendment** *(DOK level: 2–3; Content Topic, USH.c.3; Practice, SSP.1.a)* Option A freed all slaves, option B gave freed slaves citizenship, and option D was not a Civil War amendment.

14. **B. a shift from agriculture to manufacturing** *(DOK level: 2–3; Content Topic, USH.c;*

Practice, SSP.2.a) During the Industrial Revolution, many new inventions led to new technology in factories. Many people left their farms to work in factories.

15. **Sample answer: The South was being told what to do. There were many requirements for the South during Reconstruction, such as being required to ratify amendments if they wanted to be readmitted to the Union. They had little choice in how they governed, which made them feel humiliated.** *(DOK level: 2–3; Content Topic, USH.c.4; Practice, SSP.1.a)*

16. **Sample answer: I would have developed a list of things the Confederate states had to do to become part of the Union again, such as allowing African Americans to vote and preventing discrimination, much like the Union did. However, I would have offered more financial help to the South in return for their efforts. I would have tried to make Reconstruction for the South less humiliating.** *(DOK level: 2–3; Content Topic, USH.c.2; Practice, SSP.9.a)*

LESSON 4

PAGE 34

Relate to the Topic
Answers will vary with the individual.
Reading Strategy
1. Answers will vary with the individual.
2. Possible answers include dates, statistics, and types of industries involved.

PAGE 35

B

PAGE 37

B

PAGES 38–39

1. **Child labor** *(DOK level: 1; Content Topic, USH.f, E.c.4; Practice, SSP.4.a)*

2. **reformers** *(DOK level: 1; Content Topic, USH.f, E.c.4; Practice, SSP.4.a)*

3. **master** *(DOK level: 1; Content Topic, USH.f, E.c.4; Practice, SSP.4.a)*

4. **literate** *(DOK level: 1; Content Topic, USH.f, E.c.4; Practice, SSP.4.a)*

5. **apprentice** *(DOK level: 1 ; Content Topic, USH.f, E.c.4; Practice, SSP.4.a)*

6. **12** *(DOK level: 2–3; Content Topic, USH.f, E.c.4; Practice, SSP.11.a)* To find the median age, list all the ages being considered, then look for the number in the middle.

7. **It is a fact.** *(DOK level: 2–3; Content Topic, USH.f, E.c.4; Practice, SSP.7.a)* The author states that the children were hunched over sewing machines for long hours. This position would result in curved spines.

8. **The owners claimed that children could do some jobs better than adults, and it cost the owners less to hire because they paid children less than they paid adults.** *(DOK level: 2–3; Content Topic, USH.f, E.c.4; Practice, SSP.3.b)*

9. **Factory owners did not want Hine to take photographs of the conditions in which children were working. They were afraid that, the state or Congress would pass child labor laws if they saw Hine's photographs.** *(DOK level: 2–3; Content Topic, USH.f, E.c.4; Practice, SSP.3.b)*

10. **A. positive correlation** *(DOK level: 2–3; Content Topic, USH.f, E.c.4; Practice, SSP.10.a)* The average minimum age limit increased with each year, so the correlation is positive.

11. **B. dirty workplace** *(DOK level: 2–3; Content Topic, USH.f, E.c.4; Practice, SSP.6.b)* The photo shows a floor covered with litter and stains. Option A is not detectable from the photograph. Options C and D are not supported by the photograph.

12. **D. An apprentice learned more valuable skills than a factory worker** *(DOK level: 2–3; Content Topic, USH.f, E.c.4; Practice, SSP.3.d).* Option A is true but it states a similarity, not a contrast. Options B and C are false.

13. **Sample answer: The picture shows more clearly than any written description why factories are unsuitable for children.** *(DOK level: 2–3; Content Topic, USH.f, E.c.4; Practice, SSP.6.b)*

14. **Sample answer: Teenage workers should stop work by 9 P.M. on school nights. When a teenager works more than five hours, he or she should get a half-hour break.** *(DOK level: 2–3; Content Topic, E.c.4; Practice, SSP.9.b)*

LESSON 5

PAGE 40

Relate to the Topic
Answers will vary with the individual.

Reading Strategy

1. The map shows the countries involved in World War I and the side they each fought for.

2. The map allows you to see a lot of information at once. You can see the size of the countries who fought, how close to each other the countries were, and which countries were on which side.

PAGE 42

A

PAGE 43

A

PAGES 44–45

1. **alliance, neutral** *(DOK level: 2; Content Topic, USH.f.1; Practice, SSP.4.a)*

2. **Nationalism, militarism** *(DOK level: 1; Content Topic, USH.f.2; Practice, SSP.4.a)*

3. **imperialism** *(DOK level: 1; Content Topic, USH.f.2; Practice, SSP.4.a)*

4. **sphere of influence** *(DOK level: 1; Content Topic, USH.f.2; Practice, SSP.4.a)*

5. **stalemate** *(DOK level: 1; Content Topic, USH.f.2; Practice, SSP.4.a)*

6. **It made the war much bigger because it automatically drew countries into the war because they had promised to support their allies.** *(DOK level: 2; Content Topic, USH.f.1; Practice, SSP.3.c)*

7. **The fact that nationalism often comes with a feeling that one's country is better and more important than another.** *(DOK level: 2; Content Topic, USH.f.2; Practice, SSP.7.b)*

8. **stalemate; It left Russia with very few resources for its own people. The people rebelled and a new government took over.** *(DOK level: 2; Content Topic, USH.f.3; Practice, SSP.3.b)*

9. **The author portrays Woodrow Wilson as a peacemaker. He or she states that the United States only got involved in the war because its ships were being attacked and that Wilson immediately started planning to end the war.** *(DOK level: 2; Content Topic, USH.f.4; Practice, SSP.5.a)*

10. **Sample answer: It is likely that new international conflicts prompted the United States to pass the Neutrality Acts.** *(DOK level: 3; Content Topic, USH.f.6; Practice, SSP.1.a)*

11. **A. to ensure peace among nations** *(DOK level: 2; Content Topic, USH.f.5; Practice, SSP.2.a)* The League of Nations was to protect the integrity of all states, large and small. To do this, there must be peace among nations.

12. **B. a government website** *(DOK level: 2; Content Topic, USH.f; Practice, SSP.5.d)* Of all of the options, a government website is the most reliable source.

13. **C. militarism** *(DOK level: 3; Content Topic, USH.f.2; Practice, SSP.1.a)* Militarism is the building up of a military. If a country wants to be seen as strong and one that will protect itself, militarism is the best way to do this.

14. **Sample answer: Yes, there is a sense of nationalism in the United States today. You can see it in the way we treat immigrants. We also try to convince other countries to set up the same type of government that we have.** *(DOK level: 3; Content Topic, USH.f.2; Practice, SSP.9.a)*

15. **Sample answer: I would not have supported the Neutrality Acts. I would have been in favor of becoming involved if it were** necessary. I would have been concerned that if the United States had stayed out of conflict, it would have missed the chance to prevent greater conflict. *(DOK level: 3; Content Topic, USH.f.6; Practice, SSP.9.b)*

LESSON 6

PAGE 46

Relate to the Topic

Answers should refer to the team's common goal and team members' efforts to accomplish the goal.

Reading Strategy

1. the number (in millions) of women at work during the time period in question

2. the years from 1940 through 1950

PAGE 47

A

PAGE 49

A

PAGES 50–51

1. **Nazism** *(DOK level: 1; Content Topic, USH.f.9; Practice, SSP.4.a)*

2. **facism** *(DOK level: 1; Content Topic, USH.f.9; Practice, SSP.4.a)*

3. **totalitarianism** *(DOK level: 1; Content Topic, USH.f.9; Practice, SSP.4.a)*

4. **Holocaust** *(DOK level: 1; Content Topic, USH.f.10; Practice, SSP.4.a)*

5. **internment camps** *(DOK level: 1; Content Topic, USH.f.11; Practice, SSP.4.a)*

6. **decolonization** *(DOK level: 1; Content Topic, USH.f.12; Practice, SSP.4.a)*

7. **It offered jobs that had not been available before and contributed to the Allies' victory.** *(DOK level: 2–3; Content Topic, USH.f, E.c.4; Practice, SSP.3.b)*

8. **Sample answer: Many citizens had lived through World War I and did not want to become involved in another major conflict.** *(DOK level: 2–3; Content Topic, USH.f.7; Practice, SSP.2.b)*

9. Many women left their jobs or were let go. *(DOK level: 2; Content Topic, USH.f.13; Practice, SSP.3.c)*

10. If the graph showed men in the labor force during those years, it would have shown decreases during the war years and increases after the war. *(DOK level: 3; Content Topic, USH.f, E.c.4; Practice, SSP.10.b)*

11. B. France was a member of the Allies. *(DOK level: 1; Content Topic, USH.f.8; Practice, SSP.2.b)* The other options were all members of the Axis Powers.

12. A. Many women were unwilling to return to the way life was before the war. *(DOK level: 2; Content Topic, USH.f, E.c.4; Practice, SSP.10.a)* Options B and D are true but unrelated to changes on the graph. Option C is related to only one change on the graph.

13. D. men returning to their jobs *(DOK level: 2; Content Topic, USH.f.13, E.c.4; Practice, SSP.10.c)* At the end of World War II, the GI bill gave soldiers hiring privileges. Many of them came back to the jobs women had done during the war and the women became unemployed.

14. Sample answer: I would have been very angry, but I would have tried to make the best of it like many people did. *(DOK level: 2–3; Content Topic, USH.f.11; Practice, SSP.9.a)*

15. Sample answer: I believe the United States does have a responsibility to intervene and prevent another Holocaust. The United States should be a world leader in democracy and freedom and should step in when people are being persecuted. *(DOK level: 3; Content Topic, USH.f.10; Practice, SSP.9.b)*

LESSON 7

PAGE 52

Relate to the Topic
Sample answer: Cold War was not like a traditional war. There were no battles. It was a war of ideas between communism and capitalism.

Reading Strategy
Sample questions: What were relations between the United States and the Soviet Union like? How were countries allied during the Cold War?

PAGE 55

Drawing Conclusions; B
Using Visuals; B

PAGES 56–57

1. Cold War *(DOK level: 1; Content Topic, USH.g.1; Practice, SSP.4.a)*

2. containment *(DOK level: 1; Content Topic, USH.g.1; Practice, SSP.4.a)*

3. capitalism, communism *(DOK level: 1; Content Topic, USH.g.1; Practice, SSP.4.a)*

4. blockade *(DOK level: 1; Content Topic, USH.g.1; Practice, SSP.4.a)*

5. One reason is that the Soviet Union wanted to gain back lands in eastern Europe that had once been theirs. *(DOK level: 2; Content Topic, USH.g.1; Practice, SSP.3.b)*

6. Both plans show the United States taking charge and making decisions, like a world power would. *(DOK level: 3; Content Topic, USH.g.3, USH.g.5, USH.g.6; Practice, SSP.3.b)*

7. Sample answer: An article written by a Soviet in 1955 is likely to be more supportive of the Soviet Union and communism than this article. *(DOK level: 3; Content Topic, USH.g.1; Practice, SSP.8.a)*

8. the Warsaw Pact; It was formed because the Soviet Union was worried when the Federal Republic of Germany became part of NATO. *(DOK level: 2; Content Topic, USH.g.2; Practice, SSP.3.b)*

9. France, Britain, the United States, and the Soviet Union could not agree on what to do with Germany, so they divided it up. *(DOK level: 2; Content Topic, USH.g.4; Practice, SSP.3.c)*

10. B. The author feels it was a wise plan with excellent ideas. *(DOK level: 2; Content Topic, USH.g.7; Practice, SSP.5.a)* The

article refers to Johnson's plan to "build a great society." The author included this in the description of the plan to emphasize the great ideas in the plan.

11. **A. unfortunately** *(DOK level: 2; Content Topic, USH.g.8; Practice, SSP.5.b)* The word *unfortunately* indicates that the author believes it is too bad that Nixon is best remembered for a scandal and not for the good things he did.

12. **D. the fall of the Berlin Wall** *(DOK level: 2; Content Topic, USH.g.9; Practice, SSP.3.c)* Option A happened after communist governments began falling. Option B and option C had nothing to do with the fall of communism.

13. **The Soviets suffered hardships because of the destruction in World War II and wanted to punish the Germans. Americans had not suffered the same kind of hardships but wanted to avoid another war. They felt the best way to do this was to return German life to normalcy.** *(DOK level: 2; Content Topic, USH.g.1; Practice, SSP.9.a)*

14. **Sample answer: I do think the United States had a responsibility to provide assistance. I agree that without help, many countries would have been in danger of being taken over by communist governments.** *(DOK level: 2; Content Topic, USH.g.5, USH.g.6; Practice, SSP.9.b)*

LESSON 8

PAGE 58

Relate to the Topic
Sample answers: freedom of speech, freedom of religion, right to vote, right to a fair trial, right to buy arms.
Reading Strategy
1. civil rights
2. I will be looking for ways that people fought for civil rights.

PAGE 59

A

PAGE 61

B

PAGES 62–63

1. **constitutionality** *(DOK level: 1; Content Topic, USH.d.1; Practice, SSP.4.a)*
2. **segregation, intermarriage** *(DOK level: 1; Content Topic, USH.d.1; Practice, SSP.4.a)*
3. **NAACP** *(DOK level: 1; Content Topic, USH.d.3; Practice, SSP.4.a)*
4. **suffrage** *(DOK level: 1; Content Topic, USH.d.2; Practice, SSP.4.a)*
5. **The states; They made it so that African Americans were treated unfairly. Instead of keeping the races separate, but equal, they just denied African Americans access to what the whites had.** *(DOK level: 2; Content Topic, USH.d.1; Practice, SSP.3.c)*
6. **Sample answer: I think women's suffrage affected the Civil Rights Movement positively. People fighting for civil rights were likely inspired to keep fighting because they saw that women kept fighting until they gained the right to vote.** *(DOK level: 2; Content Topic, USH.d.2, USH.d.3; Practice, SSP.2.b)*
7. **Equal Protection Clause; Sample answer: It likely states that all citizens are guaranteed equal protection under the law, meaning they should be treated the same.** *(DOK level: 2; Content Topic, USH.d.3; Practice, SSP.1.a)*
8. **Sample answer: They likely justified the laws by pointing out that they were the same for both African Americans and whites and that African Americans got their own compartments, their own parks, and so on.** *(DOK level: 2; Content Topic, USH.d.1; Practice, SSP.2.b)*
9. **Sample answer: The court under Chief Justice Warren took more cases that centered on civil rights, while previous courts took more cases that centered on economic rights.** *(DOK level: 2; Content Topic, USH.d.5; Practice, SSP.3.d)*

10. Sample answer: She was a great model of how to stand up to segregation and she inspired others to do the same in a nonviolent way. *(DOK level: 2; Content Topic, USH.d.3; Practice, SSP.2.b)*

11. A. a Louisiana judge *(DOK level: 2; Content Topic, USH.d.4; Practice, SSP.2.b)* The case was brought by Homer Plessy against the judge who ruled he could be arrested for not moving from the white compartment on the train.

12. C. excellent *(DOK level: 2; Content Topic, USH.d.3; Practice, SSP.7.a)* The word promoted only tells what he did, not how he did it. The words well-known and famous are factual, so not necessarily the author's opinion. The word excellent is the author's opinion and supports the idea that the author had a positive view of Martin Luther King, Jr.

13. C. Jim Crow laws were allowed to continue. *(DOK level: 2; Content Topic, USH.d.4; Practice, SSP.1.a)* The decision in *Plessy vs. Ferguson* supported the states and their desire to keep segregation. Because of this decision, it took many years before anyone challenged it again.

14. Sample answer: If the members of the court had been more traditional and conservative, it is likely that the Civil Rights Movement would not have been supported by the court. Instead, the court would likely have continued to give more power to the states, which would have probably strengthened segregation and discrimination. *(DOK level: 3; Content Topic, USH.d.3; Practice, SSP.3.d)*

15. Sample answer: Yes, I do think discrimination exists in the United States today. I think that to change it, people need to be willing to speak up and stop it when they see it and that African Americans need to be given more opportunities. *(DOK level: 3; Content Topic, USH.d; Practice, SSP.9.b)*

LESSON 9

PAGE 64

Relate to the Topic

On Sept. 11, 2001, the World Trade Center and the Pentagon were attacked by terrorists. I think the events of Sept 11 frightened most Americans. Americans had not been attacked in the U.S. for a long time. This probably made them feel unsafe.

Reading Strategy

1. the ongoing hostilities in Iraq
2. The Iraq war was longer and more difficult than was expected.

PAGE 66

B

PAGES 68–69

1. insurgents, Taliban *(DOK level: 1; Content Topic, E.f; Practice, SSP.4.a)*

2. economic security *(DOK level: 1; Content Topic, E.f; Practice, SSP.4.a)*

3. foreign policy *(DOK level: 1; Content Topic, USH.h; Practice, SSP.4.a)*

4. entrepreneurship *(DOK level: 1; Content Topic, USH.h; Practice, SSP.4.a)*

5. emerging nation *(DOK level: 1; Content Topic, USH.h; Practice, SSP.4.a)*

6. diplomacy, preemption *(DOK level: 2; Content Topic, USH.h; Practice, SSP.4.a)*

7. The War on Terror is not a war against a specific country. The enemy is likely to change. It is more difficult to know what the enemy is planning. *(DOK level: 3; Content Topic, USH.h; Practice, SSP.3.d)*

8. It became preemptive. Instead of waiting to be attacked, the United States went on the offensive, trying to prevent possible attacks. *(DOK level: 2; Content Topic, USH.h; Practice, SSP.3.c)*

9. $4 trillion to $6 trillion *(DOK level: 1; Content Topic, E.f; Practice, SSP.42.a)*

10. Sample answer: Economic stability leads to a happy and content population. People have what they need. They are able to survive. If this is the case, there are fewer reasons for conflict, so the country is

more likely to be politically and socially stable. *(DOK level: 3; Content Topic, E; Practice, SSP.1.a)*

11. **C. It was rushed.** *(DOK level: 2; Content Topic, USH.h; Practice, SSP.5.b)* The author describes how the Iraq War hurt U.S. relations with other countries because other countries wanted to wait longer for diplomacy to work, but the United States moved more quickly.

12. **B. Economic security correlates to political stability.** *(DOK level: 3; Content Topic, E.f; Practice, SSP.10.c)* The article states that a country that is economically secure is more likely to be politically stable, but it does not state if one of these is the cause of the other, so you can only describe the two events as correlating to each other.

13. **A. Economics plays a large role in conflict.** *(DOK level: 3; Content Topic, E.f; Practice, SSP.7.b)* The article states that most conflicts are rooted in economics.

14. **Sample answer: I would have been pleased to hear he was prepared to fight back against the terrorists. It happened very close to 9/11 and I think I would still have been angry about 9/11. I would also have been alarmed that the United States was going to end up fighting another war like Vietnam.** *(DOK level: 3; Content Topic, USH.h; Practice, SSP.9.b)*

15. **Sample answer: I think that Al-Qaeda and the Taliban needed to be ousted in Afghanistan, but I do not believe the United States should have invaded Iraq. Diplomacy should have been used and war started only if absolutely necessary. It was not worth the cost.** *(DOK level: 3; Content Topic, E.f, USH.h; Practice, SSP.9.a)*

HISTORY AT WORK

PAGE 71

1. **C. hot coals** *(DOK level: 1; Content Topic, E.h, G.b.3; Practice, SSP.1.b)* The passage indicates that hot coals were used to heat colonial irons.

2. **D. Colonial irons were smaller than modern irons** *(DOK level: 3; Content Topic, E.h, G.b.3; Practice, SSP.3.d)* Option B is not supported in the text. Options A and C are false.

3. **D. all of the above** *(DOK level: 2; Content Topic, E.h, G.b.3; Practice, SSP.1.b)* The reasons are not stated directly, but all three are reasonable explanations.

4. **Sample answer: We take the electricity we use today for granted. We think nothing of turning on the light at any hour of the day or night. Back in the colonial era, people did not have electricity. They used candles for light. It took dozens of candles to get the same amount of light we now get from a single light bulb. People had to carry the candles with them when they moved from room to room in order to light the way.** *(DOK level: 3; Content Topic, E.h, G.b.3; Practice, SSP.3.d, SSP.9.b)*

UNIT 1 REVIEW

PAGES 72–75

1. **A. to protect Spain's claim to La Florida** *(DOK level: 2; Content Topic, USH.e, E.g; Practice, SSP.3.b)* The king claimed all of La Florida, and wanted to get rid of the French colonists, so option B is incorrect. Option D is incorrect because Spain reached the Americas long before England or France even tried. The article does not support option C.

2. **B. Juan Ponce de León came to the Americas from Spain.** *(DOK level: 2; Content Topic, USH.e; Practice, SSP.3.a)* The other options, in chronological order, are D, A, and C.

3. **South Carolina** *(DOK level: 2; Content Topic, USH.c.2; Practice, SSP.6.b)*

4. **Missouri, Kentucky, Delaware, and Maryland** *(DOK level: 2; Content Topic, USH.c.1; Practice, SSP.6.b)*

5. **Texas, Louisiana, Arkansas, Mississippi, Tennessee, Alabama, Georgia, Virginia, North Carolina, South Carolina, and Florida.** *(DOK level: 2; Content Topic, USH.c.4; Practice, SSP.6.b)*

6. **D. They separated the Union and the Confederacy.** *(DOK level: 2; Content Topic, USH.c.1, USHc.2; Practice, SSP.3.b)* None of the border states were along the northern Union or southern Confederacy borders, so options A and B are incorrect. They did not all separate the states from the western territories so option C is incorrect.

7. **C. The government feared that Japanese Americans might be spies for Japan.** *(DOK level: 1; Content Topic, USH.f.11; Practice, SSP.3.b)* Options A and D were not causes of the internment. The article does not support option B.

8. **B. The internment of Japanese Americans was an injustice.** *(DOK level: 3; Content Topic, USH.f.11; Practice, SSP.1.a)* The U.S. government apologized many years later and gave survivors money for damages, thus admitting the injustice. Options A and C are incorrect because the opposites were true. Option D is true, but it is not a conclusion supported by the article.

9. **1945** *(DOK level: 2; Content Topic, E.c.4, Practice, SSP.6.c)*

10. **Union membership steadily decreased as time passed.** *(DOK level: 2; Content Topic, E.c.4; Practice, SSP.10.b)*

11. **World War II; War production increased when more workers, including women and African Americans, joined the labor force. So more workers joined unions. Production increased even more after the United States entered the war in 1941. The war ended in 1945.** *(DOK level: 2; Content Topic, E.c.4; Practice, SSP.6.b)*

12. **C. about 25%** *(DOK level: 3; Content Topic, E.c.4; Practice, SSP.11.a)* Add the percentages for each year shown on the graph and then divide the sum by the total number of data values to find the mean or average.

MINI-TEST UNIT 1

PAGES 76–77

1. **D. was in a confrontation with British soldiers** *(DOK level: 2; Content Topic, USH.b.1; Practice, SSP.3.c)* (Analysis) The passage indicates that Crispus Attucks was killed because he was in a crowd that was fired upon by British soldiers.

2. **D. as a memorial to the Revolution** *(DOK level: 2; Content Topic, USH.b.1; Practice, SSP.3.b)* (Analysis) Attucks was remembered as "the first to defy, the first to die," which indicates that he is remembered as the first to die in the American Revolution.

3. **D. 1931–1940** *(DOK level: 2; Content Topic, G.d.1; Practice, SSP.10.a)* (Analysis) Comparing the two bars on the graph shows that the number of immigrants coming to the United States and the number of emigrants leaving the United States were the closest in the decade 1931–1940.

4. **B. marched for jobs and against discrimination** *(DOK level: 2; Content Topic, USH.d.3; Practice, SSP.6.b)* (Comprehension) The people in the picture are demonstrating, and the signs are about the right to work for all people.

5. **A. We must unite to fight for our rights.** *(DOK level: 3; Content Topic, USH.d.3; Practice, SSP.5.a)* (Analysis) This picture shows individuals united in a cause. They are holding signs that are about the right to work, have shelter, and be free from discrimination.

6. **D. Supreme Court decisions are based on specific sections of the Constitution.** *(DOK level: 3; Content Topic, USH.a.1; Practice, SSP.3.c)* (Application) The paragraph explains that Justice Marshall's decision in *Marbury v. Madison* established that the Supreme Court had the final authority on the constitutionality of laws. This would need to cite specific sections of the U.S. Constitution when making decisions.

7. **B. *Marbury* v. *Madison* ensured that the judicial branch became an equal partner**

with the other two branches. *(DOK level: 3; Content Topic, USH.a.1; Practice, SSP.1.a)* (Evaluation) This is the only option supported by the paragraph. The paragraph states that this decision made the Court the final authority on which laws are constitutional and clarified the power of the judicial branch over the legislative branch, which makes laws, and the executive branch, which enforces the laws.

UNIT 2: GEOGRAPHY AND THE WORLD

LESSON 10

PAGE 80

Relate to the Topic
Sample answer: Large kingdoms and companies offer more power, more profit, and less competition than smaller ones do.

Reading Strategy
1. the location of the Great Wall of China
2. about 1,000 miles (about two lengths of the scale)

PAGE 82

A. s

B. d

PAGE 83

B

PAGES 84–85

1. **barbarian** *(DOK Level: 1; Content Topic: G.a; Practice: SSP.4.a)*
2. **peasants** *(DOK Level: 1; Content Topic: G.a; Practice: SSP.4.a)*
3. **dynasty** *(DOK Level: 1; Content Topic: CG.a; Practice: SSP.4.a)*
4. **civilization** *(DOK Level: 1; Content Topic: G.a; Practice: SSP.4.a)*
5. **empire** *(DOK Level: 1; Content Topic: CG.a; Practice: SSP.4.a)*
6. **Shi Huangdi had the wall built to mark and protect China's northern border.** *(DOK Level: 2; Content Topic: G.a; Practice: SSP.3.b)*

7. **They built up the army instead of the wall.** *(DOK Level: 2; Content Topic: CG.a; Practice: SSP.3.b)*
8. **The Mongols put themselves and foreigners into high positions. The Chinese also resented the way their Mongol rulers tolerated people who did not follow traditional Chinese ways.** *(DOK Level: 2; Content Topic: CG.a; Practice: SSP.3.c)*
9. **Mean: 49; Median: 45; Mode: 45** *(DOK Level: 2; Content Topic: G.b.5; Practice: SSP.11.a)*
10. **A. Chinese professor who studies the Great Wall** *(DOK Level: 3; Content Topic: G.d.2; Practice: SSP.5.d)* Options B, C, and D may have knowledge of the Great Wall but not as much as a professor who studies the Great Wall.
11. **D. Building the Great Wall was better than building an army.** *(DOK Level: 3; Content Topic: CG.a; Practice: SSP.7.a)* Options A and B are facts that can be found in other sources. Option C is also a fact compared to option D because you can see by looking at sections of the wall which is in the worst condition. Option 4, however, is an opinion. Not all people will agree that building the Great Wall was better than building up the army.
12. **D. Qin, Sui, Tang, Ming** *(DOK Level: 2; Content Topic: CG.a.1; Practice: SSP.3.a)* Qin was the first emperor that worked on the Great Wall. Then the dynasties of Sui, Tang, and Ming followed.
13. **Answers should point out that aircraft can go over the wall to deliver invaders and bombs.** *(DOK Level: 2–3; Content Topic: G.b.3; Practice: SSP.3.c)*
14. **Sample answers: Lincoln Memorial and the Hoover Dam. Both are awe-inspiring because of their sizes, and the imagination and effort that went into their making.** *(DOK Level: 2–3; Content Topic: G.b.5; Practice: SSP.3.d)*

LESSON 11

PAGE 86

Relate to the Topic

Sample answer: Life would be less pleasant and life might be shorter.

Reading Strategy

1. inventions from a certain age or time period
2. Sample answer: As I read, I will be looking for information about new devices and new ways of doing things.

PAGE 88

A, D, E, C, B

PAGE 89

Sample answers:

A. Dr. Edward Jenner observed that milkmaids who had had cowpox did not catch smallpox.

B. He experimented by injecting a boy with cowpox and later injecting him with smallpox.

C. The results of the experiment were that the boy was protected from smallpox, vaccination was invented, and eventually, smallpox was eliminated.

PAGES 90–91

1. **smallpox** *(DOK Level: 1; Content Topic: E.h; Practice: SSP.4.a)*
2. **orchestra** *(DOK Level: 1; Content Topic: E.h; Practice: SSP.4.a)*
3. **vaccination** *(DOK Level: 1; Content Topic: E.h; Practice: SSP.4.a)*
4. **chronometer** *(DOK Level: 1; Content Topic: E.h; Practice: SSP.4.a)*
5. **century** *(DOK Level: 1; Content Topic: E.h; Practice: SSP.4.a)*
6. **immune** *(DOK Level: 1; Content Topic: E.h; Practice: SSP.4.a)*
7. **The harpsichord makes sounds by plucking strings, and the piano makes sounds by hitting strings.** *(DOK Level: 2; Content Topic: E.h; Practice: SSP.3.d)*
8. **He believed everyone had the right to enjoy life, liberty, and property, so people began exploring new inventions to enjoy.** *(DOK*

Level: 2; Content Topic: CG.b.1; Practice: SSP.2.b)

9. **Timepieces with pendulums would not be very portable and people's movements would make them inaccurate. Harrison's clock was small and worked by springs.** *(DOK Level: 3; Content Topic: E.h; Practice: SSP.1.a)*

10. **He got the idea from observing that milkmaids who had cowpox never got smallpox. He then injected a healthy boy with cowpox, which prevented him from getting smallpox.** *(DOK Level: 2; Content Topic: E.h; Practice: SSP.3.b)*

11. **D. Terrorists have used smallpox as a weapon.** *(DOK Level: 2; Content Topic: E.h; Practice: SSP.7.b)* The article states that there are fears that terrorists could use smallpox as a weapon, but the article does not describe any evidence that they have used smallpox as a weapon.

12. **C. rich and complex art** *(DOK Level: 2; Content Topic: E.h; Practice: SSP.5.a)* The other words describe the music, but do not indicate a point of view like option C.

13. **B. from nature** *(DOK Level: 1; Content Topic: CG.b.1; Practice: SSP.2.a)* Locke's ideas were called natural rights because he believed they were given by nature.

14. **Sample answer: the piano, which produces sound when the hammers inside hit the strings** *(DOK Level: 2; Content Topic: E.h; Practice: SSP.9.c)*

15. **Sample answers: AIDS, leprosy, cancer, the common cold. Sample reasons; how deadly the diseases are, how painful they are, or how common they are.** *(DOK Level: 2–3; Content Topic: E.h; Practice: SSP.9.b)*

LESSON 12

PAGE 92

Relate to the Topic

Sample answer: Some people might appreciate the advice but not the idea that someone else claims to know what is good for them. They also worry about how the selfishness of this idea will impact others if everyone is only looking out for himself or herself.

Reading Strategy

1. Mexico's gross national product
2. any two of the following: mining, manufacturing, oil, transportation

PAGE 93

A

PAGE 95

B

PAGES 96–97

1. **capital** *(DOK Level: 1; Content Topic: E.b; Practice: SSP.4.a)*
2. **liberals** *(DOK Level: 1; Content Topic: E.b; Practice: SSP.4.a)*
3. **Duties** *(DOK Level: 1; Content Topic: E.b; Practice: SSP.4.a)*
4. **conservatives** *(DOK Level: 1; Content Topic: E.b; Practice: SSP.4.a)*
5. **diplomat** *(DOK Level: 1; Content Topic: E.b; Practice: SSP.4.a)*
6. **democracy** *(DOK Level: 1; Content Topic: G.b.1; Practice: SSP.4.a)*
7. **It was unstable and chaotic with 75 changes in leadership.** *(DOK Level: 2; Content Topic: G.b.1; Practice: SSP.2.a)*
8. **Wealthy investors were not willing to invest in the country because it did not have strong leadership.** *(DOK Level: 2; Content Topic: G.b.3; Practice: SSP.3.b)*
9. **It shows correlation. The amount of gold mined increased and so did the amount of silver, but one did not cause the other, so there is no causation.** *(DOK Level: 3; Content Topic: G.b.4; Practice: SSP.10.c)*
10. **B. about $20,000,000** *(DOK Level: 2; Content Topic: G.b; Practice: SSP.11.a)* The median number is the middle number of a data set. If the data set has an even number of values, the median is the mean of the two middle values.
11. **B. Manufacturing doubled while Díaz was in office.** *(DOK Level: 3; Content Topic: G.b.3; Practice: SSP.6.a)* Options A, C, and D are contradicted by the table.

12. **A. Americans invested more money than the combined investment from Europeans.** *(DOK Level: 2–3; Content Topic: E.b; Practice: SSP.10.a)* The facts in the graph contradict options B, C, and D.
13. **Sample answer: They would not have used so many of their resources. They would have conserved for future generations so they do not run out.** *(DOK Level: 2–3; Content Topic: G.b.2; Practice: SSP.9.b)*
14. **Sample answer: People likely damaged the environment with all of the mining and manufacturing. Today, there would be regulations that companies need to follow to do as little damage to the environment as possible.** *(DOK Level: 2–3; Content Topic: G.b.4, G.b.5; Practice: SSP.9.a)*

LESSON 13

PAGE 98

Relate to the Topic

Answers should defend your position with a statement of your values or beliefs.

Reading Strategy

1. the shape of Africa
2. Possible answer: She looks sad and frustrated, possibly from being oppressed.

PAGE 99

1. they needed land and livestock to start farms
2. B

PAGE 101

A

PAGES 102–103

1. **parliament** *(DOK Level: 1; Content Topic: CG.a; Practice: SSP.4.a)*
2. **apartheid** *(DOK Level: 1; Content Topic: CG.a; Practice: SSP.4.a)*
3. **civil rights** *(DOK Level: 1; Content Topic: CG.a; Practice: SSP.4.a)*
4. **Racist** *(DOK Level: 1; Content Topic: CG.a; Practice: SSP.4.a)*
5. **republic** *(DOK Level: 1; Content Topic: CG.a; Practice: SSP.4.a)*

6. **sanctions** *(DOK Level: 1; Content Topic: CG.c.3; Practice: SSP.4.a)*

7. **Different black African groups lived in South Africa, then the Dutch came, and then the Dutch were followed by the British.** *(DOK Level: 2; Content Topic: G.d.3; Practice: SSP.2.b)*

8. **Apartheid happened when one culture (the white Boers) believed they were superior to another culture (the black Africans).** *(DOK Level: 2; Content Topic: G.d.2; Practice: SSP.3.b)*

9. **Sample answers: They no longer had freedom to move where they wished. They could not get a good education. Their privacy was violated because they had to carry passbooks with personal information.** *(DOK Level: 2; Content Topic: CG.a; Practice: SSP.2.a)*

10. **The author does not approve of apartheid. He or she portrays the whites as being very unfair to the blacks.** *(DOK Level: 2; Content Topic: CG.a; Practice: SSP.5.a)*

11. **D. They tried to open nongovernment schools for black children.** *(DOK Level: 2; Content Topic: CG.a; Practice: SSP.1.b)* Option A indicates the ANC valued self-defense. Option B indicates that it valued human rights. Option C indicates it valued cooperation.

12. **C. They are weary.** *(DOK Level: 3; Content Topic: CG.a; Practice: SSP.6.b)* The woman does not appear proud or lazy. Her eyes show she is likely tired, or weary. Rather than careless, she appears to have many cares.

13. **D. to show that whites have no place in Africa** *(DOK Level: 3; Content Topic: G.c.2, G.d.3; Practice: SSP.6.b)* The cartoon clearly shows that black Africans are the true inhabitants of Africa, and therefore whites have no place there.

14. **Sample answer: The number would be lower because the Boers would want to make themselves look better by saying**

they did not arrest so many blacks. *(DOK Level: 3; Content Topic: G.c.2, G.d.3; Practice: SSP.8.a)*

15. **Sample answer: I would end all apartheid laws still in force.** *(DOK Level: 2–3; Content Topic: CG.a; Practice: SSP.9.a)*

LESSON 14
PAGE 104
Relate to the Topic
Your answer should recap a recent world news report involving conflict in a foreign country.
Reading Strategy
1. **Sample question: Who are peacekeepers?**
2. **Sample question: Where are the countries that make up the Middle East?**

PAGE 106
A
PAGE 107
A
PAGES 108–109
1. **mediator** *(DOK Level: 1; Content Topic: CG.b.7; Practice: SSP.4.a)*
2. **neutral** *(DOK Level: 1; Content Topic: CG.b.7; Practice: SSP.4.a)*
3. **charter** *(DOK Level: 1; Content Topic: CG.b.7; Practice: SSP.4.a)*
4. **deadlocked** *(DOK Level: 1; Content Topic: CG.b.7; Practice: SSP.4.a)*
5. **provinces, cease-fire** *(DOK Level: 1; Content Topic: CG.b.7; Practice: SSP.4.a)*
6. **Observers are unarmed and few in number. Peacekeeping forces are lightly armed and can number in the thousands.** *(DOK Level: 2; Content Topic: CG.b.7; Practice: SSP.3.d)*
7. **Sample answer: It is likely that the cultural groups living in far flung parts of the country were different from the one in power, which can lead to tension.** *(DOK Level: 3; Content Topic: G.c.2; Practice: SSP.3.b)*
8. **Fighting drove the farmers from their fields, which were producing very little**

anyway because of a three-year drought. *(DOK Level: 2; Content Topic: G.b.4; Practice: SSP.3.c)*

9. **B. The UN is made up of many different nations.** *(DOK Level: 2; Content Topic: CG.b.7; Practice: SSP.7.b)* The photo does not provide enough information to draw the hypotheses stated in options A, C, and D.

10. **B. The United Somali Congress overthrew Siad.** *(DOK Level: 2; Content Topic: G.c.2; Practice: SSP.3.a)* All other options happened after this one.

11. **D. They may feel a need to help people of their culture.** *(DOK Level: 2; Content Topic: G.c.2; Practice: SSP.1.a)* Peacekeeping troops must be fair and not take sides. This is too difficult if one's own culture is one of the sides.

12. **Sample answer: It is an opinion. I disagree because the UN troops were successful in that they protected civilians.** *(DOK Level: 2; Content Topic: CG.b.7; Practice: SSP.7.a)*

13. **Sample answer: If I took the side of one friend, the other will be less willing to let me help find a solution to the dispute.** *(DOK Level: 2–3; Content Topic: CG.b.7; Practice: SSP.9.b)*

LESSON 15

PAGE 110

Relate to the Topic
Answers should describe specific actions, such as organizing friends to pick up trash.

Reading Strategy

1. You may already know about the glaciers, sea animals, oil, or other features of the Alaskan environment.

2. You may know about the Alaskan pipeline or about transporting oil in ocean-going tankers.

PAGE 111

Sample answer: The definition written will depend on the context of the selected word in the article.

PAGE 113

Sample answer: The oil spill was the largest any group had ever cleaned up; oil is a difficult substance to remove from water or the gravel beaches.

PAGES 114–115

1. **sound** *(DOK Level: 1; Content Topic: G.c.1; Practice: SSP.4.a)*

2. **environment** *(DOK Level: 1; Content Topic: G.c.1; Practice: SSP.4.a)*

3. **glacier** *(DOK Level: 1; Content Topic: G.c.1; Practice: SSP.4.a)*

4. **crude oil** *(DOK Level: 1; Content Topic: G.c.1; Practice: SSP.4.a)*

5. **iceberg** *(DOK Level: 1; Content Topic: G.c.1; Practice: SSP.4.a)*

6. **The currents were moving to the southwest. The spill traveled south along the coast.** *(DOK Level: 3; Content Topic: G.c.3; Practice: SSP.6.b)*

7. **The author was more frustrated with the oil spill in the beginning of the article when talking about it shortly after it happened. He or she softens later in the article since many animals have returned but is still frustrated because the environment has changed and the recovery is slow.** *(DOK Level: 2–3; Content Topic: G.b.5; Practice: SSP.5.c)*

8. **A sound has land on many sides. This means the oil does not have anywhere to spread out. It just washes up on shore.** *(DOK Level: 3; Content Topic: G.c.3; Practice: SSP.3.c)*

9. **A. Exxon Mobil paid $5 billion to Alaska fisherman.** *(DOK Level: 2; Content Topic: G.b.5; Practice: SSP.3.a)* Options B, C, and D all happened before Exxon Mobil paid Alaskan fisherman.

10. **D. The cleanup helped some living things in the environment.** *(DOK Level: 2; Content Topic: G.b.5; Practice: SSP.5.a)* The article contradicts options A and C. No information in the article supports option B.

11. Sample answer: Tourists probably stayed away from refuges and beaches spoiled by oil. As a result, hotels in the area probably fell on hard times and laid off workers. *(DOK Level: 3; Content Topic: G.b.5, G.c.3; Practice: SSP.6.1, SSP.1.a)*

12. Your answer should address whether or not the cost of the tax for the oil-spill cleanup fund is likely to be passed along to gasoline customers through higher gas prices. *(DOK Level: 2–3; Content Topic: G.b.5, E.d.5; Practice: SSP.9.a)*

LESSON 16

PAGE 116

Relate to the Topic

Possible answers: I ate bread, which is made from wheat, and cheese, which comes from milk, given by grazing cows. Preserving productive land is important because it is a source of food and of the jobs of the people who work on it.

Reading Strategy

1. desertification, drylands
2. irrigated land, rainfed cropland, range land

PAGE 118

1. B   2. A

PAGE 119

A

PAGES 120–121

1. displaced *(DOK Level: 1; Content Topic: G.d.1; Practice: SSP.4.a)*

2. overgrazing *(DOK Level: 1; Content Topic: G.b.5; Practice: SSP.4.a)*

3. topsoil *(DOK Level: 1; Content Topic: G.c.1; Practice: SSP.4.a)*

4. desertification *(DOK Level: 1; Content Topic: G.b.5; Practice: SSP.4.a)*

5. Ecotourism *(DOK Level: 1; Content Topic: G.b.2, E.c.1; Practice: SSP.4.a)*

6. drought *(DOK Level: 1; Content Topic: E.c.1; Practice: SSP.4.a)*

7. Rural areas typically have lots of farmland to grow crops. This means they have huge areas of land with few trees to hold the soil, so the soil is more likely to erode. *(DOK Level: 3; Content Topic: G.d.3; Practice: SSP.3.c)*

8. The type of land with the highest percentage of damage is the driest land. It is a case of causation. Very little rainfall leads to desertification. *(DOK Level: 2–3; Content Topic: G.b.5; Practice: SSP.10.b, SSP.10.c)*

9. zero tillage farming *(DOK Level: 2; Content Topic: G.b.2; Practice: SSP.2.b)*

10. D. Range land has suffered more damage than cropland. *(DOK Level: 3; Content Topic: G.b.5; Practice: SSP.6.b, SSP.10.a)* In all six regions, range land shows the highest percentage of damage.

11. A. Desertification refers to land; drought refers to the weather. *(DOK Level: 3; Content Topic: G.b.5; Practice: SSP.3.d)* Drought is a long period of unusually dry weather; desertification is turning of productive land into desert.

12. B. in a rural area with many farms with livestock *(DOK Level: 2; Content Topic: G.d.4; Practice: SSP.3.c)* Overgrazing is a cause of desertification.

13. Answers should include the fact that it often is poor people who practice the farming and herding methods that damage the land the most and lead to desertification and that poor people often live together in large groups on small amounts of land. *(DOK Level: 3; Content Topic: G.b.5, G.d.3; Practice: SSP.2.b)*

14. Answers might suggest some compensation for the farmers whose land would be replanted with trees. *(DOK Level: 2–3; Content Topic: G.b.2; Practice: SSP.9.b)*

GEOGRAPHY AT WORK

PAGE 123

3 trains; numbers 18, 126 and 150.

12:29 p.m.; 9:44 a.m.

Baltimore *(DOK Level: 1–2; Content Topic: G.b.3; Practice: SSP.1.b)*

UNIT 2 REVIEW
PAGE 124–127

1. **C. to get water for their crops and animals** *(DOK Level: 2; Content Topic: G.b.3; Practice: SSP.6.b)*

2. **A. Grassland covers much of the North Central Plains** *(DOK Level: 2; Content Topic: G.b.4; Practice: SSP.6.b)*

3. **As the key shows, these states are marked with a symbol of a cow.** *(DOK Level: 2; Content Topic: G.c.1; Practice: SSP.6.b)*

4. **Alaska, Wyoming, North Dakota, Louisiana, and Mississippi** *(DOK Level: 2; Content Topic: G.c.1; Practice: SSP.6.b)*

5. **C. how many states are top producers of both oil and cattle** *(DOK Level: 2; Content Topic: G.c.1; Practice: SSP.2.a, SSP.6.b)*

6. **D. fleet of ships** *(DOK Level: 2; Content Topic: USH.e; Practice: SSP.4.a)* The other options are false.

7. **B. He named an inexperienced nobleman as fleet commander.** *(DOK Level: 3; Content Topic: USH.e; Practice: SSP.1.b)* The other options are true, but only option B showed faulty logic that high rank makes up for ability and experience.

8. **Sample answer: Because England is an island, its navy would have been its strongest defense. King Philip II was too confident in his nation's strength. Spain required an experienced seaman to plan the attack.** *(DOK Level: 2–3; Content Topic: USH.e; Practice: SSP.1.a)*

9. **Spain used ships to carry riches from the distant parts of its empire back to Spain. So Spanish rulers established settlements on coasts where the riches could be loaded onto the ships.** *(DOK Level: 2–3; Content Topic: USH.e; Practice: SSP.6.b)*

MINI-TEST UNIT 2
PAGES 128–129

1. **C. Almost all of these countries became independent within a fifteen-year period.** *(DOK Level: 2; Content Topic: G.b.1; Practice: SSP.6.b)* (Analysis) From 1811 to 1825, nine of the ten countries shown gained their independence.

2. **D. moving is a matter of survival** *(DOK Level: 2; Content Topic: G.d.1; Practice: SSP.1.a, SSP.3.b)* (Analysis) Push factors force people out, suggesting that they face death if they remain in the existing conditions. Thus, moving is a matter of survival.

3. **D. Americans moving west to settle their own farms during the 1800s** *(DOK Level: 2; Content Topic: G.d.1; Practice: SSP.2.b)* (Application) The opportunity to farm and own one's land is a pull factor. Options A, B, and C are examples of push factors.

4. **D. has 54% of the total volume of the Great Lakes** *(DOK Level: 2; Content Topic: G.c.1; Practice: SSP.6.b)* (Evaluation) With over half the total volume of the Great Lakes, Lake Superior is larger, in terms of volume, than the four other Great Lakes combined.

5. **C. How did the EU develop into more than an economic association?** *(DOK Level: 3; Content Topic: E.c.11; Practice: SSP.2.a)* (Comprehension) The passage traces how the association now known as the EU developed from an economic association to an organization that cooperates on political and other issues as well.

6. **D. Members never disagree about policy.** *(DOK Level: 2; Content Topic: E.c.11; Practice: SSP.7.b)* (Analysis) The word never identifies a hasty generalization. Even though the member nations have agreed to cooperate, there is no reason to believe that they always agree on policy issues.

UNIT 3: CIVICS AND GOVERNMENT

LESSON 17

PAGE 132

Relate to the Topic

Sample answer: I recycle aluminum cans at work but have no storage space at home for other items.

Reading Strategy

1. Sample answers: recycling; getting rid of trash
2. Sample answer: society; everyone throwing away trash

PAGE 134

B

PAGE 135

A

PAGES 136–137

1. **landfill** *(DOK Level: 1; Content Topic: G.b.5; Practice: SP.4.a)*
2. **federal government** *(DOK Level: 1; Content Topic: CG.c.3; Practice: SSP.4.a)*
3. **recycling** *(DOK Level: 1; Content Topic: G.b.2; Practice: SSP.4.a)*
4. **groundwater** *(DOK Level: 1; Content Topic: G.b.4; Practice: SSP.4.a)*
5. **Constitution** *(DOK Level: 1; Content Topic: USH.a.1; Practice: SSP.4.a)*
6. **Hazardous wastes** *(DOK Level: 1; Content Topic: G.b.5; Practice: SSP.4.a)*
7. **In the U.S., different levels of government, including federal, state, and local governments, all share the power to tax.** *(DOK Level: 2; Content Topic: E.d.5; Practice: SSP.3.b)*
8. **Possible answer: Yes, I think the author recycles and composts. He or she states that governments face a "trash crisis" and talks about the negative impacts of landfills, such as "the poisons pollute groundwater."** *(DOK Level: 3; Content Topic: G.b.2; Practice: SSP.5.a)*

9. **As time goes by, the recycling rate increases.** *(DOK Level: 2; Content Topic: G.b.2; Practice: SSP.10.b)*
10. **The trash has to be sorted.** *(DOK Level: 2; Content Topic: G.b.2; Practice: SSP.3.a)*
11. **B. People should generate less trash.** *(DOK Level: 2; Content Topic: G.b.2; Practice: SSP.7.a)* Option D does not take into account the symbolism of the massive amounts of trash. The cartoonist may agree with options A and C, but the main idea is one of excess.
12. **D. Local governments have set up different ways to get people to recycle.** *(DOK Level: 2; Content Topic: G.b.2; Practice: SSP.2.a)* The paragraph does not support option A. Options B and C are conclusions one might reach from reading the entire article, not just the one paragraph.
13. **C. take out a loan** *(DOK Level: 2; Content Topic: CG.c.3, CG.c.4; Practice: SSP.1.a)* Options A and B are powers given only to the federal government. Option D is a power given only to state governments. Taking out a loan is borrowing money, which is listed as a shared power in the article.
14. **Mean: 16.6%, Median: 10.1%, Mode: 6%** *(DOK Level: 2; Content Topic: G.b.2; Practice: SSP.11.a)*
15. **Sample answer: I recycle newspapers and magazines; I could collect aluminum cans that litter parks and streets.** *(DOK Level: 1–2; Content Topic: G.b.5; Practice: SSP.9.c)*

LESSON 18

PAGE 138

Relate to the Topic

Your answer should describe what the action was, which branch was responsible for it, and how you felt about the action.

Reading Strategy

1. checks and balances in government
2. Sample answer: The diagram gives information about how the different branches of government exert checks to balance each other.

PAGE 140

C

PAGE 141

A

PAGES 142–143

1. **judicial branch** *(DOK Level: 1; Content Topic: CG.c.1; Practice: SSP.4.a)*

2. **separation of powers** *(DOK Level: 1; Content Topic: CG.b.61; Practice: SSP.4.a)*

3. **executive branch** *(DOK Level: 1; Content Topic: CG.c.1, CG.c.6; Practice: SSP.4.a)*

4. **Constitutionalism** *(DOK Level: 1; Content Topic: CG.b.3; Practice: SSP.4.a)*

5. **legislative branch** *(DOK Level: 1; Content Topic: CG.c.1; Practice: SSP.4.a)*

6. **checks and balances** *(DOK Level: 1; Content Topic: CG.c.1, CG.b.5; Practice: SSP.4.a)*

7. **Sample answers: print money, make treaties, declare war** *(DOK Level: 2; Content Topic: CG.c.3; Practice: SSP.2.b)*

8. **It gives the power to the people.** *(DOK Level: 2; Content Topic: CG.b.2; Practice: SSP.2.b)*

9. **The President and some members of Congress thought that the line-item veto would help control wasteful spending and thus lower the federal deficit.** *(DOK Level: 2; Content Topic: CG.b.5; Practice: SSP.3.c)*

10. **The Supreme Court declared it unconstitutional.** *(DOK Level: 2; Content Topic: CG.c.1, CG.b.5; Practice: SSP.3.a)*

11. **B. Each branch of government checks the power of the other branches.** *(DOK Level: 2; Content Topic: CG.c.1, CG.b.5; Practice: SSP.6.b)* Options A and C are opinions, not facts. Nothing in the diagram is related to option D.

12. **A. veto laws.** *(DOK Level: 2; Content Topic: CG.c.1, CG.c.2; Practice: SSP.1.a)* Option B is the role of the judicial branch. Options C and D are roles of the legislative branch.

13. **B. Some governors with line-item veto power had success in limiting spending.** *(DOK Level: 3; Content Topic:*

CG.b.5; Practice: SSP.7.b) Option A does not specifically support the hypothesis that it would save money. Options C and D are not facts but are hopes that supporters of the law had.

14. **Separation of powers divides the government's power into three equal branches with different functions. The checks and balances system gives each branch powers to check actions of the other two branches.** *(DOK Level: 2–3; Content Topic: CG.b.5, CG.b.6; Practice: SSP.3.d)*

15. **Sample answer: They fit together because it is important for the majority that rules to remember the rights of the minority. If they do not, the government could become one-sided, and no longer be a democracy.** *(DOK Level: 3; Content Topic: CG.b.4; Practice: SSP.9.a)*

LESSON 19

PAGE 144

Relate to the Topic

Answers will vary. You may think of being defended from foreign attack and being free to speak your mind and practice your religion. You may think of voting and volunteering your time as ways of giving back to the country.

Reading Strategy

1. **Sample answer: I have heard the term used in a television news program about freedom of religion.**

2. **Answers should relate to personal experiences such as participating in political, religious, or social gatherings.**

PAGE 146

A

PAGE 147

B

PAGES 148–149

1. **Bill of Rights** *(DOK Level: 1; Content Topic: CG.d.1, CG.b.8; Practice: SSP.4.a)*

2. **warrant** *(DOK Level: 1; Content Topic: CG.d.1, CG.d.2; Practice: SSP.4.a)*

3. **Justice** *(DOK Level: 1; Content Topic: CG.d.1; Practice: SSP.4.a)*

4. **amendment** *(DOK Level: 1; Content Topic: CG.d.1; Practice: SSP.4.a)*

5. **Due process** *(DOK Level: 1; Content Topic: CG.d.1; Practice: SSP.4.a)*

6. **rule of law** *(DOK Level: 1; Content Topic: CG.b.7; Practice: SSP.4.a)*

7. **Answers should include two of the following: the freedom to speak and write what one thinks, to assemble with other people, to worship freely; freedom of the press; the right to petition the government.** *(DOK Level: 2–3; Content Topic: CG.d.1, CG.b.8; Practice: SSP.2.a)*

8. **Sample answer: Rule of law is what keeps a society safe and working together and guarantees everyone's rights. Without rule of law, rights would be less protected.** *(DOK Level: 3; Content Topic: CG.b.7; Practice: SSP.2.a)*

9. **Possible answer: There would not have been a Second Amendment debate at that time because everyone owned guns. The author would have been completely in favor of the Second Amendment.** *(DOK Level: 3; Content Topic: CG.d.1, CG.d.2; Practice: SSP.5.c)*

10. **B. Attacking guaranteed rights is as much a danger as terrorism.** *(DOK Level: 3; Content Topic: CG.d.1, CG.b.8; Practice: SSP.6.b)* The cartoon shows the Bill of Rights being line-item vetoed by the president and the caption describes the Patriot Act. These ideas together suggest that weakening the Bill of Rights in order to combat terrorism is as much a danger to Americans as terrorism is.

11. **B. Congress** *(DOK Level: 1; Content Topic: CG.c.5; Practice: SSP.2.a)* Only Congress or the state legislatures may propose an amendment to the Constitution.

12. **D. It is more persuasive than a notice.** *(DOK Level: 2; Content Topic: CG.d.2; Practice: SSP.8.a)* The flyer and the notice would be about the same topic, but written from two different perspectives.

A notice would just be a statement of facts about the meeting but a flyer would try to persuade readers to come to the meeting and support the community center.

13. **Sample answer: Due process helps ensure that innocent people are not convicted of crimes, and that justice is equal for all Americans.** *(DOK Level: 2; Content Topic: CG.d.1; Practice: SSP.3.b)*

14. **Answers should suggest ways of giving time and talent to help improve one's community.** *(DOK Level: 2; Content Topic: CG.d.2; Practice: SSP.9.c)*

LESSON 20

PAGE 150

Relate to the Topic

Answers should include the date of the last election held in your community and a description of a candidate, campaign, or issue that was important or noteworthy from that election.

Reading Strategy

1. political party, political action committees

2. Possible answer: Both relate to the process of electing people to office.

PAGE 151

B

PAGE 153

A

PAGES 154–155

1. **campaign** *(DOK Level: 1; Content Topic: CG.e.3; Practice: SSP.4.a)*

2. **media** *(DOK Level: 1; Content Topic: CG.e.3; Practice: SSP.4.a)*

3. **political action committees** *(DOK Level: 1; Content Topic: CG.e.2, CG.e.3; Practice: SSP.4.a)*

4. **politics** *(DOK Level: 1; Content Topic: CG.e.3; Practice: SSP.4.a)*

5. **primary election** *(DOK Level: 1; Content Topic: CG.e.3; Practice: SSP.4.a)*

6. **political party** *(DOK Level: 1; Content Topic: CGe.1, CG.e.3; Practice: SSP.4.a)*

7. **general election** *(DOK Level: 1; Content Topic: CG.e.3; Practice: SSP.4.a)*

8. **A voter must be at least 18 years old, a citizen, and a resident of the state where he or she votes.** *(DOK Level: 2; Content Topic: CG.e.3; Practice: SSP.2.a)*

9. **The author feels that the right to vote is one of the most important rights and states that it is a right that many groups of Americans worked hard to win.** *(DOK Level: 2 Content Topic: CG.e.3; Practice: SSP.5.b)*

10. **Sample answer: To help candidates who have the same values as they do get elected to office.** *(DOK Level: 2; Content Topic: CG.e.1; Practice: SSP.1.a)*

11. **D. A magazine includes information about only one candidate for senator.** *(DOK Level: 2; Content Topic: CG.e.3; Practice: SSP.1.b)* Options A, B, and C are ways that the media try to present a balanced picture of a campaign.

12. **B. to support candidates who share the group's views** *(DOK Level: 2; Content Topic: CG.e.2, CG.e.3; Practice: SSP.3.c)* The special interest groups want to elect people who have the same or similar views. So option A is incorrect. There is no evidence to support option C or D.

13. **D. The high cost of political campaigns has raised concern among many Americans.** *(DOK Level: 3; Content Topic: CG.e.3; Practice: SSP.7.a)* All the other options express opinions.

14. **Sample answer: No, I think money from interest groups may give one candidate an unfair advantage over another candidate. Interest groups may also deceive the public.** *(DOK Level: 2–3; Content Topic: CG.e.2; Practice: SSP.9.a)*

15. **Sample answers: I would negotiate a deal with the major television stations to get a better rate for political campaign ads and would limit the number of weeks during which candidates can campaign.** *(DOK Level: 2–3; Content Topic: CG.e.3; Practice: SSP.9.b)*

LESSON 21

PAGE 156

Relate to the Topic

Sample answer: I pay gasoline tax, sales tax, and income taxes now; perhaps I will pay property tax in the future.

Reading Strategy

1. Both relate to federal tax monies.
2. how the government collects and spends money for running the country

PAGE 158

1. A
2. B

PAGE 159

B

PAGES 160–161

1. **Income taxes** *(DOK Level: 1; Content Topic: CG.c.4; Practice: SSP.4.a)*
2. **Entitlements** *(DOK Level: 1; Content Topic: CG.b.9; Practice: SSP.4.a)*
3. **budgets** *(DOK Level: 1; Content Topic: E.d.4; Practice: SSP.4.a)*
4. **revenue** *(DOK Level: 1; Content Topic: E.d.4, E.d.5; Practice: SSP.4.a)*
5. **excise taxes** *(DOK Level: 1; Content Topic: E.c.2; Practice: SSP.4.a)*
6. **Property taxes** *(DOK Level: 1; Content Topic: CG.c.4; Practice: SSP.4.a)*
7. **to collect the money needed to run the government and to provide services for citizens** *(DOK Level: 2; Content Topic: CG.b.9; Practice: SSP.3.b)*
8. **No, the graphs do not show causation or correlation. The taxes from which revenue comes do not either cause or correlate with the areas where taxes are spent.** *(DOK Level: 3; Content Topic: E.d.4, E.d.5; Practice: SSP.10.c)*
9. **B. personal income taxes, social security/social insurance taxes, corporate income taxes** *(DOK Level: 2; Content Topic: CG.b.9; Practice: SSP.6.c, SSP.10.a)* The percentages are 50%, 33%, and 10% respectively.

10. **A. a tax lawyer** *(DOK Level: 3; Content Topic: E.d.4; Practice: SSP.5.d)* All of the options listed would be qualified to speak about taxes, but a tax lawyer, whose job it is to understand taxes thoroughly, would be the most credible.

11. **B. Individual states decide which kinds of taxes to levy.** *(DOK Level: 3; Content Topic: CG.b.9; Practice: SSP.1.a)* According to the information, the majority of states levy income taxes and many also levy sales taxes. However, since some states do not levy these taxes, the information supplies adequate support for the idea that individual states decide which taxes to use to raise revenues.

12. **Businesses contribute to the revenue for a state by paying corporate taxes and employing workers, who pay state income taxes.** *(DOK Level: 2; Content Topic: E.c.2; Practice: SSP.2.b, SSP.9.a)*

13. **Answers should support their opinion on whether the government is spending its tax revenues wisely.** *(DOK Level: 2–3; Content Topic: E.d.5; Practice: SSP.9.a)*

LESSON 22

PAGE 162

Relate to the Topic

Topics in public policy I have heard about recently include healthcare, the environment, social security and Medicare, and education.

Reading Strategy

1. health expenditures as a share of GDP for different countries

2. It is arranged from left to right from greatest share of GDP to least share of GDP.

PAGE 163

B

PAGE 165

A

PAGES 166–167

1. **employee benefit** *(DOK Level: 1; Content Topic: CG.f; Practice: SSP.4.a)*

2. **deductible** *(DOK Level: 1; Content Topic: CG.f; Practice: SSP.4.a)*

3. **Medicare** *(DOK Level: 1; Content Topic: CG.f; Practice: SSP.4.a)*

4. **preventive care** *(DOK Level: 1; Content Topic: CG.f; Practice: SSP.4.a)*

5. **premium** *(DOK Level: 1; Content Topic: CG.f; Practice: SSP.4.a)*

6. **Public policy** *(DOK Level: 1; Content Topic: CG.f; Practice: SSP.4.a)*

7. **Preventive care can catch an illness in early stages when it is easier to treat. Preventive care also helps to save money because it costs less to treat diseases in the earlier stages than the later stages.** *(DOK Level: 2; Content Topic: CG.f; Practice: SSP.1.a)*

8. **They can no longer be denied insurance based on pre-existing conditions like their illness.** *(DOK Level: 2; Content Topic: CG.f; Practice: SSP.3.c)*

9. **Sample answers: obesity and how to reduce the obesity rate, how to get more uninsured on health insurance, making sure health insurers are fair.** *(DOK Level: 2; Content Topic: CG.f; Practice: SSP.2.b)*

10. **D. how much the program costs** *(DOK Level: 2; Content Topic: CG.f; Practice: SSP.5.b)* The author lists the many advantages of the Affordable Care Act, but does not describe their costs. In so doing, the author shows his or her bias in favor of the Act.

11. **C. Canada** *(DOK Level: 1; Content Topic: CG.f; Practice: SSP.10.a)* According to the graph, Canada also spends about 8% of its GDP public funds on healthcare.

12. **C. The Affordable Care Act will greatly benefit Americans.** *(DOK Level: 2; Content Topic: CG.f; Practice: SSP.7.b)* Options A, B, and D are not supported by the article. The article does not state how costly it will be. The article does not specifically state how long it took the Affordable Care Act to become law. It also states that the Affordable Care Act almost didn't become a law, meaning it was not favored by most Americans, but by enough to get it passed into law.

13. **Sample answer: There are many different people with different opinions involved**

in the debate. Insurance companies were operating more freely before the law so they likely worked to prevent legislation from being passed in the past. *(DOK Level: 3; Content Topic: CG.f; Practice: SSP.9.b)*

14. **Sample answer: I would prefer the system in which healthcare is provided for everyone. This would mean there would be no uninsured and everyone's needs would be met.** *(DOK Level: 3; Content Topic: CG.f; Practice: SSP.9.c)*

CIVICS AT WORK

PAGE 169

1. **C. to distribute election flyers at Stone Elementary School** *(DOK Level: 1; Content Topic: CG.e; Practice: SSP.1.b)* Anita names the task in the first sentence of her memo.

2. **B. giving flyers about the election to interested adults** *(DOK Level: 2; Content Topic: CG.e; Practice: SSP.1.b)* Distributing flyers is an example of free speech, a right guaranteed by the First Amendment.

3. **C. the local law specified she must be that distance from the entrance** *(DOK Level: 3; Content Topic: CG.e; Practice: SSP.1.b)* Anita mentions the distance right after referring in her memo to "all the laws that you explained to me."

UNIT 3 REVIEW

PAGES 170–173

1. **Answers should include two of the following: they both involve rape, the police questioned both men without advising them of their rights, neither man had a lawyer present during questioning** *(DOK Level: 3; Content Topic: CG.b.8; Practice: SSP.3.d)*

2. **C. before they question the suspect** *(DOK Level: 2; Content Topic: CG.b.8; Practice: SSP.1.a)* The point of the Miranda rights is that they are told to the suspect before he or she says anything to incriminate themselves,

so the police need to notify the suspect before they question him or her.

3. **D. "hopefully" and "finally" in the last sentence** *(DOK Level: 3; Content Topic: CG.f; Practice: SSP.5.b)* The author states his or her opinion in the last sentence. The other options are from factual statements in the article.

4. **C. to approve again** *(DOK Level: 2; Content Topic: CG.f; Practice: SSP.4.a)* To reauthorize means to authorize again, or approve again. In the case of legislation, it means to approve money to be spent on a program.

5. **public library and auto registration office** *(DOK Level: 2; Content Topic: CG.d.2, CG.e.3; Practice: SSP.2.a)*

6. **A person must be at least 18 years of age to vote.** *(DOK Level: 1; Content Topic: CG.d.2, CG.e.3; Practice: SSP.1.b)*

7. **D. Votes can make a difference in all kinds of elections.** *(DOK Level: 2; Content Topic: CG.d.2, CD.e.3; Practice: SSP.1.a)* According to the article, the outcome of past elections might have been different if more people voted.

8. **the schools** *(DOK Level: 2; Content Topic: CG.b.8; Practice: SSP.6.b)*

9. **The man with the hat represents the military.** *(DOK Level: 3; Content Topic: CG.b.8; Practice: SSP.6.b)*

10. **C. The right to privacy is threatened because the government can get information.** *(DOK Level: 3; Content Topic: CG.b.8; Practice: SSP.6.b)* The cartoon suggests that the military uses school records to collect key information about Americans.

MINI-TEST UNIT 3

PAGES 174–175

1. **B. Rebels assaulted federal workers.** *(DOK Level: 2; Content Topic: USH.b.3; Practice: SSP.1.b)* (Evaluation) The paragraph points out that protesters rioted and violently attacked federal agents, tarring and feathering them.

2. **B. the Bill of Rights** *(DOK Level: 2; Content Topic: CG.d.1, CG.d.2; Practice: SSP.3.d)* (Comprehension) The protestors were allowed to protest because of the freedom of speech and assembly that is guaranteed in the Bill of Rights.

3. **B. demonstrators protesting U.S. involvement in a war** *(DOK Level: 3; Content Topic: CG.d.2; Practice: SSP.3.d, SSP.6.b)* (Application) There are two rights being shown in the image—the right to vote and the right to free speech and assembly. Of the options, demonstrators protesting involvement in a war is most like the people urging others to vote for them.

4. **D. The king has restricted the powers of colonial governors.** *(DOK Level: 3; Content Topic: CG.b.2, CG.b.7; Practice: SSP.7.a)* (Evaluation) This fact appears in the third paragraph. All of the other options express likes, dislikes, and other points of view.

5. **A. Some colonists were very angry with the King of Great Britain.** *(DOK Level: 2; Content Topic: CG.b.2, CG.b.7; Practice: SSP.7.b)* (Evaluation) This disappointment is expressed in the list of repeated injuries and usurpations in the quotation.

6. **C. During election season, attack ads insult television viewers.** *(DOK Level: 3; Content Topic: CG.e.3; Practice: SSP.6.b)* (Comprehension) Slinging mud on someone is an expression that means "speaking negatively of someone." The conversation between the pigs shows they are watching a political ad. Pigs enjoy rolling in mud, so the depiction of viewers as pigs suggests that viewers are being demeaned.

7. **D. be ashamed of the nastiness in negative political campaigns** *(DOK Level: 3; Content Topic: CG.e.3; Practice: SSP.6.b)* (Analysis) By implying that viewers who tolerate negative campaign ads are acting like pigs, the cartoon is trying to persuade viewers to feel shame.

UNIT 4: ECONOMICS
LESSON 23

PAGE 178

Relate to the Topic

Sample answer: I got my haircut. I decided that I could not wait any longer. I did not have much money for a haircut, so I went to a salon that cost less.

Reading Strategy

1. **how business profits should be viewed**
2. **Her opinion is that businesses benefit from contributions made by society through taxes (such as roads and education) and so businesses should give back some of their profit to help others.**

PAGE 180

B

PAGE 181

B

PAGES 182–183

1. **comparative advantage** *(DOK Level: 1; Content Topic: E.c.8; Practice: SSP.4.a)*
2. **entrepreneur** *(DOK Level: 1; Content Topic: E.c.7; Practice: SSP.4.a)*
3. **interdependence** *(DOK Level: 1; Content Topic: E.c.11; Practice: SSP.4.a)*
4. **incentives** *(DOK Level: 1; Content Topic: E.c.2; Practice: SSP.4.a)*
5. **Profit** *(DOK Level: 1; Content Topic: E.c.6; Practice: SSP.4.a)*
6. **specialization** *(DOK Level: 1; Content Topic: E.c.9; Practice: SSP.4.a)*
7. **Sample answer: Ayn Rand believes that entrepreneurs who have worked hard to build their businesses deserve everything they have. She insists that people starting**

businesses have helped the economy by providing jobs for others and that they have not gotten where they are at the expense of others. Senator Warren believes that companies that are making billions of dollars should be giving more back because they did not build their businesses by themselves. Everyone had a hand in getting their businesses built because of all of the help from taxpayers. *(DOK Level: 3; Content Topic: E.c.6, E.c.7; Practice: SSP.5.a, SSP.8.a)*

8. A positive incentive rewards people while a negative incentive punishes people. *(DOK Level: 2; Content Topic: E.c.2; Practice: SSP.3.d)*

9. No, a person who is not looking for a job is not available for work. *(DOK Level: 2; Content Topic: E.d.10; Practice: SSP.4.a)*

10. A. As the number of people who are unemployed increases, the unemployment rate increases. *(DOK Level: 3; Content Topic: E.d.10; Practice: SSP.10.b)* The unemployment rate is a measure of the number of people who are unemployed. So as the number of people who are unemployed rises, so will the unemployment rate.

11. C. Specialization leads to interdependence. *(DOK Level: 2; Content Topic: E.c.9, E.c.11; Practice: SSP.3.c)* Incentives lead to purchases, which can lead to profits, but it is not as directly connected as specialization and interdependence. Comparative advantage is more closely related to specialization than interdependence. Entrepreneurship leads to profits rather than profits leading to entrepreneurship.

12. C. Country X should produce wheat. *(DOK Level: 3; Content Topic: E.c.8; Practice: SSP.2.b)* Comparative advantage means that a country should produce products that they can produce at a lower cost than anyone else. Hours of labor cost money. The country that can produce wheat in fewer labor hours should produce wheat. This is country X.

13. Sample answer: I would like to be my own boss. Entrepreneurs are able to make many of the decisions for their business on their own. I would like this aspect of entrepreneurship. *(DOK Level: 2; Content Topic: E.c.7; Practice: SSP.9.a)*

14. Sample answer: Inflation means a higher price for goods and services for everyone, including businesses. A small business may need to raise its prices if the rate of inflation is high because that means the business also has to pay higher prices for the goods it needs to run its business. *(DOK Level: 3; Content Topic: E.d.8; Practice: SSP.3.c)*

LESSON 24

PAGE 184

Relate to the Topic

Sample answer: Cheerios® brand breakfast cereal has lasted because the manufacturer has created other flavors besides the basic recipe. Legos® brand blocks are durable, promote creativity and fine motor skills, and have universal appeal to children.

Reading Strategy

1. farms in the United States

2. changes in numbers of farms in the nation and changes in the average size of those farms

PAGE 185

A

PAGE 187

B

PAGES 188–189

1. **free enterprise system** *(DOK Level: 1; Content Topic: E.d.1, E.d.2; Practice: SSP.4.a)*

2. **subsidies** *(DOK Level: 1; Content Topic: E.d.5; Practice: SSP.4.a)*

3. **market** *(DOK Level: 1; Content Topic: E.c.1; Practice: SSP.4.a)*

4. **demand** *(DOK Level: 1; Content Topic: E.d.1; Practice: SSP.4.a)*

5. **cooperative** *(DOK Level: 1; Content Topic: E.d.3; Practice: SSP.4.a)*

6. **efficiency** *(DOK Level: 1; Content Topic: E.c.10; Practice: SSP.4.a)*

7. **New methods of farming allow farmers to increase the amount of crops produced, so they can make more money on their crops without increasing the price.** *(DOK Level: 2–3; Content Topic: E.c.10, E.c.11; Practice: SSP.2.a)*

8. **No, they are not produced in the United States.** *(DOK Level: 3; Content Topic: E.d.9; Practice: SSP.2.a)*

9. **These relationships give farmers a secure market for their products so they can plan and be financially stable.** *(DOK Level: 1; Content Topic: E.d.3; Practice: SSP.2.b)*

10. **C. 2,500,000** *(DOK Level: 2; Content Topic: E.c.9, E.c.10; Practice: SSP.11.a)* The average is the sum of the data points divided by the number of data points. It is closest to 2,500,000.

11. **A. Farms will be close to the same size as in 2010, and there will be about the same number of them.** *(DOK Level: 3; Content Topic: E.c.4, E.d.1; Practice: SSP.10.a)* The graphs show that the decline in the number of farms and increase in their size have slowed considerably, making it likely that the numbers will be similar ten years later.

12. **D. It provides subsidies to farmers.** *(DOK Level: 2; Content Topic: E.d.7; Practice: SSP.1.a)* The main goal of subsidies is to provide security to farmers in the case of market failures.

13. **Sample answer: The author states that subsidies cost the government billions of dollars each year, and indicates that they should be carefully studied to see if they are effective. This shows the author is uncertain if subsidies are worthwhile.** *(DOK Level: 3; Content Topic: E.d.5; Practice: SSP.5.a)*

14. **Sample answer: Competition makes cellular phone services lower their prices. I choose the service with low prices. If less competition existed, prices for cellular phone calls might be higher, and my phone bill would probably go up.** *(DOK Level: 2; Content Topic: E.c.3; Practice: SSP.1.a)*

LESSON 25
PAGE 190
Relate to the Topic
Sample answer: From talking with my siblings, I've learned that using a credit card for weekly expenses can lead to overspending.
Reading Strategy
1. Answers should name someone who has a spending plan and tries to follow it.
2. Sample answer: Look for the lowest interest rate and make sure the monthly payments are affordable.

PAGE 192
B
PAGE 193
B
PAGES 194–195

1. **opportunity cost** *(DOK Level: 1; Content Topic: E.c.5; Practice: SSP.4.a)*

2. **net income** *(DOK Level: 1; Content Topic: E.d.4; Practice: SSP.4.a)*

3. **interest** *(DOK Level: 1; Content Topic: E.e.1; Practice: SSP.4.a)*

4. **annual percentage rate** *(DOK Level: 1; Content Topic: E.e.3; Practice: SSP.4.a)*

5. **fixed expense** *(DOK Level: 1; Content Topic: E..d.4; Practice: SSP.4.a)*

6. **budget** *(DOK Level: 1; Content Topic: E.d.4; Practice: SSP.4.a)*

7. **flexible expense** *(DOK Level: 1; Content Topic: E.d.4; Practice: SSP.4.a)*

8. **Sample answer: The author is biased against smoking, drinking, and expensive entertainment. The author describes these as items that people do not really need. The author likely believes money spent on these items should be saved instead.** *(DOK Level: 3; Content Topic: E.d.4, E.e.2; Practice: SSP.5.b)*

9. The certificate of deposit will pay more interest, but you have to leave your money in the bank for a certain amount of time. *(DOK Level: 2; Content Topic: E.e.2; Practice: SSP.3.d)*

10. Sample answer: Create and follow a spending plan. Consider all the costs involved in a purchase before deciding. Do not borrow money often. Read and understand the terms of a loan. *(DOK Level: 2; Content Topic: E.d.4; Practice: SSP.2.a)*

11. C. People should not spend money on smoking or alcohol. *(DOK Level: 2; Content Topic: E.d.4; Practice: SSP.7.a)* The words "should not" are clues that this is the author's opinion and not a fact. The other statements are facts.

12. A. a financial advisor *(DOK Level: 3; Content Topic: E.e.2, E.d.4; Practice: SSP.5.d)* Option B, a loan officer, would be too biased. Option C, a bank manager, would also be slightly biased. Option D, a tax collector would have specialized knowledge of taxes but not necessarily budgeting.

13. D. It spends less on health care than it does on electricity, gas, telephone, and other utilities. *(DOK Level: 3; Content Topic: E.d.4; Practice: SSP.6.a, SSP.10.a)* The graph shows that the average family spends 4.8 percent of income on health care, compared with 5.9 percent on utilities.

14. Sample answer: Lenders make money when a person takes out a loan for many years because interest is charged every month. When the loan is paid off early, the lender will charge a penalty to gain back some of the interest money it will lose. *(DOK Level: 2; Content Topic: E.e.1; Practice: SSP.1.a)*

15. Sample answer: Lenders make money on loans. Their goal is not to protect the interests of the borrower but their own interests. Consumer credit laws exist so lenders cannot use unfair practices.

The article describes the hidden costs of loans and, without consumer credit laws, lenders would take even more advantage of consumers. *(DOK Level: 2–3; Content Topic: E.e.3; Practice: SSP.9.a)*

LESSON 26
PAGE 196
Relate to the Topic
Sample answer: I bought several boxes of cookies when they were on sale and cookies are a want; I did not buy a gold chain because of the price and the chain was a want.
Reading Strategy
1. the information on the price of baseball cards
2. The table might focus on supply and demand, using baseball cards as an example.

PAGE 198
A
PAGE 199
A
PAGES 200–201
1. inelastic supply *(DOK Level: 1; Content Topic: E.d.1; Practice: SSP.4.a)*
2. profit *(DOK Level: 1; Content Topic: E.d.1; Practice: SSP.4.a)*
3. elastic supply *(DOK Level: 1; Content Topic: E.d.1; Practice: SSP.4.a)*
4. scarce *(DOK Level: 1; Content Topic: E.d.1; Practice: SSP.4.a)*
5. inelastic demand *(DOK Level: 1; Content Topic: E.d.1; Practice: SSP.4.a)*
6. elastic demand *(DOK Level: 1; Content Topic: E.d.1; Practice: SSP.4.a)*
7. supply *(DOK Level: 1; Content Topic: E.d.1; Practice: SSP.4.a)*
8. Sample answer: The author might believe that the boy should have paid the fair price for the card. *(DOK Level: 2; Content Topic: E.d.1; Practice: SSP.5.c)*

9. Sample answer: Elastic stretches. When a supply or demand is elastic, it moves either up or down in reaction to a price change. *(DOK Level: 2; Content Topic: E.d.1; Practice: SSP.1.b, SSP.4.a)*

10. The store owner took the boy who bought the card to court. *(DOK Level: 2; Content Topic: E.d.1; Practice: SSP.3.a)*

11. D. The new owner of the Ryan card will make a profit. *(DOK Level: 2; Content Topic: E.d.1; Practice: SSP.3.b)* Option A is a fact, not a prediction. The paragraphs do not support a prediction of option C. Option B is wrong because the opposite is likely to happen.

12. D. The shorter supply of Clemens' Fleer Update card caused the higher price. *(DOK Level: 3; Content Topic: E.d.1; Practice: SSP.10.c)* The best explanation is one of causation. The decreased supply of the 1984 card compared to the 1985 card is responsible for the higher price.

13. B. $5.00 *(DOK Level: 2; Content Topic: E.d.1; Practice: SSP.11.a)* The mode of a set of data is the value that appears most often. $5.00 appears twice in the data set. The other values all only appear one time.

14. If demand is high, this will make supplies more scarce. So companies will enter the market to sell products, hoping to make profit by meeting the demand. If demand is low, companies will leave the market if they cannot sell enough of the product to make a profit. *(DOK Level: 3; Content Topic: E.c.1; Practice: SSP.3.c)*

15. Sample answer: I would advise against investing in baseball cards. Many companies make baseball cards, and the value of the cards may fail to rise in the future. *(DOK Level: 3; Content Topic: E.c.5; Practice: SSP.9.b, SSP.9.c)*

ECONOMICS AT WORK

PAGE 203

1.
Calla lily	in season
Carnation	out of season
Delphinium	out of season
Hyacinth	out of season
Poppy	in season
Tulip	in season

(DOK Level: 2; Content Topic: E.d.1; Practice: SSP.6.a)

2. B. Calla Lily—$2.25 per stem *(DOK Level: 2; Content Topic: E.d.1; Practice: SSP.6.c)* The fact that the price of the Calla lily is near the highest price paid suggests that it is in short supply and thus, out of season.

3. Sample answer: I have noticed how the price of grapefruit fluctuates in the grocery store. Around October, the price of grapefruits begins to fall, and it gets really low in December and January. As spring approaches, the price begins to climb again. This makes me think that grapefruits are in season in fall and winter and out of season in spring and summer. *(DOK Level: 3; Content Topic: E.d.1; Practice: SSP.9.c)*

UNIT 4 REVIEW

PAGES 204–207

1. D. people concerned about the environment *(DOK Level: 2; Content Topic: E.d.1, E.d.2; Practice: SSP.3.c)* Cornstarch helps plastic decompose, which helps the environment. Corn has always been considered a food so options A and B are incorrect. Option C is incorrect because this group could possibly be hurt by the new uses of corn.

2. A. Demand for corn is likely to increase. *(DOK Level: 3; Content Topic: E.d.1; Practice: SSP.1.a)* According to the article, the new products will increase the demand for corn so option B is incorrect. The supply is likely to increase also, so options C and D are incorrect.

3. Sample answer: They had $200 less to spend on wedding photographs. *(DOK Level: 3; Content Topic: E.c.5; Practice: SSP.6.b)*

4. Sample answer: The wedding photographer cost less money than they had budgeted.

They had less money to spend because they spent more on their rings. So their incentive was to spend less on the photographer, which allowed them to save money and stay within budget. *(DOK Level: 2; Content Topic: E.c.2; Practice: SSP.1.a)*

5. **B. The Lees spent about an average amount on flowers but less than average on music.** *(DOK Level: 3; Content Topic: E.d.4; Practice: SSP.6.a)* According to the graph, flowers and music each represent 9 percent of the average wedding budget. The table shows that the Lees spent 9 percent on flowers but only 3 percent on music.

6. **The seller is using bait-and-switch advertising.** *(DOK Level: 2; Content Topic: E.e.3; Practice: SSP.1.b)*

7. **The seller is using the special-pricing method.** *(DOK Level: 2; Content Topic: E.e.1, E.e.3; Practice: SSP.1.b)*

8. **B. Be alert to unlawful practices.** *(DOK Level: 2; Content Topic: E.e.1, E.e.3; Practice: SSP.7.b)* According to the article, buyers should be wary of selling methods used by some sellers. The article does not state that all sellers are dishonest, so option A is incorrect. Option C is incorrect, because although it may sometimes be true, it is not supported by the article. Option D is incorrect because the article implies customers should check prices.

9. **Sample answer: They specialize in providing services for the poor, who have less money and who borrow smaller amounts of money.** *(DOK Level: 3; Content Topic: E.d.3, E.e.1, E.e.2; Practice: SSP.2.a, SSP.3.d)*

10. **Sample answer: The author states in the last sentence that even though the rates are high, they are still less than those from informal moneylenders which indicates the author still is in favor of them.** *(DOK Level: 2; Content Topic: E.e.1; Practice: SSP.5.a)*

11. **D. The transaction costs are higher because there are many loans.** *(DOK Level: 2; Content Topic: E.e.1, E.e.2; Practice: SSP.3.c)* The cost of all the transaction fees increases the cost of the microloans. The article does not provide information on the other three options.

MINI-TEST UNIT 4

PAGES 208–209

1. **A. to help shoppers compare the value of similar items in order to decide which to purchase** *(DOK Level: 3; Content Topic: E.d.2; Practice: SSP.1.a)* (Comprehension) Unit prices allow an equal basis for comparison of products.

2. **B. The unit prices would increase.** *(DOK Level: 2; Content Topic: E.d.8; Practice: SSP.3.c)* (Application) Inflation is the increase of prices compared to money available over time. Inflation is seen in increasing prices.

3. **C. Between 2000 and 2012 home prices in both San Francisco and Los Angeles rose and then fell.** *(DOK Level: 2; Content Topic: E.d.1, E.d.8; Practice: SSP.10.a)* (Analysis) Between 2000 and 2012, home prices in the San Francisco and Los Angeles regions rose significantly and then fell by 2012.

4. **D. As in 1999, cash and checks were used for most purchases in 2005.** *(DOK Level: 2; Content Topic: E.e; Practice: SSP.6.a, SSP.10.a)* (Evaluation) The table shows that cash and checks made up more than half of all transactions in both years: 72.1 percent of transactions in 1999 and 61 percent in 2005.

5. **C. Personal check transactions will decrease while debit card transactions increase.** *(DOK Level: 2; Content Topic: E.e; Practice: SSP.10.a)* (Evaluation) The table shows a significant decrease in the use of personal checks between 1999 and 2005. During the same time, the use of debit cards increased by about the same percent.

6. **C. Bears have sluggish periods and bulls sometimes charge or stampede.** *(DOK Level: 2; Content Topic: E.d.6; Practice: SSP.2.b)* (Application) The paragraph describes a bear market as a time when prices go down and the economy is slow or sluggish, like a bear in winter; during a bull market, on the other hand, stock prices are going up and the economy is generally fast-paced, like a charging bull.

7. **B. poor earnings predictions from major companies** *(DOK Level: 2; Content Topic: E.d.6; Practice: SSP.3.c)* (Analysis) Poor earnings would discourage investors and create pessimism, leading investors to sell or at least to not buy stock. This could lead to a bear market.

POSTTEST

PAGES 211–222

1. **D. their physical appearance and poise** *(DOK Level: 2; Content Topic: CG.e.3; Practice: SSP.3.d)* (U.S. History: Analysis) Based on the information and the photograph, John F. Kennedy appeared to be the more attractive and poised candidate.

2. **C. Televising the debates prompted voters to be influenced by the candidates' appearance.** *(DOK Level: 2; Content Topic: CG.e.3; Practice: SSP.1.a)* (U.S. History: Comprehension) Televising the debates allowed millions of Americans to compare each candidate's physical appearance, as well as his political views. The election outcome implies that enough voters were influenced by Senator Kennedy's poise and good looks that he was able to win the election against the more experienced Vice-President.

3. **C. Agents must be prepared for unhappy travelers.** *(DOK Level: 2; Content Topic: E.c.4; Practice: SSP.5.a)* (Economics: Evaluation) If the author had given an accurate glimpse of what it would be like to be a ticket agent, he or she would have included negative aspects, such as dealing with unhappy customers.

4. **B. It must be ratified by three-fourths of the states.** *(DOK Level: 2; Content Topic: CG.c.5; Practice: SSP.3.b)* (Civics and Government: Comprehension) The Tenth Amendment distinguishes between the power of the federal government and the power of the states, granting all powers to the states that are not specifically given to the federal government or prohibited to the states. The tension between federal government power and states' rights has been an ongoing source of conflict in U.S. history.

5. **D. Three of the world's oceans border the continent of Antarctica.** *(DOK Level: 3; Content Topic: G.c.3; Practice: SSP.6.b)* (Geography and the World: Application) The map shows that Antarctica is bordered by the South Pacific, South Atlantic, and Indian oceans.

6. **C. nationalatlas.gov** *(DOK Level: 2; Content Topic: G.c.3; Practice: SSP.5.d)* (Geography and the World: Analysis) The most credible source listed is a .gov website, which is an official government website. Although the textbook will likely have the correct map, the .gov website is a definitive source.

7. **A. They had deep ties to their land.** *(DOK Level: 2; Content Topic: USH.b.7; Practice: SSP.3.c)* (U.S. History: Analysis) In the letter quoted in paragraph 2, the tribe members indicated how deep their ties to their land were when they compared the land to the mother who gave them birth, stating that leaving the land would be like rejecting their birth mother.

8. **B. Congress authorized the government to take Native American lands.** *(DOK Level: 3; Content Topic: CG.b.4; Practice: SSP.1.b)* (Civics and Government: Analysis) Congress passed a law giving the federal government the right to take land away from the Native Americans who lived in the East. The law does not allow the government to take land from other groups of Americans.

9. **B. In 1838, the federal government forcibly removed the Cherokees from their lands.** *(DOK Level: 3; Content Topic: CG.b.4; Practice: SSP.5.b)* (Civics and Government: Analysis)

10. **B. a decrease in the unemployment rate in the 1930s** *(DOK Level: 2; Content Topic: E.a; Practice: SSP.2.a)* (Economics: Analysis) Economic indicators, such as the unemployment rate, indicate how an economy is doing. A lower unemployment rate indicates a stronger economy. A lower unemployment rate during the 1930s would be a result of the New Deal as opposed to World War II.

11. **D. Washington politicians are too involved with big corporations.** *(DOK Level: 2; Content Topic: CG.c3; Practice: SSP.7.a)* (Civics and Government: Analysis) A conflict of interest is defined as a conflict between a person's private interest and his or her public obligations. A politician who has a conflict of interest with a corporation may not fulfill his or her obligation to pass fair laws, but may instead vote for laws that favor corporations. The janitor in the cartoon implies that all politicians in Washington have conflicts of interest with corporations; thus, the cartoonist thinks that Washington politicians are too involved with corporate interests.

12. **B. Don't let a petitioner rush you into signing something you don't support.** *(DOK Level: 2; Content Topic: CG.e.3; Practice: SSP.1.b)* (Civics and Government: Evaluation) The word "rush" indicates that the person trying to get you to sign a petition may try to hurry you into signing, which means they may use aggressive tactics to get your signature.

13. **B. Don't sign any petitions because your signature might be stolen.** *(DOK Level: 2; Content Topic: CG.e.3; Practice: SSP.7.b)* (Civics and Government: Analysis) It is faulty reasoning to think that you should not sign any petitions simply because you have to take precautions to prevent your signature from being stolen.

14. **B. seventeen years after the magazine cover was published** *(DOK Level: 2; Content Topic: G.d.2; Practice: SSP.3.a)* (Geography and the World: Analysis) The girl did not give Steve McCurry her name when he took the photograph. But, seventeen years later, a National Geographic team was able to find family members who identified her.

15. **D. 1943** *(DOK Level: 2; Content Topic: USH.f.8; Practice: SSP.6.b)* (U.S. History: Analysis) According to the timeline, the first surrender of an Axis power took place in 1943. From this, you can conclude that 1943 marked a turning point in the war against the Axis powers.

16. **powers** *(DOK Level: 2; Content Topic: CG.b.6; Practice: SSP.7.b)* (Civics and Government: Comprehension) Separation of powers is the division of powers among the three branches of government so that no one branch becomes too powerful.

17. **socialism** *(DOK Level: 2; Content Topic: CG.a; Practice: SSP.4.a)* (Civics and Government: Application) A country in which there is little or no private property has employed the socialist system; as the description states, in socialism, "the means of production, distribution, and exchange are mostly owned by the state."

18. **autocracy/despotism** *(DOK Level: 2; Content Topic: CG.a; Practice: SSP.4.a)* (Civics and Government: Application) A country that has one ruler or a single ruling party is ruled by "a supreme, unlimited authority." Thus, this country's government is based on the political philosophy of autocracy or despotism.

19. **anarchism** *(DOK Level: 2; Content Topic: CG.a; Practice: SSP.2.b)* (Civics and Government: Application) This clear statement of opposition to government and to all types of authority is an example of anarchism.

20. **C. More immigrants were from Europe in the 1960s and 1970s, but by 1990 more Latin American and Asian immigrants lived in the United States.** *(DOK Level: 3; Content Topic: C.d.1; Practice: SSP.10.a)* (U.S. History: Analysis) The graph shows that European immigration was much higher than Asian and Latin American immigration between 1960 and 1980, but that European immigration was surpassed by Latin American immigration in the early 1980s and by Asian immigration in the early 1990s.

21. **B. Expenditures for public safety account for about half of the city's budget.** *(DOK Level: 3; Content Topic: E.d.4; Practice: SSP.6.c)* (Economics: Evaluation) The graph on the right shows that public safety expenditures, which would include police, firefighting, and paramedic operations, account for about half of the city's expenditures. In other words, the city is spending about half of its revenue on these public safety services.

22. **A. he may require the Opinion, in writing, of the principal Officer in each of the executive Departments, upon any Subject relating to the Duties of their respective Offices** *(DOK Level: 2; Content Topic: CG.c.2; Practice: SSP.3.b)* (Civics and Government: Evaluation) The cabinet members are the President's closest advisors. They help the President make decisions and they each head an executive department.

23. **Students should describe whether or not they feel President Lincoln was following rule of law when he made the Emancipation Proclamation. They should also describe the political philosophies Lincoln may have been following such as natural rights philosophy and individual rights. They should support their answer with evidence from the article or background knowledge.** *(DOK Level: 3; Content Topic: CG.b.1; Practice: SSP.9.a)* (Civics and Government: Analysis)

abolitionist a person who is against slavery

adequacy sufficiency; enough to be considered acceptable

alien a person living in the United States who is not an American citizen

alliance a formal treaty between nations to cooperate for specific purposes

Allies all the nations who fought Germany and its supporters in World Wars I and II

amendment an addition or change

annual percentage rate (APR) the percent of interest a lender charges per year

apartheid a policy in South Africa that separated black Africans from white society

appeal to bring a court decision from a lower court to be reexamined in a higher court

appeasement an attempt to avoid conflict

apprentice someone who learns a trade from an expert called a master

apprenticeship a period of training that includes on-the-job training

aquifer an underground layer of rock or earth that holds water

assumption a statement accepted as true without proof; a belief

bachelor's degree a degree earned after a four-year college education

bar graph a graph used to make comparisons

barbarian a person considered to be inferior and ignorant

bill a proposed law

Bill of Rights the first ten amendments to the United States Constitution, listing the rights of individuals

bloc a group of nations that acts together for military, political, or economic purposes

blockade a restriction of travel and or supplies in or out of a place

boycott to protest by refusing to use a service or to buy a certain item

broadcast the sending of a radio or TV program by radio waves

budget a detailed plan showing earnings and expenses over a period of time

campaign a series of events designed to get people to vote a certain way

candidate a person who runs for public office

capital money, assets, or property used for investment

capitalism an economic system in which the means of production are owned privately

cash crop a crop grown for sale rather than for personal use

cause why something happens

cease-fire a pause in fighting

century a period of 100 years

charter a plan that sets up an organization and defines its purpose

checks and balances the idea that each branch of a government has powers that limit the other branches' powers

child labor the practice of using children as workers

chronometer a very accurate clock

circle graph graph used to show parts of a whole; also known as a pie chart

civics the branch of political science that deals with the rights and duties of citizens

civil rights freedoms guaranteed to citizens, including the right to be treated equally

civil war a war between people who live in the same country

civilization the society and culture of a particular group, place, or period

climate the general weather of a region over a long time

Cold War the struggle for world power between the United States and the Soviet Union

colony a settlement or group of settlements far from the home country

communicate to exchange information

communism a political and economic system that does away with private property and places production under government control

comparative advantage the advantage gained in being able to produce something at a lower cost than anyone else

compare to tell how people, events, or things are alike

composting producing rich organic matter by letting food waste and plants decay

computer an electronic machine for processing, storing, and recalling information

conclusion a logical judgment based on facts

Confederacy the southern states during the American Civil War

conquistador Spanish word meaning "conqueror"

conservative a person who wants to maintain traditional and established values and practices

Constitution the plan for the United States government, proposed in 1787

Constitutionalism the idea that a government can and should be limited in its powers

constitutionality the characteristic of being constitutional

consumer a person who buys and uses goods and services

containment a policy to prevent the spread of communism to other nations

context 1) the rest of the words in a sentence 2) one particular situation

contrast to tell how people, events, and things are different

cooperative people who join together to ensure the best price for their products

crude oil untreated oil

culture customs or way of life

currency a kind of money

current part of any body of water that flows in a definite direction

deadlocked unable to agree; a tie vote

decolonization the process of colonies becoming independent

deductible a set amount that a person pays in medical costs in a year before insurance will cover any costs

deflation a decrease in prices relative to money available

demand the amount of goods or services consumers are willing to buy at a certain price at a given time

democracy a system of government in which the power to make choices belongs to the people

desertification the turning of productive land into desert

detail small piece of information

diagram a drawing that shows steps in a process or how something is organized

diplomacy negotiating

diplomat a person who handles relations between nations

discrimination the unequal and unfair treatment of a person or group

displaced forced to leave ones home, often by climate change, natural disaster, or war

drought a long period of unusually dry weather

due process steps in the legal process that protect the rights of an accused person

duty a tax collected on goods brought into a country and sometimes on goods sent out of a country

dynasty a family of rulers whose generations govern one after another over a long time

e-mail a message a writer sends electronically using a computer

economic security the state of having a stable income to support a standard of living now and into the future

economics the study of how people use their resources to meet their needs

ecotourism travel that appeals to people with environmental interests

effect what happens as the result of a cause

efficiency the state of being productive without wasting time, money, or energy

elastic demand a willingness to buy that increases or decreases as the price of a good or service changes

elastic supply an amount of a good or service that increases or decreases as the price changes

elevation the height of the land above sea level

Emancipation Proclamation the statement made by President Abraham Lincoln declaring freedom for slaves in states fighting against the Union during the American Civil War

emerging nations countries that are on their way to becoming industrialized

empire a group of widespread territories or nations under a single ruler or government

employee benefits extra employee compensation that comes with a job

entitlement a governmental program, such as food stamps or veterans' pensions, available to people who meet its requirements

entrepreneur a person who starts his or her own business

entrepreneurship the starting of a new business

environment all of the living and nonliving things that make up a place

equator an imaginary circle exactly halfway between the North and South poles

estimate to guess an amount based on past experience

excise tax tax on a specific item, such as cigarettes, alcohol, or gasoline

executive branch the branch of government that carries out the laws

export 1) to send and sell a nation's goods to other nations 2) a good produced in one country and sent to another country for sale

fact a statement of something that can be proved

fascism a system in which the government is ruled by a dictator

federal deficit the amount of money the national government spends in excess of its income

federal government the government with authority over the entire United States

fixed expenses costs that stay the same each month

flat tax an income tax under which everyone pays the same percentage of his or her wages

flexible expenses costs that vary from month to month

foreign policy policies that a nation follows when it deals with another nation or nations

free enterprise system an economic system in which buyers affect which goods and services are produced

free trade importing and exporting without political barriers, such as tariffs or taxes

general election a regularly scheduled election for state, local, or federal officials

geography the study of Earth's places and peoples

glacier a huge mass of ice that moves slowly over land

glossary an alphabetical listing of important words and their definitions

government the system of laws and political bodies that make it possible for a nation, a state, or a community to function

graph a drawing that is used to compare numerical information

gross domestic product (GDP) the total market value of all the finished goods and services produced within a country's borders in a specific time period

gross national product (GNP) the money value of all goods, services, and products of a nation's industries

groundwater an underground source of water, such as a spring, well, pond, or aquifer

gun control legal limits on the sale of guns to the public

hasty generalization a broad statement based on little or no evidence

hazardous waste something thrown away that is harmful to the environment

Holocaust the persecution and murder of nearly six million Jews by the Nazis

iceberg a huge block of floating ice that has broken off from a glacier

immigrant a person who moves from his or her homeland to another country

immune protected against a disease

impeach to accuse a public official of misconduct; sometimes to additionally remove that public official from office

imperialism the policy of acquiring and keeping colonies

implied suggested, but not stated outright

import 1) to bring in or purchase goods from another country 2) a good brought into a country from another country

incentive a reason for action

income tax a tax on a person's earnings

indentured servant a person who works for a set period of time in exchange for something of value, such as fare to another country

indict to formally charge someone with a crime

inelastic demand a willingness to buy that is not affected when the price of a good or service changes

inelastic supply an amount of a good or service that cannot change

inference an idea a person figures out based on details in given material and on what the person already knows

inflation a rise in prices relative to money available

insurgent a person who forcefully opposes the government

interdependence the idea that the businesses in an economy are dependent on each other

interdependent several parts, such as nations, relying on one another to be successful

interest the fee paid for borrowing money

intermarriage a marriage with spouses of two different races

interned to be forced to live in a camp away from home

Internet a network of computers connected by telephone lines

internment camps residential camps where people were held against their will during wartime

internship a temporary job assignment

isolationism the policy of a country isolating itself from other nations

job rotation a system that trains workers in many tasks so they can step into other jobs when the need arises

job shadowing following a worker on a typical day to observe his or her job responsibilities

judicial branch the branch of government that interprets laws

judicial review the federal courts' power to determine whether a law or an executive action follows the Constitution

justice 1) fair and equal treatment under the law 2) a judge who serves on the Supreme Court

landfill a place where trash is buried

laser a narrow beam of intense light

latitude distance north or south of the equator

legislative branch the branch of government that makes laws

legislature a group of persons that makes the laws of a nation or state

liberal a person who supports political change

line graph a graph using lines to show how something increases or decreases over time

literate able to read and write

logic a systematic method of thinking that is based on reasoning correctly

longitude distance east or west on Earth, measured from the Prime Meridian in Greenwich, England; also called meridians

main idea the topic of a paragraph, passage, or diagram

market 1) a place where buyers and sellers meet 2) potential customers for a product or service

master an experienced tradesperson

media agencies of communication, such as television, radio, newspapers, and magazines

mediator a person who settles differences between persons or groups

Medicaid government insurance for low-income individuals and families

Medicare government insurance for the elderly

mentoring teaching a less experienced person about a job through example and discussion

meridians the lines on a map or globe that are used to measure distances east and west on Earth; lines of longitude

microchip a tiny electrical circuit

migrate to move from one place to another

militarism the policy of maintaining a large military

minutemen American colonists who were ready to fight at a minute's notice

mission a settlement centered around a church, established for the purpose of winning people over to a religion

NAACP National Association for the Advancement of Colored People

nationalism loyalty to one's own country

navigator a person who charts the position and course of a ship during a voyage

Nazism the belief that white races were or are better than all other races

negative incentive punishment for making a certain choice

net income money left after taxes are paid

neutral refusing to be on one side or the other

nominate to choose a candidate to run for an elected office

opinion a statement that expresses what a person or group thinks or believes

opportunity cost the cost of choosing one thing over another

orchestra a large group of people who play a variety of musical instruments together

ordinance a law or regulation

overgrazing the practice of letting too many animals feed on an area's grasses or of letting animals feed in one place for too long

override to cancel the executive branch's veto or rejection of a proposed law

parallels the lines on a map or globe that are used to measure distances from the equator; lines of latitude

parliament a lawmaking body

peasant a poor person who owns or rents a small piece of land that he or she farms, especially in poorer countries

pendulum a suspended weight, usually in a clock, that swings back and forth at regular intervals

persuasive intended to encourage people to have a certain opinion or to take a certain action

point of view how someone feels or thinks

political action committee (PAC) a group that gives money to candidates who have interests similar to its own

political cartoon a drawing that expresses an opinion about an issue

political map a map that focuses on showing boundaries, such as those between countries or states

political party a group of people who have similar ideas about public issues

politics ideas and actions of government

positive incentive a reward for making a certain choice

precipitation moisture that falls to Earth as rain, snow, or some other form

predicting outcomes trying to figure out what the results of events will be

preemption the concept of launching an attack in order to prevent a suspected attack

premium the monthly fee paid for health insurance coverage

preventive care care, such as regular checkups, to maintain health

primary election an election to choose delegates to the nominating convention at which a political party decides on candidates to run for office in the general election

prime minister the head of a parliament

probable cause good reason to link a suspect with a crime and to make an arrest

profit to make money by selling something at a higher price than the original cost

progressive tax a plan under which the percentage of a person's wages paid as income tax increases as the wages increase

property tax tax on the value of something that a person owns

protectionist supporting tariffs on imports to protect a nation's own producers of goods and services

province a political region in some countries that is similar to a state in the United States

public policy the system of laws and actions on a particular topic

pueblo Native American settlements with apartment-like buildings

quality circle a group of workers who check the quality of products and services they produce

quota a set limit of something such as imports

racist favoring one race of people over another

ratify to confirm or approve

recycling reusing solid and non-solid waste for the same or new purposes

reformer a person who works to change things for the better

region an area that differs in one or more ways from the places around it

register to complete a form with such things as name, address, and date of birth in order to vote

reparations money paid to make up for damages, such as suffering during wartime

repeal to take back or do away with something, such as a law

republic 1) a self-governing territory usually headed by a president 2) a government in which the power is given to elected officials who represent the people

revenue income collected or produced

rule of law the idea that everyone must follow laws and the laws must be fair and equal

sales tax tax on a purchase

sanction an economic or military measure used to force a nation to stop violating an international law or human right

scale a set of marks that compares the distance on a map to actual distance

scarce describes a limited supply of something that is in demand

segregation separation

self-defense to defend oneself or one's property

separation of powers a system that divides the functions of government among independent branches so that no one branch becomes too powerful

sequence a series of events that follow one another in a particular order

service industry business that employs people who meet the needs of other people

smallpox a deadly disease that has been virtually eliminated through vaccination

soft money money donated to a political party for supposedly nonpolitical uses, and which is not subject to the limitations on campaign contributions

sound a long, wide ocean inlet

specialization focusing on what one does best

sphere of influence an area in which one nation wields power over another

stalemate deadlock

strike to stop work in protest

subsidy assistance in the form of money

suffrage the right to vote

summarize to reduce a large amount of information into a few sentences

supply the amount of goods and services sellers are willing to offer at certain prices at a given time

switchboard a device for controlling, connecting, and disconnecting many telephone lines within one building or location

table a type of list that organizes information in columns and rows

Taliban an extreme Islamic government that ruled Afghanistan from 1996 to 2001

tariff a tax on imports

technology the tools and methods used to increase production

telecommunications ways to send messages over long distances

timeline an illustration that shows when a series of events took place and the order in which they occurred

topic sentence the specific sentence in a paragraph that contains its main idea

topsoil the soil on Earth's surface, in which the roots of most plants usually take hold

totalitarianism a system in which the government controls every aspect of life

trade deficit the value of the nation's imports that exceeds the value of the nation's exports

transistor a small device that controls the flow of the electricity in electronic devices

tree line the beginning of an area where temperatures are too cold for trees to grow

tropics the area on Earth that receives almost direct rays from the sun year-round

tundra a treeless region with a thin layer of soil over permanently frozen earth

unemployment a measure of the number of unemployed persons in the United States

Union the northern states during the American Civil War

U.S. history history of the area now known as the United States of America

vaccination an injection that protects a person from a disease

values ideas or qualities that people feel are important, right, and good

vegetation the plants that grow naturally in an area

veto to refuse to sign a bill into law

warrant a document that permits a police search in connection with a crime

work ethic the belief in the value of work, demonstrated through commitment to job responsibilities

world history history of all of the people and nations of Earth